S0-BFD-788

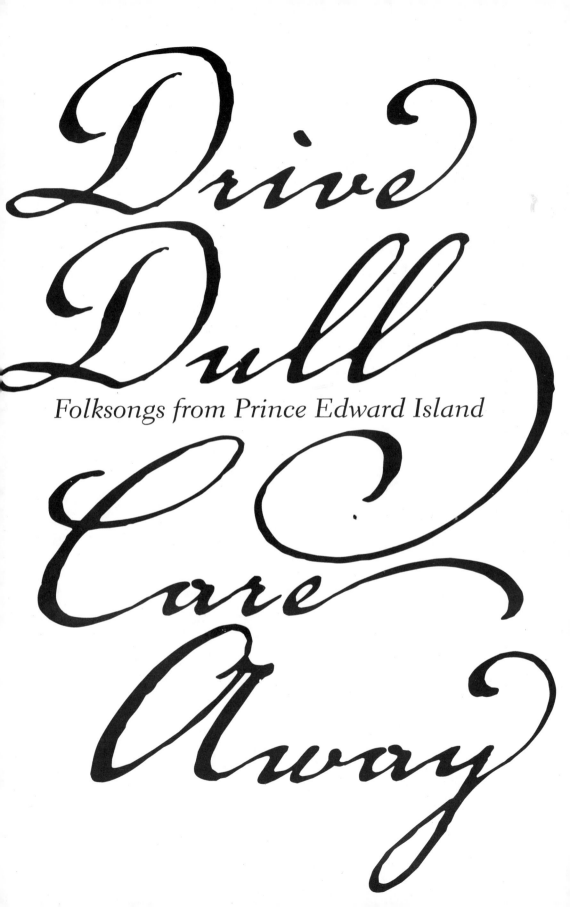

Drive Dull Care Away

Folksongs from Prince Edward Island

Drive Dull Care Away

*Folksongs From
Prince Edward Island*

Edward D. "Sandy" Ives

Institute of Island Studies
Charlottetown, Prince Edward Island
1999

"Away, away, away, away—
We will drive dull care away!
And while we're here
with our friends so dear
We'll drive dull care away!"

—as sung by Charlie Gorman (p. 81)

This one is for

Bobby

consistent critic
and
constant companion,
who thinks I should have dedicated it to

Mary Cousins

© 1999 by Edward D. "Sandy" Ives
ISBN 0-919013-34-1

Editors: Laurie Brinklow, Edward MacDonald
Layout/Design: UPEI Graphics
Printing and Binding: Williams & Crue Ltd., Summerside,
   Prince Edward Island, Canada
CD Production: Shane Bryanton

Published with the kind assistance of the Prince Edward Island Council
of the Arts and the Canadian-American Center, University of Maine.

Canadian Cataloguing in Publication Data

Ives, Edward D.

   Drive dull care away

   Includes bibliographic references and index.
   ISBN 0-919013-34-1

1. Folk songs — Prince Edward Island.   I. Title.   II. University of
Prince Edward Island. Institute of Island Studies.

ML3563.7.P7I95 1999   782.42162'009717   C99-950029-5

Institute of Island Studies Publishing Committee

John Cousins (Chair)	Allan Hammond
Harry Baglole	Michael Hennessey
Laurie Brinklow	Catherine Innes-Parker
David Cairns	Deirdre Kessler
John Crossley	Edward MacDonald
Donna Giberson	Ian MacQuarrie

The Institute of Island Studies
Faculty of Arts
University of Prince Edward Island
Charlottetown, Prince Edward Island
Canada C1A 4P3
tel: 902.566.0956
fax: 902.566.0756
e-mail: iis@upei.ca

Contents

Illustrations

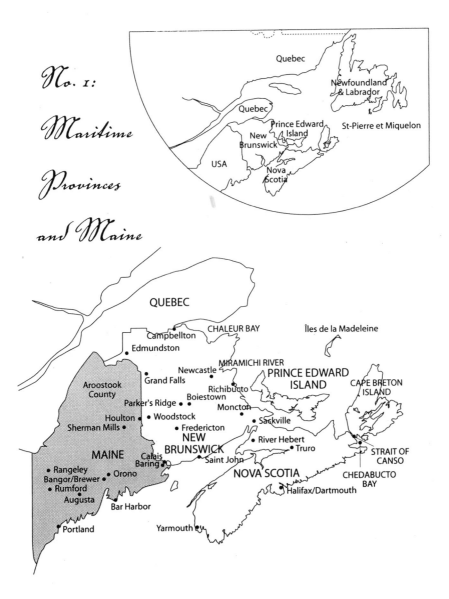

No. 1:

Maritime

Provinces

and Maine

Quebec

Newfoundland & Labrador

Quebec

Prince Edward Island

New Brunswick

St-Pierre et Miquelon

USA

Nova Scotia

QUEBEC

Campbellton

CHALEUR BAY

Îles de la Madeleine

Edmundston

MIRAMICHI RIVER

Newcastle

PRINCE EDWARD ISLAND

Grand Falls

CAPE BRETON ISLAND

Aroostook County

Richibucto

Boiestown

Parker's Ridge

Moncton

Houlton

Woodstock

Sherman Mills

Fredericton

Sackville

NEW BRUNSWICK

River Hebert

MAINE

Calais

Baring

Saint John

Truro

STRAIT OF CANSO

Rangeley

Orono

NOVA SCOTIA

CHEDABUCTO BAY

Bangor/Brewer

Rumford

Halifax/Dartmouth

Augusta

Bar Harbor

Portland

Yarmouth

No. 2: Western & Central Prince Edward Island

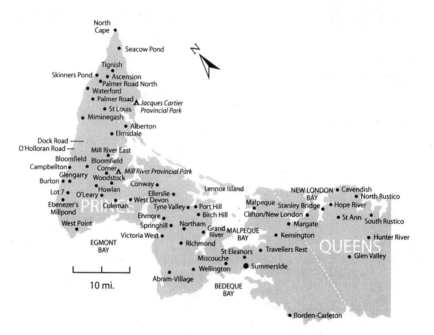

North Cape
● Seacow Pond
Tignish ●
Skinners Pond ● ● Ascension
● Palmer Road North
Waterford ●
● Palmer Road ▲ Jacques Cartier
● St Louis   Provincial Park
● Miminegash
● Alberton
● Elmsdale
Dock Road ——
O'Holloran Road ——
Mill River East
Bloomfield   Bloomfield
Campbellton ●   Corner ▲ Mill River Provincial Park
Glengarry   Woodstock
Burton ●   Conway ●   Lennox Island
Lot 7 ●   Howlan ●
O'Leary ●   Ellerslie ●   NEW LONDON ● Cavendish
● West Devon   BAY   ● North Rustico
Ebenezer's   Coleman   Tyne Valley ● ● Port Hill   Malpeque ● Stanley Bridge ● ● Hope River
Millpond   ● Birch Hill   Clifton/New London ●   ● St Ann
West Point ●   Enmore ●   ● Margate   South Rustico
Springhill ●   Northam ●   Grand MALPEQUE   ● Hunter River
Victoria West ●   River BAY   ● Kensington
EGMONT   ● Richmond   ● Travellers Rest   ● Glen Valley
BAY   St Eleanors ●   QUEENS
Miscouche ●
● Wellington ● Summerside
Abram-Village ●   BEDEQUE
BAY
10 mi.
● Borden-Carleton

Gulf of St. Lawrence

Northumberland Strait

No.3: Central & Eastern Prince Edward Island

- Selkirk
- Groshaut/St Charles
- Souris
- St Peters
- Farmington
- Morell
- Morell Rear
- Dundas
- Poplar Pt
- Mount Stewart
- Annandale
- St Georges/Narrows Creek
- North Rustico
- **KINGS**
- DeGros Marsh
- Pooles Corner
- South Rustico
- Georgetown
- Hunter River
- **QUEENS**
- Panmure Island
- Glen Valley
- Montague
- Charlottetown
- Orwell Cove
- Iona
- Murray Harbour
- Murray River
- Point Prim
- Wood Islands

10 mi.

Gulf of St. Lawrence

Northumberland Strait

No. 4: Sandy Ives in 1957.

No. 5: Sandy Ives interviewing retired woodsman Jack Holland at the First
Miramichi Folksong Festival, Newcastle, New Brunswick,
September 1958.

Introduction

The Island and Its People

PRINCE EDWARD ISLAND IS A CURVED SLICE OF LAND from three to thirty-five miles wide and about one hundred and twenty miles long, lying along the southern rim of the Gulf of St. Lawrence and separated from the mainland of New Brunswick and Nova Scotia by the narrow waters of Northumberland Strait. It is an island of low rolling hills and plains, and its characteristic red soil is nostalgically familiar to all who have seen it. The shoreline alternates sandstone cliffs and gentle beaches and is heavily indented with deep tidal inlets and large shallow bays. Up until 1997 the standard way to reach the Island was by ferry from either Cape Tormentine, New Brunswick, or Caribou, Nova Scotia, but in 1997 the Confederation Bridge was completed, allowing trucks and cars direct access.

French explorer Jacques Cartier is often credited with "discovering" this island, which the native Mi'kmaq called *Abegweit*, in 1534. It was a French possession called *Île St. Jean* until it was ceded to the British by the Treaty of Paris in 1763. The British divided the Island up into sixty-seven townships or "lots" of about 20,000 acres each, which were granted to various people who had claims against the Crown (still today we speak of places as "Lot Seven" or "Lot Eleven"), and in 1799 they changed the name from the Island of St. John to Prince Edward Island in honour of George III's fourth son (and father-to-be of Queen Victoria). The Fathers of Confederation met in Charlottetown in 1864, but Prince Edward Island did not itself join the Dominion until 1873.

Although tourism is now challenging farming as the Province's leading industry, the Island's culture is still basically agricultural; almost half of its 136,500 people live in rural areas, if not on active farms, and the farms themselves occupy about seventy-five per cent of the land. In some areas, fishing is the main occupation, but even some of the fishermen are part-time farmers. There is little industry and almost no manufacturing.

The Celtic heritage is strong. About a third of the Island's people today can claim Scottish descent, and most of those can speak of their Highland ancestry. While the Irish now make up only about a fifth of the population, in the late nineteenth century they were far more important, the Highlanders and Irish together accounting for about two-thirds of the people. As for the first-arriving French Acadians, they continue to be very much a presence, most of them living in Prince County (Cape Egmont and west and north of Cascumpec Bay) and around Rustico, but there are other small enclaves elsewhere on the Island.[1] In addition, of course, there were English settlers, and while they may have been the least important as far as numbers went they seem to have occupied a rather privileged position both economically and socially. And there are still a few hundred Mi'kmaq up on Lennox Island and in several other small reserves.[2]

My Fieldwork and Its Historical Background

I should begin by saying that my fieldwork on Prince Edward Island has been neither broad nor deep when compared with that carried on by collectors like Helen Creighton and W. Roy Mackenzie in Nova Scotia or Kenneth Peacock in Newfoundland.[3] It all began with my search for information on the life and work of the lumberwoods songmaker Larry Gorman, not with any attempt to make a comprehensive collection of folksongs for their own sake. I started by publishing letters in newspapers like *The Guardian* and the *Journal-Pioneer* asking specifically about Gorman, and then I followed up on the people who responded. As time went on I broadened my search to include other poets like Joe Scott and Lawrence Doyle, but my focus stayed pretty steadily on local songs and songmaking.[4] It could be said, then, that better than half the songs in this book came to me by the purest serendipity—that is to say while I was looking specifically for something else.

---

[1] For a good survey of the French-language folksong tradition on Prince Edward Island, see Georges Arsenault, *Complaintes acadiennes de l'Île-du-Prince-Édouard* (Ottawa: Les Éditions Leméac, 1980).

[2] For an excellent and readable historical geography of P.E.I. containing 155 maps illustrating such matters as population distribution, cultural origins of the settlers, specific characteristics of farming and fishing operations, values of farms, and sizes of holdings, see Andrew Hill Clark, *Three Centuries and the Island* (Toronto: University of Toronto Press, 1959).

[3] In her long career Helen Creighton published a half-dozen solid collections of Nova Scotia songs. For Mackenzie, see his *Ballads and Sea Songs from Nova Scotia* (Harvard, 1928). See also Kenneth Peacock's three-volume set, *Songs of the Newfoundland Outports* (Ottawa, 1965). In addition, the late Kenneth Goldstein was editing his collection of 4,500 songs from Newfoundland at the time of his death.

[4] For the results, see my *Larry Gorman: The Man Who Made the Songs* (Bloomington: Indiana University Press, 1964; reprinted Fredericton, N.B.: Goose Lane Editions, 1993); *Lawrence Doyle: The Farmer-Poet of Prince Edward Island*, Maine Studies No. 92 (Orono: University Press, 1971); *Joe Scott: The Woodsman-Songmaker* (Champaign: University of Illinois Press, 1978).

Not only was the scope of my inquiry limited, so was the time I could devote to fieldwork; thus none of my Island sojourns were long ones. In 1957 I was there for about a month, in 1958 for a week, in 1963 for exactly two days, in 1965 for maybe two weeks, and in 1968 and 1969 for a week each. Both my limited time and tight focus can go a long way toward explaining why certain well-known categories of song don't appear in this collection. It probably explains, for instance, why I found no "obscene" or "dirty" songs, and it may also help to explain why I found so very few Child ballads.[5]

On the other hand, since my fieldwork centred on local songmaking—and admittedly I spend a great deal of time on local songs in this book—is it possible that in reacting against the earlier scholarly emphasis on the Child ballads I have overemphasized the importance of local songs? Certainly that is possible, even probable, but I ask readers to keep in mind that I do not offer this book as in any way a definitive work on the folksongs of Prince Edward Island. The chances are it is reasonably representative of the Island's English-language folksong tradition, but—being simply one man's look-in set in the narrative of his looking—I can claim no more for it than that. If the definitive work is ever to come, someone else will have to compile it.

Yet it just happens that my emphasis on local songmaking throws into rather clear relief the interplay between two song traditions: the local and the regional. Lawrence Doyle's songs, for example, are hardly known at all outside of a few townships in northeastern Kings County, while Joe Scott's ballads are known not only in all three counties on P.E.I. but in New Brunswick, Nova Scotia, Maine, and New Hampshire as well. Actually, what this involves is less a regional tradition (though it was confined to a region) than an occupational one: that of the lumbercamps of the late nineteenth and early twentieth centuries.

I have told elsewhere, especially in *Joe Scott*, both how thousands of young men from the rural Maritimes came to work in the Maine lumberwoods and how during those years there was a vigorous singing tradition in the camps. These young men learned the songs that were sung there and took them home, where, as Edmund Doucette points out, people would make a real effort to learn these "new" songs. Thus Wesley Smith learned Joe Scott's "Guy Reed" (written in western Maine) before he even left the Island to go into the woods, and Billy Bell learned "The *Cumberland's* Crew" back home in

---

[5]For the benefit of the general reader, a Child ballad is one of the 305 ballads included by Professor Francis James Child in his monumental five-volume collection, *The English and Scottish Popular Ballads* (Boston: Houghton Mifflin, 1882-98). Such ballads were long considered the "aristocrats" of British balladry, and the finding of versions of them was given special importance. For one of the best descriptions of them available, see Gordon Hall Gerould, *The Ballad of Tradition* (Oxford University Press, 1932).

Enmore almost sixty years before I recorded it at his home in Brewer, Maine. Both songs were certainly brought to P.E.I. by men who had learned them in the woods, but both Smith and Bell learned them locally, and that—together with the fact that "PIs"[6] were often acknowledged to be the best singers in the camps—points to a solid singing tradition at home. This woods/local mix is exciting, and I will be referring to it again and again.

The Present Collection

Back in 1964 I published *Twenty-One Folksongs From Prince Edward Island*,[7] which I intended to be a representative sample of the songs I had found on my first three trips to the Island, and, while it is long out-of-print, it still serves that purpose well today. In a way, the present book can serve the same purpose, bringing the earlier one up-to-date, and indeed anyone familiar with *Twenty-One Folksongs* will recognize how shamelessly I have reproduced sections of it this time around.[8] But I intend a good deal more than a simple re-do here. The whole perspective has changed, and the songs are set in quite a different context, an autobiographical one in which I counterpoint two strains that are usually played quite separately: with the one hand I present a rather straightforward collection of songs from Prince Edward Island; with the other, I tell the story of how and why these songs were collected. Actually, I have used this approach here and there in all my earlier books, but now I have carried it to its logical conclusion, making it the organizing principle for the whole work.

Since the significance of this shift may not be clear to the general reader, perhaps a little history of folksong scholarship will be helpful. The time-honoured way of presenting a regional collection of songs has been to give the songs and any commentary on them separately. The songs themselves would be arranged either by academic genres (Child ballads, British broadsides, American and Canadian ballads, local songs) or by theme (love, murder, war, disaster, humour, etc.), and there would be scholarly headnotes telling what is known about the distribution, sources, and analogues of each one. Any information on the general cultural context or on the singers themselves would be placed in an introduction, while the specific

---

[6]"PI" was, and still is, a common Maine designation for someone from Prince Edward Island. At first it was a term of disparagement, but it has largely lost that note. Even PIs use it to describe themselves.

[7]*Northeast Folklore* V (Orono, Maine: Northeast Folklore Society, 1963).

[8]I have also raided *Larry Gorman, Lawrence Doyle, and Joe Scott* in the same way. All such incorporations are duly credited by footnote.

circumstances in which this-or-that song came to be sung for the fieldworker hardly ever appeared at all.[9] Such an arrangement worked well for several generations of fieldworkers, allowing them to treat the songs as discrete entities that could be arranged in a generally accepted and logical framework. It made the whole enterprise appear scientific or (at least) respectably objective and free of the taint of the anecdotal, with its concomitant risk of the sentimental.[10]

But a straightforward collection that neither presents the songs in some kind of interpretive frame nor gives us a sense of the part the songs played in the lives of the people who sang them no longer butters even the most academic of parsnips, and while such collections seemed adequate to me at first (after all, what else was available?), increasingly I found them wanting as my interest in cultural and historical context—especially in the people who created and sang the songs—grew. My three book-length studies of songmakers show that emphasis plainly, as do my two published collections (*Twenty-One Folksongs* and *Folksongs of New Brunswick*[11]), where I arranged the material neither by genre nor by subject but by singer. I wanted to show the songs embedded in the lives and memories of the people who sang them for me—to show them in their natural matrix, as it were.[12]

In the present work, I have gone a large step further in that direction by showing how I was very much a part of that matrix—in fact, a controlling part, since the songs were only sung because I asked for them. In no way can I claim to have been a detached and impartial observer; I was always a young man with an agenda, and that agenda changed some over time. I knew what I was looking for and had some general ideas about what else I might find along the way, and along that way I was surprised, delighted, disappointed, exhilarated, discouraged, and moved by what I did and did not find. Then, too, like everyone else, I'm partial to some people, can't stand others, and when it came to the songs these people would sing me I had definite—if developing— ideas about what was "good," what was "genuine"—in a word,

---

[9]For an exception, see Dorothy Scarborough, *A Song Catcher in Southern Mountains* (New York: Columbia University Press, 1937; reprinted AMS, 1966). W. Roy Mackenzie printed the story of his search in a separate book, *The Quest of the Ballad* (Princeton University Press, 1919). See also John Avery Lomax, *Adventures of a Ballad Hunter* (New York: Macmillan, 1947).
[10]See Chapter Three, "Folksong Collections in Great Britain and North America," in D. K. Wilgus, *Anglo-American Folksong Scholarship Since 1898* (Rutgers University Press, 1959), pp.122–239, for more detail.
[11](Fredericton, N.B: Goose Lane Editions, 1993).
[12]Others, before and since, have used this approach. See Byron Arnold, *Folksongs of Alabama* (Birmingham: 1950), and Edith Fowke, *Traditional Singers and Songs from Ontario* (Hatboro, Pa. and Don Mills, Ont.: 1965). For an excellent and detailed study of this singer/song relationship, see Ellen J. Stekert, "Two Voices of Tradition" (University of Pennsylvania doctoral dissertation, 1965). See also Roger D. Abrahams (ed.), *A Singer and Her Songs* (Baton Rouge, La.: 1970).

what was and was not "folksong."

Since all of these things had their effect, not only on what I found but also on how I thought about what I found, setting the songs in an autobiographical memoir seemed to make a good deal of sense. Social and cultural description would come through immediate concrete examples rather than through introductory generalizations, allowing readers to evaluate the data in the context of its collection and, aided by a comprehensive index, draw conclusions of their own. I recognized that such a scheme had serious drawbacks—notably that of making the book appear less an organized whole than a mere self-indulgent gallimaufry—but I decided to take the risk and go with it. Besides, it furnished me a natural way to tell some good stories and at the same time pay tribute to the real heroes of my adventures: the singers themselves.

Perhaps I should say a word about the three sources I have used in putting the narrative together: tape-recorded interviews, journals, and memory. Recordings of the songs need no comment here, but right from the beginning I tried to leave the recorder on between songs to capture as much as I could of what singers had to say about them. That didn't always work (sometimes, for instance, singers would ask me to shut down as soon as they finished singing), but even under the best of circumstance there is always much that, for one reason or another, doesn't get on the tape, and that's where journals come in. While in the field I have always tried to write up my impressions of an interview as soon as possible after it, and for the most part I succeeded in doing that, but there are unfortunate gaps. Sometimes I was in a hurry, sometimes I was just plain lazy, and there are even places where, decades later, I discover I can't find notes I damn well remember having written. I have had leisure to regret these lapses, but fortunately I am gifted with an extremely sharp and retentive memory, and even more fortunately—since she was with so much of the time—I have been able to draw on my wife Bobby's recollections, too. In addition, listening to a tape or reading a journal entry always seems to trigger memories I never even knew were there. It is safe to say, though, that very little in this book comes purely from my unaided memory.[13]

A final note in passing. I hope I'll be forgiven for not jumping into the bramble bush of a full-scale definition of folksong—a very brambly bush indeed. Let's just say folksongs are songs like the ones in this book—songs passed on chiefly by oral tradition in small-group, face-to-face situations—

---

[13]For an excellent study of long-term memory, see Alice M. and Howard S. Hoffman, *Archives of Memory: A Soldier Recalls World War II* (Lexington: University Press of Kentucky: 1990).

and leave it at that. But how about *Prince Edward Island* folksongs? All I mean is songs that were *sung* here. Almost two-thirds of the songs in this book quite obviously originated off-Island, some of them in England, Scotland, or Ireland, others in the United States, but so long as Island people sang them we should consider them Island folksongs. Were I to limit my selection simply to songs originating on P.E.I. or songs about P.E.I., this book would give a very skewed sampling of the Island folksong tradition.

Other P.E.I. Collections

While preparing my earlier *Twenty-One Folksongs* for publication I naturally looked for English-language collections that might have preceded mine, and the results were disappointing. Some earlier collecting work had been done among the Acadian French, but the collecting of English-language material had scarcely begun. Dr. Helen Creighton had made at least two trips to the Island and had done collecting in all three counties, but her harvest was small. Christopher Gledhill, then Provincial Director of Music for Schools, had collected about thirty items in both English and French, mostly from West Prince, but neither his nor Creighton's work was available in published form. That gave my small volume the distinction of being the first published collection of folksongs to be devoted entirely to Prince Edward Island. Considering the amount of material that had been published on both Nova Scotia and Newfoundland — not to mention Maine — over the preceding four decades, I found that distinction rather surprising, but there it was.

Fortunately the pace picked up some after 1963. Two books appeared in 1973, the Island's Centennial Year. First of all, Gledhill published *Folk Songs of Prince Edward Island*, fifteen songs from his aforementioned collection (with piano accompaniment added), and Randall and Dorothy Dibblee brought out *Folksongs from Prince Edward Island*, a useful collection of fifty-four songs, mostly from Kings and eastern Queens. In addition, several folksingers have brought out useful and enjoyable records, and two of them deserve special mention here: *When Johnny Went Plowing for Kearon*, featuring John Cousins (Mary Cousins' son) and Tommy Banks (a farmer from Annandale), and *Island Folk Festival* . Both are certifiably close-to-the-bone, and it is from the second of these that I have taken the four songs included in Chapter Eight.[14]

---

[14]John Cousins and Tommy Banks. *When Johnny Went Plowing for Kearon.* LP record (Charlottetown: P.E.I. Museum and Heritage Foundation, 1976). *Island Folk Festival.* LP record (Belfast, P.E.I.: Fox House, Charlottetown: Institute of Island Studies, 1985).

Change

It is safe to say that the old folksong tradition described in this book no longer plays an important part in the lives of present-day Islanders. Even those who still know and care for the old songs find fewer and fewer occasions to sing them. Rural electrification—a sort of vanguard of urbanization—brings with it better radio reception than that available from the old and erratic wet-battery sets. It also brings television and (not to be discounted) good reading light. In the same way, improved roads have made communities less dependent on their own resources, especially in the arts (a trip to town for a movie was no longer a big deal, for instance). Thus the occasions when people used to sing and listen to the old come-all-ye's have been more and more taken up with other activities—often in other venues—and the universal human needs for narrative and song are otherwise fulfilled.

Yet these old songs are tenacious of life, and we will probably find people who know and treasure them for some time to come. What the future will bring remains perpetual possibility until it happens. There will be change, and inevitably there will be loss, but just as inevitably newness will come to be, and we can be of good cheer when we see how singers like Clifford Wedge made old songs new again or how Alton MacLean and Allan Rankin make new songs built on the old ways. The end is not yet.

A Note on the Editing

All song texts are given *verbatim*. In the general narrative, quoted material marked with an asterisk is given *verbatim* from tape-recorded interviews. All omissions are indicated with standard ellipsis marks (. . .). Material in square brackets is of two kinds: italicized words are either "stage directions" or words I have added to make the sense of a passage clear; non-italicized material indicates that the recording is not clear but the given words are as close as I can come to what I heard. Where I do not mark a quotation with an asterisk, I am reconstructing what was said either from my journals or from memory.

As for the music, rather than trying to present some sort of tune outline or other generalized form, I have given a sample stanza from each song in some detail, hoping that this method will give the reader both "the tune" and some idea of how that tune was presented, which is to say the "style." Transcribing traditional music raises many problems, not the least of them being whether a particular note should be given metrical value or simply put in as a grace note. I can only hope I have been reasonably consistent. On several of the tunes I have made no attempt at establishing a consistent meter but have marked the piece *parlando rubato* and used dotted bar lines to indicate the ends of phrases.

I have set each tune so that its final falls on g, rather than transcribing it in the key in which I heard it performed. Not everyone—especially those cursed with "perfect pitch"—will be happy with this practice, but I have my reasons for selecting it. First, it makes it easier for the reader to compare one tune with another. Second, and most important, it is my experience that the whole concept of "key" has no place in folk tradition. Traditional singers place a tune where it is comfortable for them at the time, and that may not be where it had been comfortable the time before—or the time before that. Even so, just for the record, I have preceded each tune with a catch-signature to show where this particular singer placed it this particular time. Third, I assume that most readers of this book are like me in not being able to read music at sight—not easily anyway (I always have to figure out where "doh" is and work from there)—and it saves time and trouble not to have to deal with a multitude of key signatures, especially, as I have just pointed out, when the original tradition doesn't fuss with key at all. My advice to anyone wanting to sing a song from the "score" they find here is to do just exactly what the original singer did: place it where it's comfortable.

I have another suggestion for those who want to sing these songs: don't try to "explain" or "dramatize" what is going on in the song by getting louder or softer, speeding up or slowing down, or colouring your voice to show fear or anger or surprise. Save that for pop music or grand opera; it is no part of our folksong tradition. Let the words do all the work. Listen to the enclosed compact disc, and you'll see what I mean.

The Compact Disc

Not all that long ago—and not for the first time in my life either—a friend questioned the aesthetic worth of these songs I have spent my life studying. He agreed they had value as social and cultural data. But as art? My response was that had he been with me to hear them sung in parlour or kitchen, not only would he not need an answer but he probably never would have asked the question. True enough, really, but not very helpful, because we can't go back to that moment. "Fled is that music."

In this book I have tried through narrative and description to help the reader experience the life of a time and place and what it was like for me briefly to be an intrusive part of it. I have also carefully transcribed the songs themselves—words and music—and certainly that is one way of presenting them, but inevitably it leaves out a lot. Missing are the voices themselves—what the songs sounded like when sung by this person in that room—and that is something the recordings I made at the time can go a long way toward supplying. Even they, of course, will not take us all the way back to that nexus, but, listened to in the context of the narrative I have built up for them in the book, they'll get us as close as we're ever going to get.

In listening to the fourteen selections I have placed on the accompanying compact disc, keep in mind that they represent neither studio nor professional recordings. Often they were makeshifts—made with the best ambience and mike placement I could manage at the time and with whatever equipment I could then afford. In 1957 and 1958, that equipment was a huge Webcor home recorder and the little crystal mike that came with it; by 1963 I had moved up to a Wollensak T-1500 with an Electro-Voice 664 mike; then in 1965 and thereafter I was using a UHER 4000 Report L with its standard M516 mike, though occasionally I switched to a Roberts 192 (a Japanese knockoff of the big Ampex 600 series). What surprises me today, though, is how good some of the very early recordings still seem to be, but, deaf as I now am, and sentimental as I've always been, perhaps I'm not really in a position to pass that judgment any more.

Acknowledgments

It remains for me to thank some of the institutions and individuals who have helped me see this work to completion, and first and foremost must come the University of Prince Edward Island's Institute of Island Studies. Harry Baglole, its Director, got the whole idea of this book going some years ago, and his continued support and enthusiasm—and that of his Publications Coordinator Laurie Brinklow—have been extremely important to me, always. Ed MacDonald has served as my official Editor, and a most consistent and careful one he has been, for sure. Not only that, but his knowledge of Island history has saved me from many gaffes, both major and minor. But the fact is that the three of them—Baglole, Brinklow, and MacDonald—have teamed with me in a way where it would be unrealistic to separate their functions. We've worked together, and it's been great.

Here at the University of Maine, I owe thanks to the Canadian American Center, especially to its Director Stephen Hornsby, not only for long-standing encouragement but for a generous and enabling subvention. The University's Research Funds Committee has been very generous over the years with a series of travel and equipment grants, but I wish particularly to thank its predecessor, the Coe Research Fund Committee and its Secretary Dr. Geddes Simpson. In 1957 they awarded me two grants totaling $850. I know that sounds piffling these days, but at that time it amounted to better than twenty per cent of my salary as an Instructor in English. Those grants were a grubstake: they got me going, and they kept me alive!

Other organizations have been helpful, notably, of course, the John Simon Guggenheim Memorial Foundation. Their award to me of a fellowship for 1965–66 was, like those early Coe grants, worth far more than money. Judy McCulloh of the University of Illinois Press has once again shown herself a friend by involving her press in the distribution of this book; and thanks, too, to Goose Lane Editions in Fredericton, New Brunswick, and Tangle Layne Distribution in Prince Edward Island, for their help in the same task. Steve Green, Archivist for the Maine Folklife Center, prepared digital copies of songs from the Northeast Archives of Folklore and Oral History, and Indiana University's Archives of Traditional Music was very prompt in supplying me with digital copies of songs I had entrusted to their care almost four decades ago. Joe Hickerson of the Archive of Folk Culture (Library of Congress) was, as always, helpful in my searches for obscure sources and analogues.

Dr. Gordon Bowie autographed the tunes from my original transcriptions and made many suggestions—all of which I followed—for changes and improvements. Shane Bryanton has been chiefly responsible for preparing the final version of the compact disc and Matthew MacKay led us through the design and layout of the book with style and patience. Jim Hornby has graciously allowed me to reproduce material from *Island Folk Festival*, the record he produced of the 1982 Westisle Folk Festival. I am also grateful to Steve Roud, Bill McNeil, and Neil Rosenberg for help in tracking down sources and the like—a never-ending and always cooperative chore. David Taylor read the manuscript and made several valuable suggestions. Steve Bicknell prepared readable early versions of the maps from my barely readable rough copy; Glenda Clements-Smith prepared the final versions.

My debts to those Islanders who spent untold hours talking with me and singing for me are too numerous and too weighty to mention here. May their very presence in this book stand as token of my gratitude; the simple fact is there could have been no book without their generosity. But there are two other people whose help deserves special mention. John Cousins' knowledge of the history and folkways of West Prince is prodigious, and he has shared it with me the way only friends can share, both enriching my knowledge and setting me right about many small matters. Thanks, John.

And then there's my old pal George Carey, who read over the manuscript a couple of times and reacquainted me with certain hard truths about writing. If I didn't always follow his advice, there was never a time when I didn't listen up real good. So thanks, too, to you, George.

No. 6: A rather typical Maine lumbercamp crew, showing the teamsters with their horses, the cook in his apron, etc. Photographers used to travel from camp to camp taking these photos, usually on Sunday, which would have been the only day the men were in camp during daylight hours. Then they'd return a few weeks later to sell the pictures to the men. *P106.* (Note: this photo has been flipped on the cover for design purposes.)

Beginnings

I'VE ALWAYS LOVED MAPS. As a kid back in the early thirties I had a huge antique wall map of the United States and the Dominion of Canada hanging next to my bed, and I used to prowl it by the hour. Half of Oklahoma was still designated "Indian Territory," and I remember my excitement on discovering Niagara Falls—the same place pictured on the Shredded Wheat box! But Canada was special. There were great white areas there (actually a cracked and faded brown) marked "Unexplored," and I'd say over wonderful names like Moose Jaw, Winnipeg, Keewatin, Yellowknife, Whitehorse, Ungava. I loved the idea of that huge northern nation, and I liked its being a Dominion. Not that I knew what that was, but I knew it was something different. Early on, then, I had a pretty good idea of where things were up there, and I'd take imaginary trips, running my finger from, say, St. John's to Calgary. But somehow I missed Prince Edward Island entirely.

I first heard of it years later when a friend of my sister's was going to a family reunion up there and wanted Ruth to go along. Prince Edward Island. . . . I remembered places like Prince Charles Island and Prince of Wales Island from my childhood map travels—blank spaces in the blue Arctic waters—and I wondered if Prince Edward Island could possibly be one of those, perhaps in the Labrador Sea or even Baffin Bay. But Ruth's trip never came off, and, like a good American, I forgot all about Canada in general and Prince Edward Island in particular. Until, that is, I came to Maine from New York in the mid-1950s to teach English at the State University.

I had long been interested in folksongs. I played the requisite guitar and had the mostly standard repertoire picked up from Burl Ives records and Carl Sandburg's *The American Songbag,* and for some years I'd had—among a rather large circle of college friends and friends of college friends—something of a reputation as a performer at parties and the like. Therefore—having discovered shortly after my move to Maine that I'd have to do something to bring my income up to the poverty level—I set up a sideline as a folksinger. It worked, and I kept busy, but while my standard repertoire was adequate for high-school assemblies, I soon saw that something was missing when I sang for older and more local audiences. "Do you know any of the old woods songs?" I'd be asked, or "How about 'Peter Emberly'?" To fill this void, I turned to books like Eckstorm and Smyth's *Minstrelsy of Maine*, Doerflinger's *Shantymen and Shantyboys*, and Barry's *The Maine Woods Songster*,[1] and before I knew it I was hooked on reading whatever I could lay my hands on that had to do with the old lumberwoods.

Everything I read made the point that in the late nineteenth and early twentieth centuries thousands of young men from the Maritime Provinces came down to work either in the Maine woods or in the concomitant saw and paper mills, and it became clear to me that they brought their songs with them. One man in particular caught my attention. His name was Larry Gorman; they called him "the man who makes the songs"; he came from Prince Edward Island; and he spent his last years in nearby Brewer. I wanted to know all I could about him, and since I soon exhausted the documentary record in the fall of 1956, I went public with a letter in the *Bangor Daily News* and a brief spot on local television where I sang a couple of his songs. Letters came in and the phone began ringing, the common message being that if I wanted to find out about Larry Gorman I'd have to go to Prince Edward Island. "All them good singers were PIs," I was told by one old woodsman, "every one of them, and you're just going to have to go down there."

I was willing to be persuaded, especially as many old Islanders rhapsodized, with that faraway look in the eyes, on what a beautiful place it was. Some years later Joe McKenna, who grew up in an Island family in Rumford, Maine, caught that look, that note, perfectly in his book, *The Sign of the Stag*. As a child, he heard the oldsters talk about it. "It was a place far away," he decided. "I would never get there. It was a place like heaven or the garden behind the moon."[2] He did get there, of course. And so did I. But only after I'd had time in Maine to see how those from the Island never entirely left it behind, and how the old songs took them back there. None showed that better than Billy Bell of Brewer.

His sister Jeanette Shields called me in response to my appeal over local television. "He remembers Larry Gorman," she said. "They both worked at the pulp mill there in South Brewer. Give him a call."

I did. Yes, he remembered him alright. "I don't know how much I can tell you," he added, "but I remember him, and I know some of them old come-all-ye's."

I wasn't at all sure what a come-all-ye was, but we decided to get together

---

[1] Fannie Hardy Eckstorm and Mary Winslow Smyth, *Minstrelsy of Maine* (Boston and New York: Houghton Mifflin, 1927); William M. Doerflinger, *Shantymen and Shantyboys* (New York: Macmillan, 1951); Phillips Barry, *The Maine Woods Songster* (Cambridge: Powell Printing Co., 1939).
[2] James E. McKenna, Joseph R. McKenna, Peter A. McKenna. *The Sign of the Stag: A Chimera* (Orono, Maine: *Northeast Folklore* XXXII: 1997). The book is written in the first person of the Rev. Joseph McKenna.

at his place that Thursday night (December 13, 1956). On the way I picked up Mrs. Shields at her home in Bangor.

Bell had been born in Enmore, P.E.I., in 1887, but he came to Maine in the early 1900s and soon got a job at "The Eastern" pulp mill in South Brewer. In the years to follow he worked at many things, mostly in the local mills, though he had worked in the woods some and done a stretch in France in the First World War. He'd been retired since 1952 and was not in good health, having had "the darned asthma" for a number of years, but he sang over with some difficulty what he remembered of a couple of Gorman's songs. At one point, his sister spoke up. *"I was telling him on the way over," she said, "how when I was a youngster and folks would come to the house to visit, you know, and they always got Billy to sing. And most always they asked him to sing 'The *Cumberland's* Crew.' And I can remember how tortured I used to be when he used to sing that, and he'd come to the part 'Slowly they sank 'neath Virginia's dark waters.' And I could just see those poor things going down. I'd just sit there and cringe. I *despised* that song!"

I was curious. *"Do you know the song?" I asked.

*"Oh Lord yes," said Bell, "but it's as long as a sleigh track! I don't know as I can sing it. I've got this darned asthma 'til sometimes I'm kind of hoarsed up. I couldn't sing anyway, but—well, if I was good—"

I felt he really wanted to try. *"Can you—see if you can just sing me enough stanzas to give me the tune, and then just recite it?"

*"Well, if I was in good shape like I am sometimes I could, but see, I'm kind of hoarsed up." Even so, he began, and sailed right through that whole long ballad memorializing the sinking of the Union sloop-of-war *Cumberland* by the Confederate ironclad *Merrimac* off the Virginia shore in early 1862.

That was my first taste of a come-all-ye and of real traditional singing, and while I have heard many wonderful things in the years since that evening, none has been more wonderful than that. Things were quiet for a moment; then we expressed our approval. *"That's all right," said Mrs. Shields. "That doesn't make me grieve quite so much as it did when I was a young girl. Do you wonder," she added, turning to me, "when I was a child and used to have to listen to those old songs that I was scared to go up to bed without a light?"

We all laughed. *"Where did you learn that?" I asked.

*"Down P.I. about fifty years ago," he said. "Must be all of that. Yeah, it would have to be, because I was nineteen when I left there and for God's sake I'm seventy now!"

*"Was there much singing back on P.E.I?" I asked.

*"There was," said Mrs. Shields, "and there is."

The Cumberland's Crew

♩. = 40 approx.

Oh ship-mates, come ral-ly and join in my dit-ty Of a
ter-rr-ble bat-tle that hap-pened of late. Let each good Un-ion tar shed a
tear of sad pi-ty As they list to the once gal-lant *Cum-ber-land's* fate. On the
eighth day of March told this ter-rib-le sto-ry And ma-ny a tar to this
world bade a-dieu; But our flag it was wrapped in a
man-tle of glo-ry By the he-ro-ic deeds of the *Cum-ber-land* crew.

1.

Oh shipmates, come rally and join in my ditty
Of a terrible battle that happened of late.
Let each good Union tar shed a tear of sad pity
As they list to the once gallant *Cumberland's* fate.
On the eighth day of March told this terrible story,
And many a tar to this world bade adieu;
But our flag it was wrapped in a mantle of glory
By the heroic deeds of the *Cumberland* crew.

2.

On that ill-fated day about ten in the morning,
The sky it was clear and bright shone the sun;
The drums of the *Cumberland* sounded a warning,
Bidding each gallant seaman to stand by his gun.
An ironclad frigate down on us came bearing,
While high in the air her rebel flag flew;
A pennon of treason she proudly was waving,
Determined to conquer the *Cumberland* crew.

3.

Then up spoke our bold captain with stern resolution,
Saying, "Boys, of this monster do not be dismayed.
We are sworn to support our beloved Constitution,
And to die for our country we are not afraid.
We fight for our country, our cause it is glorious;
To the stars and the stripes we will ever stand true.
We'll die at our post, or we'll conquer victorious!"
Was answered with cheers from the *Cumberland* crew.

4.

Then our noble ship fired her guns' dreadful thunder,
Her broadsides like hail on the rebels did pour;
The sailors gazed on filled with terror and wonder,
For our shot struck her side and glanced harmlessly o'er.
But the pride of our Navy could never be daunted,
Though the dead and the dying our decks they did strew;
The flag of our Union how proudly she flaunted,
Sustained by the blood of the *Cumberland* crew.

5.

Three hours we fought them with stern resolution
'Til those rebels found cannon could never decide;
The flag of succession [*Secession*] had no power to gall them,
Though the blood from her scuppers it crimsoned the tide.
Then she struck us amidships, our planks she did sever,
Her sharp iron prong pierced our noble ship through;
But still as they sank 'neath the dark rolling waters,
"We'll die at our guns!" cried the *Cumberland* crew.

6.

Then slowly she sank 'neath Virginia's dark waters,
Their voices on Earth will ne'er be heard more;
They'll be wept by Columbia's brave sons and fair daughters—
May their blood be avenged on Virginia's shore.
In their battle-stained graves they are silently lying,
Their souls have forever to each bade adieu;
But the star-spangled banner above them was flying—
It was nailed to the mast by the *Cumberland* crew.

7.

Now Columbia's sweet birthright of freedom's communion—
Our flag never floated so proudly before;
The spirits of those who died for our Union
Above its broad folds now exaltingly soar.
And when our sailors in battle assemble—
God bless our dear banner, the red, white, and blue;
Beneath its broad folds we'll cause tyrants to tremble,
Or we'll die at our guns like the *Cumberland* crew.

*"That was the one amusement," said Bell. "If, years back—and I guess it's the same yet—if there was a bunch of people gathered into any house— you know, they didn't have much entertainment—and everybody was to help entertain. If he could sing a song he sang it. If he couldn't, he played the fiddle, and if somebody else couldn't sing or play the fiddle he'd get up and stepdance. And everybody had to do his bit."

That's the old "kaylee" or visiting tradition that goes right back to the old Irish *ceili* (or *ceilidh* in Scots Gaelic). I was to hear about it often in the years to come, and it had followed the Island families wherever they settled. It was the pattern in Brewer for a while, though it had fallen into disuse, and Bell hadn't sung much for the past twenty years or so. But "The *Cumberland's Crew*" had been his favourite song.

Bell's wife and Mrs. Shields went out in the kitchen to fix a lunch (another fixture, I was to learn, of any P.E.I. visit: it's always offered and you can't refuse), while Bell wanted to recite "The *Flying Cloud*" for me. I started to put on a new tape. "Oh the hell with that," he said, and started right off. He recited with the same pacing and sensitivity with which he sang. And once again, he'd learned that song, as he said, "down home."

Billy Bell was the first Islander I met, but actually Art Dalton's was the first letter I received in response to my *Bangor Daily News* letter. Someone had clipped it and sent it over to him in Rumford, and he got right to work on an answer, quoting bits of Gorman's songs and graces, suggesting people I should contact, and of course telling me that I simply had to go down to the Island. I was already planning a trip that summer, but meantime I knew I had to get over to Rumford and have a talk with this man.

The huge Oxford Paper Company mill dominated this western Maine town. It always has. In fact, that is why there's a town here at all, and that's what had drawn thousands of young Islanders here in the early years of this century. Even today there are whole PI neighbourhoods in the houses and tenements climbing the steep enclosing slopes leading down to the river. I marveled at the breakneck grade of Penobscot Street as I sought out Number 115, and that was my opening conversational gambit as I was ushered in by a cardigan-sweatered man in his late sixties with a vigourous handshake and a ready nervous laugh.

It was a dull January afternoon, and the little parlour, dominated as it was by a huge old upright piano with a fiddle case on top, seemed rather gloomy except for the dozen or so family photographs scattered around. But Dalton himself was anything but gloomy. He'd recently retired as a police sergeant. He'd left P.E.I. thirty-six years ago (about 1921) and had been on the Rumford police force for twenty-three years. *"I must know everybody," he said. "Good heavens yes! I'll go across the bridge to town over there, and I've got to keep looking over. If I don't I'll be waving with both hands. Everybody calls me by my first name and I don't know who the Sam Hill they are!"

Dalton was born in Burton, Lot Seven, P.E.I., and didn't leave until he was about twenty-five. Larry Gorman had left Lot Seven years before, but Dalton's father had known him well, having worked alongside him for years, and he'd told Art much about him. He was fascinated. *"His poetry rhymed so beautifully," he said. "That's why I remember so much of it. I always loved poetry, and anything that rhymed good, that's how I happened to remember as much as I did about it." He also remembered the parties where the old songs would be sung. *"Oh it was popular long ago," he said. "Everyone would sing that could sing. I remember in my young days going to dances. When the dance would stop, 'course there was always a big spread, all everything you could eat for all them to sit around and sing songs. Charlie Gorman, he was a great fella to sing. He knew all the old songs, you know, and he used to sing them."

What Dalton in fact remembered was bits of this and bits of that. I wondered did he know all of any song. *"The only one song that I remember is the one he [Gorman] made about the young fellas from Prince Edward Island, you know, when they weren't satisfied down there. I'll sing it as good as I can for you. And there'll be names in it. Sherlock and Clark, they were cobblers, you know, and the old-fashioned grips they used to have long ago, they called those kennebeckers." With that introduction he moved over to the piano and began to sing.

The Boys of the Island

1.
You sporting young fellows of Prince Edward Island,
Come listen to me and I'll tell you the truth;
From a lumberman's life it is my intention
To advise all young men and sensible youth.

2.
Now the boys on the Island on the farms are not happy;
They say, "Let us go; we are doing no good!"
Their minds are uneasy, continually crazy
For to get o'er to Bangor and work in the woods.
So a new suit of clothes is prepared for the journey,
A new pair of boots made by Sherlock or Clark,
A new kennebecker well stuffed with good homespun,
And then the young Islander, he will embark.

3.
He'll go o'er to Bangor and stand at the station —
The bushmen gaze on 'em all with a keen eye,
Saying, "Look at the clothes that young fellow is wearing,
And that will soon tell you he is a PI."
Then up in the woods, happy and contented,
Where God, man, and devil comes to them the same,
For rearing and tearing, cursing and blaspheming,
For kicking and fighting is the down-river game.

4.
In Bangor they'll poison the youth with bad whisky;
To the Devil they banish all brandy and ale,
And then on the corner they find the youth tipsy,
They'll send for Tim Leary and march him to jail.
They may talk of the laws of the mother of Moses,
I've seen better laws among heathen Chinee,
Where a man can get drunk and lay down and get sober
Beneath the deep shade of the mulberry tree.

Nothing in my past musical experience—not even Billy Bell—had prepared me for this. Here was a man singing at the top of his voice, his pitch frequently approximate, head thrown back and eyes closed as he held the high notes for all they were worth, and all to a larruping accompaniment on an untuned piano. Yet it was great. Listening to it years later I'm reminded of what the composer Charles Ives said of his father, a sometime choirmaster:

Once when Father was asked: "How can you stand it to hear old John Bell (who was the best stonemason in town) bellow off-key the way he does at camp-meetings?" his answer was: "Old John is a supreme musician. Look into his face and hear the music of the ages. Don't pay too much attention to the sounds. If you do, you may miss the music.

You won't get a heroic ride to Heaven on pretty little sounds!"[3]

Heaven would have to wait, and so, perhaps, would the garden behind the moon, but I would be on my way to Prince Edward Island as soon as school let out for the summer. I'd published a letter in *The Guardian* (Charlottetown) and responses were coming in from all over the Island, mostly from the west. The following from Mrs. Carrie Harris of Summerside is a fine sample, and a good way to close out this chapter:

> My brothers used to deal in oysters, growing the famous Malpeque Cup. [*They'd*] also buy and ship smelts and run two big lobster factories, so we always had a lot of men working who fished all summer and went away to the woods in the winter.
>
> One man was quite a long-winded singer and knew a great many songs, as Barbary Allen, The Burning Granite Mills, etc. I don't think he could read or write but learned the songs from others. We youngsters would coax and praise him, and finally he would put his elbows down on his knees, rest his head in his open hands, shut his eyes and start humming and swaying slightly. After he got his machinery warmed up, or at least got the proper pitch, he would go through a long song without pause. The men would all be lined up on benches in the cook house in their stocking feet, their heavy whole-stock leather knee-boots drying near the fire, the air so thick with smoke from the heavy old Island twist tobacco. They would all be still as mice, and when John had closed they would get up one by one and climb the stairs to their bunks, all relaxed. And it really was soothing to them after a hard day's work.

All signs pointed to a wonderful trip that would be rich in old songs, especially those that had been made by Larry Gorman. It was hard to wait until June. But, making a virtue of necessity, I somehow managed it.

---

[3] Henry Cowell and Sidney Robertson Cowell, *Charles Ives and His Music* (New York: Oxford University Press, 1955), p.24.

Nineteen Fifty-Seven

Big Jim[1]

"WELCOME TO P.E.I." read the sign I saw painted on a shed roof as the old *Abegweit* pulled into her slip that muggy misty Saturday in early June, and somehow—even through the excitement and apprehension of starting out on a new adventure—I *felt* welcomed.

I drove off the ferry. The sign up ahead offered two choices: Summerside to the left, Charlottetown to the right. Through both my letters to the Charlottetown *Guardian* and the Summerside *Journal-Pioneer* and the additional recommendations of Islanders in Maine, I already had a long list of people I wanted to see, and I knew almost all of them were "up west" well beyond Summerside, but there was this Mr. James Pendergast in Charlottetown who had seconded my *Guardian* letter with one of his own. "What Robert Burns was to Scotland, Larry Gorman was to Prince Edward Island," he had said, and he urged one and all to help me if they could. That letter had the ring of authority to it, and a number of my correspondents had obviously responded to it as much as they had to my own letter. Besides, he knew I was arriving and had offered hospitality. Therefore I headed for Charlottetown.

New Brunswick had been pretty much a continuation of Maine—woods with an occasional clearing—but what I was seeing along the TransCanada here on P.E.I. was completely different. Everything was under cultivation, with fields of fresh-plowed red earth alternating with the varied greens of new plantings, all separated by spruce hedgerows. I was coming quickly to understand that faraway look that came over Islanders in Maine when they talked about "Downhome."

One-seventy-one Dorchester Street. Mr. Pendergast (it was some time before I got around to calling him Jim) had sent me full instructions on how to reach his home, and I confess the approach shook me out of my euphoria. That part of Dorchester Street was not exactly the Prince Edward Island that gets shown on postcards, but here I was and there was nothing to do but go up on the porch and knock.

The door was already open, and through the screen I could see right down the long hall into the kitchen until that passage was blocked by the figure of

---

[1]The material in this section first appeared as an article, "Big Jim Pendergast As I Knew Him," in *The Island Magazine* 34 (Fall/Winter, 1993), pp. 28–33.

No. 7: James Pendergast at 89. *NA P758*. Photo taken March 31, 1968.

a man making his way slowly — and, it appeared, painfully — towards me with the aid of a cane. If he looks larger than life in my mind's eye now, that is because he *was* then. His shoulders filled that hallway, and it seemed an hour before he stood over me on the other side of the screen door. "Mr. Pendergast?" I said nervously.

"Yes," he said, in a voice that seemed to come from the bottom of a great barrel.

"I'm Edward Ives from Maine," I said, feeling somehow very callow and insignificant.

He said nothing for a moment or two as he beetled rather ferociously down on me in what was either incomprehension or disbelief; I wasn't sure which. Then he smiled or rather almost laughed outright. "Why," he boomed, "you're but a lad!" and immediately demanded me in, calling for his wife, who came from the kitchen with that wonderfully hospitable gesture — wiping her hands on her apron. And suddenly I felt very welcome indeed. "You're but a lad," he repeated with delight, and I must say that phrase defined our relationship for quite some time — at least as it looked from my side. In his presence I felt but a lad.

I was shown to my room on the third floor, and fifteen minutes later I was seated at supper with son Reggie and two boarders: Vic, who liked to talk, and Amby, who didn't.

As soon as the dishes were cleared, though, Jim looked over at me. "Well, come on there, young fella," he boomed. "Go up and get on your best bib and tucker. We're going to visit some of the split-tailed aristocracy of this town!"

I wasn't at all sure what that meant, and it never occurred to me to ask. I simply went up, put on a necktie and jacket, and reported below. With that stiff leg, we had a terrible time getting him established in the front seat of my old Studebaker, but we finally managed it, and off we went on our adventure. My mouth was dry.

After taking me to meet Frank Walker, Editor of *The Guardian*, Jim directed me to Victoria Park, although I didn't know at the time that that's what it was. I only knew that it was green and official-looking, and Jim's instructions were bringing me closer and closer to the big house that clearly dominated it. We pulled up in front. "That's Government House," said Jim. "Just go up there and tell the Lieutenant Governor that Jim Pendergast is out here and wants to see him."

I sat there in a state of shock. I could no more imagine myself doing what Jim had just suggested than I could see myself slapping Prince Philip jovially on the back. I must have looked at him in disbelief. "Go on," he said. "I know he's in there."

At that point, I would have seen it as a blessing had he not been, but I started nervously up the steps. I should say that in all my memories of that scene, there are at least twenty steps leading to the front door, but when I went to a reception there in 1986 I did a reality check and found there were only one or two at the most. Somehow I reached the door and rang the bell. A lady appeared, obviously dressed to go out. I don't know what I said, but she smiled very pleasantly and told me when tours of the house were scheduled.

"No, no," I said, conscious that I had not been clear. "It's that there's— well, you see, there's a Mr. Pendergast out in the car and he can't get out and he wants to see the Lieutenant Governor."

She looked out at the car. "Oh, yes," she said. "Well, just a minute." And she disappeared inside.

In less than a minute, Lieutenant Governor Prowse himself appeared. "You say Jim Pendergast is here?" he said to me.

I motioned toward the car, and he bounced jauntily down the walk. "Hello there, Jim," he said cheerfully, and the next thing I knew the two of them were deep in conversation.

"Would you like to see the house while they're talking?" asked Mrs. Prowse. Under the circumstances, it seemed like a good idea, so off we went on a tour.

Ten minutes later the two men were still talking, but Jim motioned for me to join them. He had obviously explained with great enthusiasm what I was about, and there was a big shake-hands all around while His Honour assured me that if Jim Pendergast said I was all right that was plenty good enough for him. "And let me tell you," he said, "you've got the right man helping you!" If I had had any doubts about that, I was well on my way to shedding them now, as we drove back into town.

"It's early yet," said Jim, "and there's someone else you really ought to see." He directed me to Beach Grove Inn, an old men's home, where he wanted me to meet and talk with Tom Gorman, one of Larry's surviving nephews. "Go on in," he said. "I'll just wait here in the car." He sensed my reluctance to leave him alone. "Go ahead," he said. "Don't worry about me. It's just too much trouble with this leg to get in and out. I'll be all right."

I went in, found Tom Gorman, and had a good talk with him. When I came out again half an hour later, I found maybe half a dozen elderly men standing around the car talking and laughing. One of them struck a pugilistic pose and apparently floored an imaginary opponent. "Yes, yes," said Jim good-naturedly, "but we've got to be on our way now," and waved the crowd back. Just before we left, though, a very small man in carpet slippers shuffled up. "Do you remember me, Mr. Pendergast?" he said doubtfully. "I used to watch you train."

Jim looked at him for a minute. "Why, you're little Butler (I think that was the name), aren't you? Yes, yes," he said, to the man's clear delight. They talked for a minute, and then we left.

He wanted to know how my talk with Tom Gorman had gone. "Did he remember any of the songs?" he asked.

"He didn't sing any," I said, "but he worded over some of 'The Horse's Confession' for me."

"Ohh, goodness," he chuckled and started to sing a few bars of it for me in his unmistakable barreltone bass. "Did he mention 'Bachelor's Hall' or 'The Gull Decoy'?"

"He knew of them," I said, "but he didn't know them. Do you know them?"

"Just little sketches of them, that's all."

"Well," I asked, "would you sing me over what you do know when we get home?"

"Oh heavens," he laughed. "You'll find all kinds of people who know them up in West Prince. All kinds of people."

I accepted his evasion but made a note to get back to this matter later on. Meanwhile, I was curious about the little tableau I had seen. "Those guys around the car," I said. "What was that all about? You done some fighting or something?"

"Ohhh, yes," he said diffidently, "way back there I did." He chuckled. "Actually, I'm sort of a minor celebrity around these parts. Now, turn right here." And that was all I got on that subject for many years, although over and over again I was to hear stories of Big Jim's tremendous strength and fistic skill, along with some business of his having been a possible White Hope back in the Jack Johnson days. One of the last times I saw him I asked about this. "Well," he said, looking down his nose, "that's something of an exaggeration." But back to my story.

Once we returned home, I reminded him about singing over what he knew of the Gorman songs he'd mentioned in the car, and, after a spate of good-natured demurral on his part and an equal amount of good-natured coaxing on mine—in which I was joined by both Mrs. P. and son Reggie— he agreed to give it a try. I went out to the car to get my tape recorder.

Keep in mind the year was 1957, and the tape recorder I lugged around was a big Webcor reel-to-reel unit that probably weighed forty pounds, not one of the little back-pocket, battery-powered affairs we're all familiar with today. I wasn't to see my first one of those for almost ten years. Worse yet, the Webcor was cranky, and I'd had trouble with it the previous day. I muttered a prayer as I horsed it into the living room.

Everything went well, and, just as he said, he only knew sketches of

Gorman's songs, but he sang enough so I could get the tunes for three of them. After this, we went into the kitchen for a glass of milk, and then off to bed.

The next day, being Sunday, was quiet. The real fun began on Monday when the two of us headed off to West Prince. That "two of us" rather surprised me at first. Jim had given me no end of names of people that I should go see, and I assumed that when I left Charlottetown I'd go see them and that would be that. But there he came out the door, suitcase in hand, hat on head, ready for travel. I should say right here that up to that point I'd always worked alone, and I'd come to prefer it that way, but it was clear that wasn't the way it was going to be for a while. How long I didn't know, but I'd begun to learn to take things as they come, and I had to admit that up to now they had come very interestingly, for sure.

We headed west down the road, stopping to visit for a while with Austin Trainor. He knew nothing about Gorman, but he was the first person to tell me about another poet, "Jinglin' Johnny" LePage. Then, after stopping off to see a priest Jim knew, he gave me directions to the Kensington home of Mrs. Alphonse Connell, who had written me some months before that she knew one of Gorman's songs and to please come see her when I came to the Island. I went up and knocked on the door, and when she heard who I was and who was with me she immediately asked us in. "You go ahead," Jim said, "and I'll come along, once I get myself out of the car."

We went on ahead into the living room, and I started to ask Mrs. Connell about the song she had said she knew, but before we had even got seated, a short, stocky, elderly man with a modified walrus mustache came bounding into the room (bounding—there is no other word for it!). "Who was the best man here before you came?" he demanded of me ferociously, and before I could answer he started dancing around, making John L. Sullivan passes at me in the nearby air.

I did the best I could. "Why, you were, sir," I said unimaginatively.

"Damn right," he said, continuing his mock attack. Then he leapt into the air. "Life begins at eighty!" he shouted.

"Oh, Alphonse," said Mrs. Connell deprecatingly.

"It's the truth," he said, "'cause I'm eighty-eight, and they can't find a man in town to fight me! Did I hear that Jim Pendergast was here?"

"Yes," I said. "He's out in the car." And he went out, caroming off wall and doorjamb and projecting himself down the kitchen steps in a way that clearly concerned his wife as much if not more than it did me. "He's nearly blind, you know," she said. We followed at a more conservative pace.

Jim, who was extricating himself from the car, suddenly found himself under severe attack, and he responded in kind. It was quite a scene, like a bantycock worriting a bull, but there was so much shouting and leaping into the air and wheeing on Al's part, and so much snorting and good-natured bellowing and fending off on Jim's, that I despaired of any chance to talk to Mrs. Connell about Gorman or his songs. Things quieted down after a bit, and we all went in the house for tea, after which Mrs. Connell went over the song she'd written me about (it wasn't one of Gorman's, by the way). Then Al decided this was the perfect opportunity to rehearse the piece he was going to recite at the party they were going to that evening, so he went through the whole of "The True Lovers' Discussion," complete with appropriate gestures. I wasn't much interested in recitations at that time. In fact, I erased my recording of it that evening, but as I look back now, I have to say he did a damn good job of it.

Jim and I were getting ready to leave for Tyne Valley when Mrs. Connell asked if I knew where the old Gorman place had been there. I said no, and she started to give me directions. Then she had a better idea. "Alphonse knows right where it is," she said. "He could show you."

"Why, sure," said Jim. "And he could help me think of people we ought to go see."

I can't say I was charmed with the prospect. As I said earlier on, I was used to working alone. I also knew I had just so much time, and I wanted to get back on the schedule I had set for myself. I foresaw the whole thing turning into a kind of rolling reunion for my companions, in which everyone would have a wonderful time but I would get little done that was to the point. In brief, I was young and impatient, but once again I made a virtue of necessity, since there wasn't anything much I could do about it anyway. Al went for his hat, and with one more "Life begins at eighty!" we were on our way — the two of them plotting in the back seat, and me up front driving and, I'm afraid, seething over inwardly as we headed for Tyne Valley.

But first we had to stop and see Frank Sweet in St. Eleanors, who, after hearty greetings and backslappings said he didn't know much himself but thought we'd probably get something from Jacob Murray. "He's Old Jake's son, you know," he added significantly, and the others agreed that was a good idea. He turned to me. "I *used* to know some of them pieces," he said. "Stop back sometime. Maybe I can think of them." I said I would, and we were on our way again.

We stopped in half a dozen more places that afternoon. It's hard to remember them separately, but the pattern was constant. I'd be told who this was and to go knock at the kitchen door. Once I'd stated my business, Al would come along and we'd go through the who-was-the-best-man-before-he-came business. Then Jim would appear, and everyone was so overjoyed to see him that Larry Gorman would be amiably forgotten, though in every case I made a point to say I'd be back in a week or so. "Life begins at eighty!" Al would say, and we'd be off to the next place. It was eight o'clock before we headed back down the Western Road.

But then Al thought of someone. "Maybe we ought to stop and see Linus McNeill," he said.

"Why, I hadn't thought of him at all," said Jim, "and he was a lovely singer. Or was it his father? But it's just a little ways off the road. Here," said Jim to me, "turn right just beyond that store." As usual, I did as I was told.

We found Linus out in the barn, where he was washing his hands after chores. He was a big friendly man, glad to see old friends, and when Al started his shadow boxing he called him The Iron Man and even sparred with him briefly. "He's quite a lad, eh?" he said to me, laughing, and I said yes he was indeed quite a lad. But when Jim asked about songs ("We're doing some research," he'd always say), "No," Linus said, "that was my father. He knew all them songs like that 'Gull Decoy.' That was one of his favourites. But I never learned them." So after he and Al had another brief spar we were back on the road.

We got Al to his party late, but we got him there, and I assume his "True Lovers' Discussion" was the hit of the evening. Jim and I went to his son Austin's down the road, where we had a late supper and called it a day.

There is no need to describe the next couple of days, as Jim introduced me to this person and that. I won't try to tell you I didn't get fiercely impatient at times, but I had several weeks on my own to discover what a great introduction I had had to Larry Gorman's native country. Over and over it was, "Oh, you're that fella was with Jim Pendergast, aren't you?" Or if I mentioned his name, "Oh, *Jim*," they'd say, and likely I'd get some story of how he had lifted a huge anchor that no one else could budge. Everyone either knew him or knew of him, and my association with him had done a great deal to make me *persona grata* wherever I went in West Prince.

All very well. But where were all the Gorman songs I was supposed to find? "Oh heavens, you'll find all kinds of people who know them up in West Prince," Jim had assured me. "All *kinds* of people." But it wasn't working out that way. I was enjoying my visits, but as for songs it was a fragment of this one here, a bit of that one there, and that was about it. Truth to tell, I was getting a bit downhearted as each interview seemed less productive than the one before. No question about it, I could use a change of luck.

A Long Grey Day

Saturday, June 22, 1957, and the day before I had driven to Borden to pick up my wife Bobby and our son Steve, both of whom had just come up from Bangor on the train. Needless to say we were all pretty well played out by the time we got back to the cabin I had recently rented for us on Mill River, and we were looking forward to a good night's sleep. Certainly Bobby was; she was seven months pregnant and hadn't slept since the train left Bangor at three that morning. I'd been on the go here and there around the west end since early morning myself. Besides which, it had begun to rain.

It was still raining at four-thirty in the morning, which was when Steve woke up, and since he was making it perfectly obvious in his four-year-old way that he wasn't interested either in going back to sleep or in playing quietly by himself, there was nothing for it but to get up and start what promised to be a long grey day. We had a leisurely breakfast, unpacked properly, and went for a walk in the rain along the bluffs by the river, after which I alternately roughhoused with Steve and typed up some notes, until my suburban work ethic told me it was well past time to get going. Bobby packed me a sandwich (eateries of any kind were scarce on the ground in West Prince at the time), and I headed back down the Western Road to Tyne Valley, the town where Gorman had been born.

To begin, I had four people I wanted to follow up with. A check at the Northam post office told me that one was in the Charlottetown hospital, another had died, while a third lived over in Victoria West, about five miles away. My drive over there took me through some of the prettiest country I'd seen in West Prince, but the gentleman had gone to Maine to visit family there. That left me a Mrs. Ellis of Tyne Valley. When I asked at the gas station where she lived, the attendant pointed with the hose. "That's her house right over there, but she ain't in now and don't think she ever will be. Gone to Moncton to live with her son." So far, it hadn't been much of a morning. Clearly, my luck wasn't changing. And it was still raining.

I pulled off the side of the road and considered what to do next. I had plenty of prospects, but all of them involved considerable driving up or down the Western Road. On the other hand, someone the day before had recommended a Mrs. John Coughlin of Ellerslie as someone who "knew a lot of that stuff," particularly a Gorman song known as "The Arlington Maid," and since Ellerslie was only a few miles away I decided to call on her now. But it was about noon, so I ate Bobby's sandwich and, for obvious reasons, took myself a short nap.

Having gotten directions at the general store, I drove into the yard and apprehensively hailed a man who was just coming down the back steps. "Excuse me," I said, "but I'm looking for the John Coughlin place."

"I'm John Coughlin," he said, looking at my license plate. "How can I help you?"

"Well, actually I'm looking for *Mrs.* John Coughlin," I said, and told him what it was I was after.

No. 8: River-drivers working to break a jam. The man in the bow is holding the batteau ready for the drivers to escape when the jam hauls, while the stern man holds it steady in the current. *NA P344.*

He laughed. "That'd be her all right. Come on in." And he led the way.

She was a much younger woman than I had expected—maybe fifty at the most—which only means that up to then I hadn't been talking to anyone younger than seventy. Her husband explained my mission. She knew what I was looking for but didn't think she could be much help. "I just know little sketches of this one and that one," she said.

"How about 'The Arlington Maid'?" I asked. Yes, she said, and recited a couple of stanzas. Did she know the tune? She did, and sang it over.

I looked around. There was no electricity, so I tried writing it out in sol-fa, getting her to repeat each phrase over and over. It was slow work, but she obviously wanted to help and was very patient—far more patient than I was, for sure—as I botched phrase after phrase and had to get her to try again. It was a great idea, but both of us saw it wasn't working very well. "Too bad I can't use my tape recorder," I said at last. "Does anyone in the neighbourhood have electricity?"

"Well why don't we just go across to McKinnons?" she said, getting up and putting on her sweater. "They've got the electricity over there, and I'm sure they wouldn't mind."

Since it was raining hard again we drove across the road and under the breezeway of the McKinnons' new house. Mrs. Coughlin went in first, then motioned to me to come ahead. Mrs. McKinnon, a beautiful woman, ushered us into the dining room, showed me where the wall outlet was, and then went about shushing and shooing the passel of kids in the living room who began to crowd around as I set the Webcor up on the floor.

Mrs. Coughlin recited and sang over the Gorman pieces she recalled, but since that only took about ten minutes I asked about other songs, naming a few. When I asked about the well-known woods song, "The Jam on Gerry's Rock," she said yes, she was pretty sure she knew that. Would she sing it for me, I asked? "It goes something like this. Now I can't sing at all in the first place, but—." And she began.

The Jam on Gerry's Rock

1.

Come all of ye brave shantyboys and list while I relate,
Concerning a young river man and his untimely fate,
Concerning a young river man so manfully and brave,
While breaking a jam on Gerry's Rock he met with a watery grave.

♩ = 104

2. It be-ing on a Sun-day, all on the sixth of May, The logs were roll-ing moun-tains high, we could not keep them a-way. "Turn out, turn out," our fore-man cried, with a heart that knew no fear. "We'll break the jam on Ger-ry's Rock and for Ev-ans Point we'll steer."

2

It being on a Sunday, all on the sixth of May,
The logs were rolling mountains high, we could not keep them away.
"Turn out, turn out!" our foreman cried, with a heart that knew no fear,
"We'll break the jam on Gerry's Rock and for Evans Point we'll steer."

3.

Oh some of them were willing, while others they were not;
For to work all on a Sunday they did not think they ought.
'Til six of our brave shantyboys did volunteer to go
To break the jam on Gerry's Rock with the foreman young Monroe.

4.

They had not rolled off many logs when the boss to them did say,
"I would have you boys be on your guard, for the jam will soon give way."
Those words were scarcely spoken when the jam did give and go.
It carried away those six brave men with their foreman young Monroe.

5.

Oh, when the comrades at the camp the sad news came to hear,
To search for their dead bodies to the river did appear;
To search for their dead bodies in sorrow, grief and woe—
All cut and mangled on the beach lay the body of young Monroe.

6.

We picked him up most carefully, smoothed back his raven hair.
They were a fair form among them whose cries did rend the air.
They were a fair form among them, a girl from Sackville town,
Whose shrieks and cries did rend the skies, for her true love had gone down.

7.

Miss Clara was a noble girl, this river man's true friend;
She dwelt with her aged mother down by the ocean bend.
The wages of her own true love the boss to them did pay,
And a generous collection she received from the shantyboys next day.

8.
But not to her enjoyment, she did not enjoy it long,
For in less than three weeks after, she was called to go,
And her dying words were to be buried by the side of young Monroe.

9.
Now come all of ye who passes by, I would have you call and see:
There's a little grave by the riverside, there grows a hemlock tree,
Where the shantyboys cut the woods all down, two lovers they laid low;
It's that Miss Clara Dimmassee and her true love Jack Monroe.

In spite of her modest disclaimer, Mrs. Coughlin definitely *could* sing, and sing damn well. I wanted to hear more, but while the McKinnon audience was interested I wasn't sure how long that interest would hold; it *was* a rainy day, and, after all, it *was* their house. Still, I wondered about maybe one more song. There was one I always hoped I'd find but so far hadn't—a rather mysterious one about a lover called back from the dead. I chanced it. "Have you ever heard 'The Lost Jimmy Whalen'?"

"Yes," she said, "and I think I know the whole of that."

"Would you sing it for me?"

She laughed, and then came the disclaimer again. "I can't sing," she said. "Never could. But I guess I can give you the air." And she started in.

What followed was beautiful. It didn't matter that she interrupted herself after the second stanza or that she bobbled the end of one line. Her voice merged with the song to create that brief presence I can only describe as high art, and it's best I don't try to say any more.

It was time to quit. The McKinnon children had been wonderfully quiet, but since I didn't want to push either my luck or theirs, I packed up the Webcor and drove Mrs. Coughlin home, planning to get together with her again before too long. But it seems that something always pre-empted me. I never got back, and I have had forty years to regret it. Even today her singing of "The Lost Jimmy Whalen" can bring tears to my eyes.

The Lost Jimmy Whalen

1.
Slowly as I strayed by the banks of the river
A-viewing those roses as evening drew nigh;
As onward I rambled I espied a fair damsel,
She was weeping and wailing with many a sigh.

2.
She was weeping for one that was now lying lonely,
Weeping for one that no mortal can save;
For the dark rolling waters lie slowly around him,
As onward they speed over young Jimmy's grave.

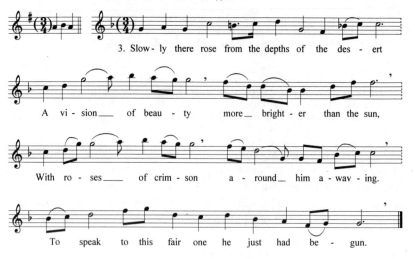

Parlando rubato ♩ = 80 approx.

3. Slow- ly there rose from the depths of the des - ert
A vi - sion___ of beau - ty more___ bright - er than the sun,
With ro - ses___ of crim - son a - round___ him a - wav - ing.
To speak to this fair one he just had be - gun.

*"There!" she said. "Is that enough to give you the tune?"

I had been so deeply into her singing that I was a little shaken by her breaking off. *"Oh," I said, "I wish you'd finish it."

She laughed. *"Oh, I never could—"

*"That's just beautiful," I said, "that's just—"

And she went on.

3.

Slowly there rose from the depths of the desert
A vision of beauty more brighter than the sun,
With roses of crimson around him a-waving.
To speak to this fair one he just had begun.

4.

"Why do you call me from red-lums [*realms*] of glory
Back to this wide world I no longer can stay;
To embrace you once more in my strong loving arms,
To see you once more I have come from my grave."

5.

"Darling," she said, "won't you bury me with you?
Do not desert me to weep and to mourn,
But take me, oh, take me along with you, Jimmy,
To sleep with you down in your cold silent tomb."

6.

"Darling," he said, "you are asking a favour
That no mortal person can grant unto thee,
For deep is the desert that parts us asunder—
Wide is the gulf lies between you and me.

7.

"But as you do wander by the banks of this river,
I will ever be near thee to keep and to guide;
My spirit will guide you and keep from all danger.
I'll guide you along from my cold silent grave."

8.

She threw herself down and she wept bitterly;
In the deepest of anguish those words she did say:
"Oh, you are my darling, my lost Jimmy Whalen;
I will sigh 'til I die by the side of your grave."

The rain had let up some, or maybe I just thought it had. I bought a bottle of root beer in the little store in Tyne Valley and, after reconnoitering both my list of names and the map, I decided to head over to Grand River to check some church records. In Gorman's time, St. Patrick's would have been the only Catholic church near enough Tyne Valley for the family to attend. If there were going to be any local Gorman records, that's where they'd most likely be. Unfortunately, that's where they weren't. Though we searched for well over an hour, neither the parish priest nor I could find a thing. As I went out to the car, it seemed to me the rain had picked up again, but perhaps it was just my disappointment. I'd been *sure* there'd be something at St. Patrick's.

The afternoon was wearing on, and I thought about heading home to Mill River, when it occurred to me that less than a week ago while trooping with Big Jim and Al we had stopped at a farm here in Grand River to see a Mrs. Cyrene McLellan, and she had said she knew one of Gorman's songs. Of course she couldn't have sung it with all the wheeing and hooraw going on then, but the farm couldn't be far from where I was at the moment, and I even thought I remembered the way. However, when I drove past the Northam post office for the second time, it was clear that I didn't. I went back to where I could see St. Patrick's Church and started over, finally stopping a boy riding by on a bike. "Can you tell me where I can find Mrs. Cyrene McLellan?" I asked, and he pointed down the road about two hundred yards. "That one on the right," he said.

I drove into the farmyard, scattering chickens and piglets galore as I reached the house. The dog woofed me furiously, but in a very friendly way, so I got out and approached the door. I saw there were no electric or phone lines leading in.

Oh well. . . .

Mrs. McLellan remembered me, and I was ushered into the hot kitchen, where everyone else was. Her husband, who had had a bad accident with his potato picker the fall before, sat painfully by the stove. The son-in-law, who had been sound asleep on the couch, tried to rouse himself enough to say hello, then lay back down again, while his wife was preparing tea for all hands.

Mrs. McLellan went back to what she had been doing, which was ironing. I'd never seen anyone do that with irons heated on the stove before, and I said so. She laughed. "You probably have a maid at home," she said. I assured her we did not.

Soon tea was ready, and the men sat down to it. I hesitated for a moment, still not entirely used to the idea that the women didn't sit down until everyone had been served. Less than a month before over in New Brunswick I had tried to wait and pull out a woman's chair at the table. I think she thought I'd gone mad. This time I simply sat myself down to a table laden with fresh bread, rolls, jam, cookies, jelly roll, two kinds of cake, pickles, poached eggs, cheese, and finally tea—dark, of course, and strong. Nothing elaborate, to be sure—just your ordinary country spread.

Inevitably, by way of everyone laughing about my previous visit with Jim and Al, the talk went to how was I making out. I said I was really just getting started, having had to find a place for my family and all, but I mentioned Mrs. Coughlin and ticked off the names of people I planned to see as soon as I could. They recognized each one ("Yes, he'd be good". . . "She'd know because. . .") and made a suggestion or two of their own, which I duly noted down. Then, as the table was being cleared, I got to work. "Didn't you say you remembered one of Gorman's songs yourself? Which one?" I asked.

"Oh, that was 'Bachelor's Hall,'" she said. "But a lot of people know that."

"Well, would you sing it for me?" I asked eagerly, and, after the traditional demurrals on her part about not really being able to sing, and the equally traditional coaxing on my part that I wish she'd try it, she sat down in a rocking chair, folded her hands in her lap, and sang—very pleasantly and very well—by far the most complete version of that song I had heard or read anywhere.

There was a general murmur of approval when she finished. "That was great," I said, "and I'd like to get that for my book. Is there a neighbour who has the electricity so I could record it? That way I wouldn't have to make you go over and over it while I write it down. And I could get the air, too."

Again demurrals, and again coaxing, in which I was enthusiastically joined by the daughter, who suggested we could go down to Linus MacDonald's in Richmond. "He takes in tourists," she explained, "and he had the electricity put in not long ago."

Mrs. McLellan gave in, not too reluctantly, it seemed to me, but she insisted on changing her dress first. A few minutes later we were on our way, and the daughter joined us.

The sign out by the road said "Dew Drop Inn/ Tourists." Mr. MacDonald ushered us into the parlour, and, after hearty introductions, I explained my mission. His face clouded a bit at the mention of Larry Gorman. "Well, now," he said, "the way I see it, every song Larry Gorman made up was an insult to somebody. Now you take that 'Peter Emberly,' for instance," he said. "Why, you see, he was just insulting Peter's father there. He shouldn't have done that." I had a moment of concern that he wouldn't let a Gorman song be sung in his house (I'd heard of such things), but then he brightened. "Just the same," he said, "it's too bad to have all those old songs just be forgotten," and he indicated we should get on with our business, which is what we did.

Just as she had done at home, Mrs. McLellan set herself down in a rocker, folded her hands in her lap, and sang. It was not an exciting voice like Mrs. Coughlin's had been, but it was clear and steady. And the song was a good one, vintage Gorman, satirizing a man who paraded a list of over fifty desirable household items—some say in a local newspaper!—in hopes of attracting a wife. It was the kind of topic Gorman did up to perfection. White sand, by the way, was a sweeping and scrubbing compound, hard to come by on this red-clay island.

Bachelor's Hall

♩. = 60

1. Young la-dies all, both short, fat and tall, On me you will sure-ly take pi-ty, For a bach-el-or's hall is no place at all, And the same I'll ex-plain in my dit-ty.

1.
Young ladies all, both short, fat, and tall,
On me you will surely take pity,
For a bachelor's hall is no place at all
And the same I'll explain in my ditty.

2.
Folks boast of a life without any wife
They tell you it would be much cheaper;
And you they'll persuade the great riches they made
By hiring a frugal housekeeper.

3.
But that's all a hoax, all those silly folk,
Their outlays are much more extensive;
And their story don't believe for they did me deceive,
And I find that it's much more expensive.

4.

If you'll listen to me or just come and see,
I'm well fitted out for housekeeping;
And the angels of love that flew as a dove
To my bedside they nightly come creeping.

5.

So now, imps divine, if you'll only be mine,
Or just take a look at my welfare;
And if you say no, it's away I will go
In order to seek a wife elsewhere.

6.[2]

[Some folks of this day will disdainfully say
Self-praise is no recommendation;
But my houses and land as you understand
Are opposite Northam flag station.

7.

I have harrows and plows, I have sheep, I have cows,
And they're a stock that I take a great pride in;
I have ten-gallon kegs all chock full of eggs,
A horse and a carriage to ride in.]

8.

I've a comb and a glass, both mounted with brass,
Some soap, a towel, and two brushes;
My mirror will show from the top to the toe,
And a mattress made out of bulrushes.

9.

I have two iron steads, I have two feather beds,
Some blankets, some quilts, and two pillows;
I have two hives of bees, I have many fruit trees,
And for ornaments two weeping willows.

10.

I've a hen and a cock, I've a stove and a clock,
I have turkeys and geese by the dozen;
I've a cat and a dog and a two-hundred hog
That I purchased last spring from my cousin.

11.

I have salt and fresh meats, I have cabbage and beets,
I've a large carving knife for the table;
Cups, saucers, and bowls, and new candle molds,
I've a frying pan, saucepan, and ladle.

12.

And a box of white sand I keep always on hand,
All packed away safe for the winter;
I've a broom and a mop to wipe every slop,
In your fingers you'll ne'er get a splinter.

---

[2]I have interpolated stanzas 6 and 7 from an earlier singing by Jim Pendergast.

13.

My story don't doubt, I'm well fitted out,
My house is both papered and plastered;
I have knives, I have forks, I have bottles and corks,
I've a lamp and a new pepper caster.

14.

But the best of all yet is my new chamber set,
My two sweet canaries in cages;
I've a bowl and a jug and another large mug
With the gilded flowers all round the edges.

15.

In the summer so gay you can see every day
My lambkins so nimbly sporting;
And the fierce iron horse with its serpentine course
You will see it go by my door snorting.

16.

I have a large farm, I've a house and a barn,
And a rich patch for rising tomatoes;
And I spared no expense in building a fence
For to keep the hogs from my potatoes.

17.

And so now, imps divine, if you'll only be mine
Or just take a look at my welfare;
And if you say no, it's away I will go
In order to seek a wife elsewhere.

18.

So now, ladies all, come each when I call,
Come Peggy, come Betsy, come Nancy;
When I see you all, both short, fat and tall,
I will surely see one that I fancy.

"You see now," said MacDonald triumphantly, "it's just like I said. Gorman was just insulting the man with that song." None of us chose to argue the point. "But lookit," he added, "would it be all right if I recited a poem on there?" He pointed at the recorder.

"Of course," I said, without any great enthusiasm, turning the machine back on. "Give her the works." And he did.

Oh why should the spirit of mortal be proud?
Like a swift fleeting meteor, a fast flying cloud,
A flash of the lightning or a break of the wave,
Man passes from life to his rest in the grave.

He recited slowly with appropriate preacher tone, significant gestures and pauses, and faraway gaze. At the time I looked on recitations as the sort of thing that had to be politely endured in hopes of "good stuff" like songs that might follow, but even then I suspicioned this might be a pretty snobbish and unproductive attitude for someone trying to be a folklorist. Anyhow, I was beginning to enjoy his performance, when suddenly he waved impatiently at the recorder and stopped in mid-verse. I shut down. "I forget," he said, shaking his head apologetically. No, he didn't want to try again. That was it. A little sadly, I packed up the Webcor, and we left.

Back at the farm I was of course invited in again, but it was getting dark and I thought I really ought to be getting back to Mill River. "Just wait a minute," Mrs. McLellan said, and went in, reappearing a moment later with a loaf of homemade bread, a bag of cookies, some rolls and a dozen eggs fresh from under the hen. "Take these home to your wife," she said, "so she won't feel she isn't among friends here."

It was still raining as I made my way up the Western Road. It had been a long grey day for sure, but without any question the most productive I'd put in yet: one Gorman song entire, fragments of three others (one with its air), and two fine old come-all-ye's sung with authority and power. Perhaps my luck *was* changing.

But something else was changing too. Up to now I had tended to think of fieldwork as "getting," a raiding of sorts in which I rescued items of value from almost certain oblivion. Today I felt that what I had received had not been so much "gotten" by me as given, and given very generously, by people whose only reward was the pleasure of sharing. I liked that way of looking at fieldwork.

I munched on one or two of Mrs. McLellan's cookies. In a little while I'd be at Mill River with my family, ready (Stephen willing) for a good night's sleep. Surely we were among friends.

Lot Seven To Miminegash: A Week Along The Shore

Monday, June 24

"KEITH PRATT, *General Merchant.* Shipper of Eggs, Blueberries, Pulpwood, and Irish Moss," the letterhead had announced, and the Red Ensign was displayed prominently in the upper left corner. He had written me some months before to say that while he himself was far too young to know much about Gorman, if I'd call at his store he'd direct me to some old-timers who should know a great deal.

I found his place easily, the storefront sign in Bloomfield Station being just as informative as his letterhead, and, as customers came and went, we spent about an hour talking about how I was doing.

"Have you seen Charlie Gorman yet?" he asked, and when I said I hadn't he gave me careful instructions on how to find him. "Henry Dalton and his family are living with him now," he added.

"How about Harry Thompson? He was in the other day and wondered if you were around yet."

"Maybe you'd better give me directions there, too," I said.

He did. "Now, has anybody mentioned Tommy Doyle to you?"

"No," I said. "Is he somebody I should see?"

"I don't know," he said. "He's pretty old—he must be nearly a hundred—and I heard the other day he wasn't well at all. But they say he and Larry Gorman were good friends. It wouldn't hurt to stop by. A couple of his daughters are home taking care of him." Again, I got careful directions.

On leaving the store, I headed for Harry Thompson's in Glengarry and quickly got lost. How that was possible with all those directions it's hard for me to understand now, but I had no idea where I was. Next thing I knew I was in O'Leary, and since O'Leary had the only restaurant for miles around I cleverly adapted to circumstances and had some lunch while I re-examined Keith Pratt's excellent map. Since my best and nearest bet now appeared to be to find Charlie Gorman and save Harry Thompson for tomorrow, I headed off for Burton on the Shore Road, and there—just a short distance beyond St. Mark's Church—was the house I was looking for.

I had written several months before about my planned trip, and he had replied that while he'd be glad to talk with me he didn't think he could be much help. I'd often heard that the family had disliked Larry—wouldn't even talk about him—and I wondered if that was his way of politely turning me off. Yet his brother Tom had seemed open enough with me. . . . At any rate, here I was, and I turned into the long lane leading up to the farmyard.

Being up on quite a rise, the house had a splendid view of Northumberland Strait. I knocked on the door, and a Mrs. Dalton ushered me into the kitchen, where Charlie—a tall, slight, bespectacled retired farmer in his early eighties—was waiting. He greeted me warmly, and since there was a fair amount of bustle in the kitchen, he suggested we move into the nearby parlour.

"Now Mr. Ives," he began, "you probably know that my father didn't approve of Uncle Larry. He wouldn't let us kids sing his songs in the house, and so I never cared much for him either. You can understand how it was; we had to live with these people Uncle Larry had songed, while he was down in Maine by that time. But that's all right now. I'll tell you all I know and won't keep anything back." That pretty well defined our relationship. We liked each other immediately and talked very pleasantly for about two hours. I tried to get him to sing over the bits of Gorman songs he knew, but there he drew the line, and since there was no electricity for my tape recorder I didn't push. "I never could sing anyhow," he said, and I let it go at that, but I was rather conscious of the fact that as a would-be "collector" I hadn't collected many songs over the past few days.

"There's a cousin of mine lives nearby," he said, "and if we paid her a visit she just might sing one or two." I jumped at the chance, and we climbed into my car and drove off.

We had been driving around for about half an hour, turning this way and that, until Charlie threw up his hands. "I know it sounds funny, Mr. Ives," he said, "because I've lived hereabouts all my life, but I'm completely lost. You couldn't lose me in a horse and wagon, but going this fast I just don't seem to recognize things at all."

I made light of it, telling him how lost I had gotten trying to find *his* place. We finally found the house we were looking for, but the niece wasn't home. We made a joke of it and headed back to Burton and the Daltons' kitchen.

We had tea, of course, and just as I was getting ready to leave Mrs. Dalton suggested I bring my wife and son over for a picnic on Sunday. "We can go down on the beach here," she said. Charlie liked the idea, and so did I, so we made plans to meet at the house Sunday about one.

Tuesday, June 25

Following the same directions I'd been given the day before, I found Harry Thompson's place in Glengarry this time with no trouble at all, and I was greeted expansively by Thompson himself, who'd been worried maybe I wasn't coming. Since he and his wife were just finishing lunch, they had me sit over for tea and a piece of pie. Then Harry lit his pipe, and, while acknowledging that Larry Gorman was about a generation before his time, for better than two hours he told me what he'd heard about him. Next to me, he was his own best audience, often exploding into laughter at some anecdote while I scribbled madly (again no electricity) to keep up with his enthusiastic and rapid-fire delivery.

We were winding down, when he thought of someone. "You know," he said, "there's some Fitzgeralds up in Waterford that are supposed to have a whole book of Gorman's songs. He used to stay with them, they say. Now, somehow I don't believe there's any book, but Gorman *did* used to stay with them, I know. Maybe we ought to pay them a visit. What do you say?"

I was just as skeptical as he was, but it didn't seem right not to check it out, so off we went.

Yes, the man said, there had been such a book but it went up in a house fire years ago. Since I had heard of such books before, and had even chased a couple around, I wasn't too disappointed, but a lead that doesn't pan out is always a bit of a downer, and Harry and I were both a bit subdued on the drive back.

44—*Sandy Ives*

"Stop here for a minute," he said, and I pulled into a local garage where two men working on a tractor were swearing at a stubborn fan belt. They stopped long enough to greet Harry, who repeated what we'd been told at Fitzgeralds. The two mechanics looked questioningly at each other for a long moment. "Well," one of them said, "if he says there isn't one, then I guess there isn't one, eh?"

We all laughed. The mechanics went back to swearing at the fan belt, and Harry and I were on our way again, perhaps just a tad more subdued than before.

"Wait a minute," he said as we came to Campbellton. "I know someone here who might be able to help you." He pointed to a small house set back toward the dunes. "Turn in here," he said.

Several children poured out the door as we pulled into the yard. They were followed by a short, rather heavy woman in house dress and apron with a child on her hip and yet another clinging shyly to her dresstail. She and Harry exchanged greetings of good-natured insult, in the course of which I was introduced to Mary Cousins—and we were immediately invited in. The kitchen table being piled to overflowing we went on into the parlour, where Elbridge and two grown sons—one sound asleep on the couch—were sitting after supper. We all found seats, Mary on the stool of the parlour organ that dominated one end of the room, and she and Harry continued their banter. "Hey Mary," he said, "you're not getting any thinner. I got a friend who's a cooper. You come along and we'll get him to stave and hoop you for a corset." I can't remember just what she said, but I do remember thinking she gave as good as she got.

It wasn't long before Harry got around to telling her what I was after. Yes, she knew about Larry Gorman, she said, but she didn't know any of his songs. On the other hand, she did know a couple of songs by another man from right around here by the name of Dan Riley—everyone called him Uncle Dan. By this time I knew enough to be interested in other songmakers, and I asked if she would sing them for me. After the traditional disavowal and the equally traditional coaxing, she agreed, and I went out to the car to get the Webcor.

Her singing was very straight. There was something of Mrs. Coughlin's hard-edged voice but nothing of her ornamental *parlando* style at all. She just sang very pleasantly the two songs I reproduce here.

The first tells the story of a famous Island murder of the last century. Mary Pickering Tuplin was killed on June 28, 1887. Her body was found shortly thereafter in the Southwest River near Margate. William Millman was indicted for her murder and brought to trial before Mr. Justice Henley on January 24, 1888. Forty-eight witnesses appeared for the Crown, eighteen for the defense. The jury brought in a verdict of "Guilty," and on April 10, 1888, Millman was hanged.[3] There is still an active tradition that he was innocent, and that another man made a deathbed confession years later. Be that as it may, here is the song as Mary sang it.

The Millman and Tuplin Song

♪ = 112

Come pull down the cur-tains, look si-lent-ly on, While I sing you the Mill-man and Tup-e-lin song.

1.
Come pull down the curtains, look silently on,
While I sing you the Millman and Tup-e-lin song.

2.
It's a tale of deep sorrow and suffering great,
Of a crime that was committed at a place called Margate.

3.
On the eighteenth of June on a calm summer's night,
When the moon in the heaven shone a pale ray of light,

4.
Young Mary walked out from her own cottage door;
Little thought she had gone to return there no more.

5.
And o'er her young spirit spread a deep ray of gloom,
For she mourned for her brother just laid in his tomb.

6.
Went to meet her young lover, who a few nights before
Said he'd make all things right when they'd meet on that shore.

7.
But a crime he committed that will ne'er be forgot;
In his hand a revolver, and the fair maid he shot.

8.
Took her out on the river, sunk her body deep down,
And he prayed in his heart she would never be found.

---

[3]See Jim Hornby, *In The Shadow of the Gallows* (Charlottetown: Institute of Island Studies, 1998), pp. 80–91.

9.
But the Judge he looked down from his throne up on high,
And he said, "For this crime now young Millman you'll die.

10.
"For my watchmen tonight I have stationed all 'round,
And when you're tried for murder your guilt will be found."

11.
So young Millman was taken just a week from that day,
And put into prison his trial to await.

12.
And there in close confinement he was left to repine
For the space of six months when he'd be tried for the crime.

13.
His trial was brought on in eighteen ninety-eight;
The counsel for his client proved eloquence great.

14.
We give him some credit for being eloquent and bright
But it's a hard thing, you know, to make wrong appear right.

15.
So friends all take warning before it's too late
And think with a shudder of that night at Margate.

The second song didn't really have a title, but over the years both Mary and I have always called it "The Uncle Dan Song," which does very nicely. The story is evidently true enough: Dan Riley was a confirmed bachelor, and, like most confirmed bachelors, he often found himself under considerable matrimonial pressure, even, according to his own account, from his dog. *"He made up a poem one time on 'The Bachelor and His Dog,'" said Mary. "Yeah, he had a dog, and he said,

He keeps a close watch o'er my chickens
Pursues both the hawk and the crows,
And one day he brought home by the dresstail
A maiden with cheeks like the rose.

He was pretending the dog was so smart he was even going to get a wife for him. He was a sly old man!" One day he was tipped off that a local widow was a-scheming for him, and he was grateful for the intelligence. The result was the following song:

The Uncle Dan Song

♩ = 98 approx.

But a sly young maid got on the plan, And she

broke the news to Un - cle Dan.

1.
Oh she minced around and waved her fan
And set her cap for Uncle Dan.

2.
But a sly young maid got on the plan
And she broke the news to Uncle Dan.

3.
Saying, "I'd really like to see you wed,
But not to her, for you're better dead.

4.
She's pulled the sod o'er one good man,
So now beware of her, Uncle Dan."

5.
He answered with a cheerful laugh,
"This bird's too old to be caught with chaff.

6.
"For I've often met the likes of her
And fended off with beak and spur.

7.
"And if that don't do, I'll use my lance
If I have to run to Spain or France.

8.
"I thank you for revealing the plan,
And I hope some day you will get a man.

9.
"Be good to him, be kind and true,
And perhaps the same will be said of you.

10.
"And if he should die and you want another man,
Just clear the road for Uncle Dan."

By this time Harry and I were beginning to feel the need to get home to our suppers, and we made moves in that direction. I packed up the tape recorder and we started for the door. Then Harry had an afterthought. "Think we ought to tell this man about the Burning Ship?" he said.

That brought the young man on the couch to a sitting position. "We saw it one night," he said. "We were coming in late. I heard of a couple of fellas who chased it one time—tried to get outside of it, but they couldn't." Others in the room nodded. Obviously this was no joke, no hoaxing of the tourist. "What's this all about?" I asked Harry.

"Oh lots of people have seen that," he said. "I did once myself. We were just getting ready for bed one night and my wife asked whose light that was showing over there, and I saw from the way she was pointing it couldn't be anybody's light, because it was all water that way. So I went over and looked, and there was a full-rigged ship in flames. It was sailing up the Strait very fast, and pretty soon it was gone. That's all I can tell you. I'm sure there's some explanation for it, but I know what I saw."

"It's supposed to show before a storm," the oldest boy said. "That's what I've heard anyway."

I wondered if there was a story connected with it. No one knew of any, but it had been seen all up and down the Strait from both sides, and it had also been seen up in the Bay Chaleur, they said. The talk went on for a few minutes; then Harry and I made our final exit.[4]

Wednesday, June 26

The day wasn't getting off to a very promising start, once again being cold and grey with a wet wind coming in off the water, and I was feeling guilty about leaving Bobby alone in that little cabin to deal with hyperactive four-year-old Steve all day. But she convinced me (it wasn't all that difficult) that I'd be more in the way than I would be a help, and, besides, that was the deal. I headed off for Miminegash to look up Edmund Doucette, with whom I'd corresponded for some months from back in Maine. It was Louise Manny over in Newcastle, New Brunswick, who first suggested I get in touch with him. He was a great fan of her Sunday afternoon "Songs of the Miramichi" radio program on CKMR Newcastle, which he could pick up on his wet-battery radio. He responded quickly and enthusiastically to my first letter and not only sent me the words to the one Gorman song he knew ("Michael O'Brien") but began scouting around the countryside gathering others, getting

---

[4]For a good account of this phenomenon, see William B. Hamilton, "Ghostly Encounters of the Northumberland Kind," *The Island Magazine* 4 (Spring-Summer, 1978), pp. 33–35. See also Catherine Jolicoeur, *Le vaisseau fantôme: legend etiologique* (Québec: Université Laval, 1970); Edward D. Ives, "The Burning Ship of Northumberland Strait: Some Notes on That Apparition," *Midwest Folklore* VIII (1958), pp. 199–203, and "More Notes on the Burning Ship of Northumberland Strait," *Northeast Folklore* 2 (Winter, 1959), pp. 53–55.

No. 9: Miminegash Run. *NAPhoto 234.*

No. 10: Fishing stages at Miminegash. *NAPhoto 916.*

as far afield as Tyne Valley when he could cadge a ride (he had no car of his own). I had recently told him approximately when I'd be coming to P.E.I., and he wrote back quickly, wanting me to be sure to understand that Miminegash was just a fishing village and though the people were poor I would of course be welcome.

Well, here I was, and there was Miminegash off to the left through the fog. All I could see from the Shore Road was a line of grey-shingled fishing stages, their roofs sawtoothed over the dunes against the leaden sky, but soon the village itself appeared—a church and then some houses along the dirt road leading down to the run. I stopped at a little store, and the proprietress stepped outside to point out Edmund's place—off the road back toward the dunes. There were half a dozen martin houses on long poles scattered around the yard and an equal number of cats gathered on the kitchen steps. I made my way through them and knocked at the door.

A stocky bespectacled man of about sixty-five answered and looked at me quizzically. "Edmund Doucette? I'm Edward Ives from Maine."

His look betokened genuine surprise. "No!" he said as he stepped back from the door. Yes, I said, that's who I was alright, at which point he invited me in.

The surprise wore off as we sat at the table and had a cup of tea. The problem, he explained, was that right from my very first letter the whole village had been speculating about me, coming to picture me as a typical cartoon professor—bent, bald, and of course bearded—and dubbing me "Edmund's Old Man." As time wore on, everyone despaired of my coming (as a matter of fact I *was* several days behind the schedule I'd set myself), but, he told me, "Two days ago my son had a dream. 'Don't worry,' he said, 'your old man's coming.'" And here—skinny, blond, close-shaven and not quite thirty-three— I most certainly was.

Edmund sat there, hat on head, smoking one cigarette after another, as we talked about this and that. He was a good talker, assured and organized, but of course I was anxious to get to the songs he knew. I asked about Gorman's "Michael O'Brien." He'd sent me the words; did he know the tune? Yes. Would he let me record it? Yes, but since there was no electricity in the house we'd have to go over to Joe Tremblay's (his brother-in-law). I started for the door. "Wait," he said, "there's something I want to show you," and he took me in the other room to a collection of painted shells (each labelled "Souvenir of P.E.I."), whittled birds and fish, and a huge full-rigged ship model. "We make them in the winter to sell to tourists," he said.

I had a feeling that as an emerging folklorist I should be interested in this activity—thirty years later I most certainly would have been!—but at the time I was after songs and that was that. One of these whittled objects, though, particularly caught my eye: a large open Bible with two names gold-lettered across the pages. "Two of my sons," he said, "both killed in Normandy. That's for the Church when I get it finished."

Joe Tremblay's was one of the biggest and finest houses in town, though even here there was no indoor plumbing and all the water came from a pump at the sink. But it had electricity and all the conveniences that brought with it—not only lights but a refrigerator, a toaster, and a radio that you could leave on all day if you wanted to. All the men were out fishing, but Mrs. Tremblay, Edmund's sister, welcomed us in and showed me where to plug in my recorder. Both she and Edmund were curious, so I played one of the few songs I had already collected—something I'd found braced prospective singers, just as playing back their own singing afterwards often pleased them.

"He wants me to sing 'Michael O'Brien,'" he said, "you know, that one about the man looking for a wife." Then, after he'd asked his sister to leave the room, he sang.

It's worth pointing out that this song exhibits three Gorman hallmarks. First, it is about a man looking for a wife. Second, like "Bachelor's Hall," it develops its theme through a list of possessions. And third, it is said to have been made up on someone who had asked Gorman to song someone else, the old "biter bit" theme. In this case Michael suggested he make up a song on his brother, Jim O'Brien, and Gorman responded that he'd never make up a song on someone who had used him as well as Jim O'Brien had.

Michael O'Brien

1.
Come all you girls both short and tall, I pray don't be so shy;
A man like me with property free—how can you pass him by?
I'm on the verge of thirty now, and tired of a single life;
It's time that I should make a vow that I should have a wife.

2.
I got house and barn, a stock and farm, and what more do they want,
With sixty acres in one block with fifty chains in front?
My house is built in the latest style and well-finished out and in,
With a heavy finishing around the eaves and a grand look-out in front.

3.
My barn is built on the medium size with tiles of the best,
And the tempest of the snow and rain from against my hay and grain.
The doors are new and painted blue, the small ones in two halves,
That I might close the lower half against my pigs and calves.

4.
I got horse and wagon, two bobsleighs, a harrow and a plow,
A fattening pig and two runabouts with five calves and a cow.

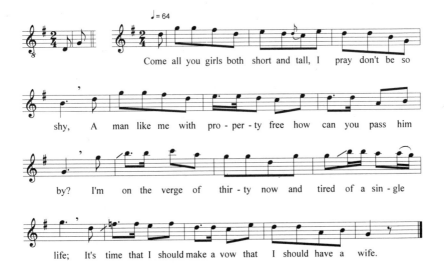

♩ = 64

Come all you girls both short and tall, I pray don't be so shy, A man like me with pro-per-ty free how can you pass him by? I'm on the verge of thir-ty now and tired of a sin-gle life; It's time that I should make a vow that I should have a wife.

I have a bull, a famous beast, your very eyes would charm;
His search was bought away down east, I think from a well-stocked farm.

5.
I got stove, pot, pans, a strainer can, a bucket, and a broom;
Stove, brush and towel, a looking-glass, a rack and a fine tooth comb.
When I get on my sporting suit, I'm quite a fancy chap,
With my brand-new dress cloth overcoat and my fine south sealskin cap.

6.
When I go to a ball or a party there's one thing makes me mad:
The girls won't keep my company, they say my breath is bad.
I'll try in vain their hearts to gain, but they won't believe my life;
So I'll take a stroll for the good of my soul and see my neighbour's wife.

"Want to hear that back?" I asked. He said he did and called his sister back into the room to listen. She liked what she heard, and said so, and while Edmund said nothing I sensed his quiet approval. We got talking about other songs. I mentioned "John Ladner." Yes, he knew it, and he even sang a stanza for me, but he wanted some time to get it together. Why didn't I come back on Sunday afternoon? Not only would he sing it for me then but he'd have his brother "Long Joe" here then and a couple of neighbours. "You'll hear some *real* singing then," he said self-deprecatingly.

"And bring your wife and little boy," said Mrs. Tremblay.

"Better bring a bottle of whisky, too," Edmund added.

It sounded like a collector's dream—several singers together, maybe reminding each other of songs, and the tape recorder going round and round all the time! "O.K.," I said, enthusiastically, "We'll be here."

It wasn't until I was part way home that I remembered I'd made that agreement with Charlie Gorman and the Daltons for a picnic that same afternoon. My heart sank. I knew the right thing was to go back and tell Edmund we'd have to make it another day. But, I convinced myself, an opportunity like this might not come again while I was on the Island. All that singing—and my time *was* running out.

I kept on driving.

Friday, June 28

Thursday I'd agreed to give a talk to the Summerside Rotary Club, so we made a day of it in town. But Friday I was back up west.

"Tommy Doyle was Larry Gorman's best friend. . . . He knew all of Gorman's songs. . . . He and Larry Gorman left the Island together. . . . He'd be the man to see, if he's still around, but God, he'd be old, a hundred maybe. . . ." It was comments like these I'd been hearing right along, but since opinion had been divided both on whether he was still alive and whether he'd be willing or able to tell me much if he was, I had delayed trying to find him. Now, with Keith Pratt's map and some assurance that he *was* alive I knew I had to try.

The house was some distance down the Shore Road from Charlie Gorman's, well back on the ridge overlooking Northumberland Strait. I checked for electric lines as I drove up the lane; there weren't any, so I grabbed a notebook and made my way to the door, surrounded and well-announced by a crowd of friendly dogs.

I was ushered into the big sitting room by one of the two daughters who were home for the summer looking after their father. I told them my mission. Yes, they had seen my letter in *The Guardian,* and had intended to write me, but their father's health had been so precarious they weren't sure he'd still be around when I arrived. As it was, he was in bed, recovering from a recent bronchitis attack and would probably never get up again. One of them went upstairs to check on him. She came down a few minutes later, motioning to me to come up with her. "He's awake," she said.

He was lying on his back, arms outside the covers, head propped up and a bib tucked under his chin. He raised one arm a little as I came in. "I'm not as smart as you," he said.

"Oh, I don't know about that," I said with a show of joviality. "I bet you're pretty smart yourself." The daughter did her best to hide a chuckle. I had yet to learn that on the Island "smart" meant physically able. But there was no reaction from the man in the bed.

"He's almost totally deaf," the daughter said. "You'll have to get up real close and shout."

I pulled up a chair and sat right next to his head. "Do you remember Larry Gorman?" I said.

He looked as if he hadn't heard, and apparently he hadn't. I tried again. "Larry Gorman! Do you remember him?"

He seemed conscious I was talking to him, but he made no response. The daughter came forward and leaned over to speak in his other ear. "This man wants to know about Larry Gorman, Father," she said.

Suddenly his eyes lit up and he began to smile. "Larry Gorman," he said, and with that he began to recite, looking up at his daughter, his voice low but for the most part clear, chuckling now and then at some line or reference. Occasionally I'd recognize a few lines of some song I'd already heard, but for the most part it was all new to me. I tried to write something down, but it was coming too fast. There was nothing I could do but listen, which is what I did. He went on for about fifteen minutes; then, as abruptly as he had begun, he stopped and closed his eyes. I listened to his shallow breathing for a moment, until the daughter motioned that we should leave.

"That must have been rather frustrating for you," she said when we got downstairs.

"Yes," I said, with the best rueful smile I could manage, "it was."

"Leave me your address," she said, "and I'll try and get him to go over as much as he can when he's a little stronger."

"That'd be great," I said, going over to a table and writing it out on a page torn from my notebook. We talked for a few more minutes. I thought back to my afternoon with Harry Thompson and Mary Cousins. "That's a great view of the Strait you have from that window," I said.

"Isn't it?" she said. "There was always a window there, but we had that big one put in about a year ago."

"I guess if the Burning Ship came along," I ventured, " you could see it from here all right."

She laughed. "You know about the Burning Ship?" she said.

"Yes," I said. "I've heard about it, but I've never seen it. Have you?"

"Oh yes!" she said quite positively. "You could even see men running around on the deck." She was still smiling, but her eyes held mine as she said that. "You probably don't believe that, do you?"

I wasn't quite sure how to respond, so I wound up with something between a giggle and a shrug.

"I wouldn't either," she said, getting me nicely off the spot she'd put me on. "I'm sure there's some explanation for it, but I know what I saw, that's all."

I thanked her for her help and said I hoped to hear from her soon, not quite believing I would (I was right. Tommy Doyle died about a week later).

No. 11: "Long Joe" and Edmund Doucette. *Photo taken July 1963.*

As I drove out onto the Shore Road, I knew I should stop at the Daltons' and explain to them and Charlie why we couldn't make the picnic on Sunday. It was not a task I looked forward to, and therefore I allowed myself to believe it would be better to wait until tomorrow, and drove on.

Saturday, June 29

It had to be done, and I hated the idea, but to make it a little easier I took Bobby and Steve along with me—sort of a substitute visit for the picnic planned for next day. "What a beautiful place," said Bobby, as we drove up the lane, and the full afternoon sun on the distant water made it even more beautiful.

Mrs. Dalton greeted us profusely. Charlie had seen us coming and had gone upstairs to shave, she explained, as she ushered us into the parlour, but he'd be down in a few minutes, if we didn't mind waiting. "No problem," I said. Then she excused herself. Five minutes later she was back in a clean dress and apron, having started the kettle boiling.

Her son Jimmy appeared, having heard the car. "Ohhh, the dirt on him!" she said in parental horror, but Jimmy and Steve disappeared happily together out into the farmyard.

We talked of this and that. I wanted to wait until Charlie came down, but then she turned to Bobby to say how glad she was she could come tomorrow. "Well, that's just the problem," I said. "Something's come up, and we're just not going to be able to make it tomorrow after all."

Her disappointment was obvious. "Oh, that's a shame," she said, "because it looks like it's going to be a nice day, too."

"I know," I said, "but—well, it's one of those things, and—I'm sorry, but there's nothing I can do."

"I know Charlie will be disappointed," she said. "He's been looking forward to it all week."

"So have we," I said, smiling my most sincere what-can-you-do-about-it smile, "but I guess that's—" and at that point Charlie walked in, clean shirt, his grey cardigan neatly safety-pinned at the neck, a smidgen of shaving cream on one ear. We shook hands, and I introduced him to Bobby, whom he greeted with that easy courtliness I was to come always to associate with him. Then Mrs. Dalton gave him the news.

"Oh, that's too bad," he said. "But we know you're busy, and—" he paused—"well, these things happen." And the talk went on to other things for about half an hour, among them the Burning Ship, which Charlie recalled seeing once as a child.

Steve and Jimmy had just come back in, and I was about to say we must be going when Charlie asked would we mind if he sang a song. "I was going to sing it tomorrow," he said. "I thought it would kind of suit the occasion, but since that's not to be—'course I can't sing anyway—I'd like to sing it now."

And he did, in true traditional style: the words coming through clearly, the rhythm relatively strict (especially within the phrase), the melody unadorned, with the last word spoken. It was a beautiful rendition, and it carried in its performance not only the conviviality and friendship of the moment but the disappointment of an awaited occasion lost. I had never heard the song before:

> Away, away, away, away,
> We will drive dull care away,
> And while we're here with our friends so dear
> We'll drive dull care away.

He was right: it *would* have suited the occasion. Fortunately, I was able to get the song on tape a year later, but it's that first singing that Bobby and I will always hear.

Sunday, June 30

Since it was a beautiful day, we were tourists all morning, driving up through Tignish to the North Cape, where we climbed the lighthouse and (since it was low tide) walked out on the long curving sandspit into the ocean. After lunch, we headed down the shore to Miminegash.

As we entered town we were greeted by eight or ten children running toward us, waving and yelling "Yay!" Obviously the word was out that something interesting was on the horizon. We pulled into the dooryard, and Edmund and his wife came down the steps with grandson Albert in tow. Albert and Steve were introduced (they got on famously right from the start) and we all piled in the car to drive the few hundred feet to the Tremblays'. I handed Edmund the bottle of scotch I had brought along. "You take care of this, O.K.?" I said. He agreed.

The Tremblay kitchen was a good big one, but it didn't seem that way as the six of us entered. Joe Tremblay, a man of about seventy, and his wife were seated at the table, along with son Jerry and daughter-in-law Audrey. But what really crowded things was the children—I counted eighteen of them, the youngest about two, the oldest (hip boots turned down, cap on backwards, rakish sideburns) about sixteen. They had probably been waiting for us ever since lunch, and not a sound from any of them.

Edmund and I went into the living room to set up the tape recorder, and the whole crowd followed, distributing themselves around the room, the grown-ups on couches and chairs, the kids wherever they could fit in. More kids appeared at windows and screen door, and women kept dropping in to the kitchen, checking on the proceedings, and then after a while dropping out again. People wanted to hear the song Edmund had sung for me, which meant I played parts of that tape over at least half a dozen times.

Everyone was there but the fellows who were supposed to do the singing, and Edmund was getting a little annoyed—going to the window, checking his watch, going to the window again—but after about half an hour, "Here they are! Come on," he said to me, and we went out to the car to greet them, shooing kids out of the way as we went.

There were four men in that car, all of them still in their dressed-down Sunday clothes (no ties, sleeves rolled part way up). Two were about my age, one about seventy (the only one wearing a hat), and a big grey-haired rawboned man of maybe sixty. This was Long Joe, and as I reached in to shake hands I was hauled into the car. "Have some moonshine," one of the young men said.

I had a hunch that a good deal could depend on how well I handled that drink. For sure, it burned going down, but no more than any straight whisky would. It was pretty good, all told, and evidently I passed my test, because the ginger-ale bottle of chaser followed without comment, and then we all went in the house. "They've been getting Joe's nerve up," Edmund said to me. "I hope he's not too drunk."

After everybody had greeted everybody, Edmund asked Long Joe to sing something. "I can't," said Long Joe, almost belligerently. "I can't sing no songs I don't know!"

"You know them, all right," said Edmund. "Here," he said, turning to me, "play him that tape." And so all of us listened once again to Edmund singing "Michael O'Brien."

Long Joe sat staring at the Webcor, listening intently, deadly serious. Then he grinned broadly and looked over at his brother. "By God, Edmund," he said, "that's *you!*"

Everyone laughed, including Joe. "Let's get another brush cut," he said, and he and his friends bolted out the door, Edmund in close pursuit.

My stomach was churning. I wanted to hear Long Joe very much, but I was also getting annoyed at all this coyness and about five minutes more of it could well have driven me to pack it in, but fortunately everyone returned, Edmund carrying my scotch and the chaser. Joe had agreed to sing, but he insisted that all the women and kids leave the room, which they did. The two bottles started around again; then Joe set himself down in front of the microphone and—right elbow on knee and right hand shading his eyes—began to sing "The Lost Babes of Halifax."

He had a great voice and was doing fine, but he broke down after a few stanzas. *"No," he said, "I just can't do it." I suggested he try again, but he waved me away. "It's no good," he said, obviously a little annoyed with himself.

Then he tried "The Miramichi Fire," but broke off after a few stanzas.

At this point Edmund took things in hand. "The trouble with you is too damn much alcohol," he said.

"No, no! It's just the stranger," said Long Joe, motioning at me. "And then I look at you and see you laughing, Ed."

"I'm not laughing," said Edmund, " but if you're going to act this way, by God *I'll* sing! I promised this man I'd sing 'John Ladner' for him, so here goes." The room was suddenly quiet, and Edmund began.

John Ladner

Parlando rubato ♩ = 60 approx.

You sym - pa - thet - ic friends draw near and lis-ten to my song,

'Til I re-late the cru-el fate of a young man dead and gone,

Who now lies si - lent in his tomb with - out a care or pain;

Prince Ed - ward Isle his na-tive soil, John Lad - in-er by name.

1.
You sympathetic friends draw near and listen to my song,
Til I relate the cruel fate of a young man dead and gone,
Who now lies silent in his tomb without a care or pain;
Prince Edward Isle his native soil, John Lad-i-ner by name.

2.
When very young he left his home relations far behind;
He hastened on o'er to Saint John employment for to find.
For work he tried but was denied, he searched but all in vain,
In deep despair he paid his fare up to the State of Maine.

3.
Arriving at the State of Maine a job was easily found,
His willing ways soon won the praise of strangers all around;
He toiled and slaved, his earnings saved, not a foolish cent he'd spend,
'Twas little did he ever think his short life soon would end.

4.

It's to the town of Madison young Ladner he did go,
He laboured there three months or more through winter rain and snow;
Contented mind, no faults to find, successful every way,
With willing heart he done his part up to his dying day.

5.

Thanksgiving morn brought joy to some, to others it brought woe,
Poor John arose, put on his clothes, and up to work did go;
To roll down logs piled up so high with steady nerve and skill,
And land them in that narrow stream that floats them to the mill.

6.

In dangerous roads he often stood but watched with careful eye,
This fatal morn he drove the same, they said who saw him die;
A dash, a crash, a fearful smash, the logs came tumbling down,
A treacherous blow soon laid him low and he in death was found.

7.

His comrades they all gathered round and drove the logs away,
With aching hearts in sorrow cried, they mourned his loss that day;
The doctor came but was too late, for he in death was cold,
His race was run, his time had come at twenty-three years old.

8.

Now, comrade, mark that bloodstained place in memory of the dead,
Look down with pity on his sad face, rise up his bleeding head;
Look down with pity on his sad face; watch danger if you can
For unexpected it might come to each and every man.

9.

Now fare you well, dear comrade John, in bitter tears we say,
Your lifeless form is boring on to that isle so far away;
You're leaving friends and those you love who once on you did smile,
A lonesome grave for you is made down on Prince Edward's Isle.

10.

The eyes that once did sparkle bright are closed in death today,
The heart that once did beat so true has ceased to beat no more
The voice that oftentimes rejoiced lies silent in the clay;
For God has called him from us all to his bright celestial shore.

There was a general rumble of approval. "Here, Edmund, you need this," said someone, passing him the bottle. He tipped it up and started it on its rounds once more (it gave out about half-way around). "That was damn good singing, Ed," said Long Joe. "I didn't know you knew that one." Edmund said nothing. Long Joe cleared his throat. "Listen," he said to me, "I'm going to try that 'Miramichi Fire' again."

The room quieted down, and I turned on the recorder. "O.K.," I said. "Go to it."

He sat very straight this time, hands on knees, beating out the time with his foot. I was really excited; it was a fabled song—one I'd been told was "a good one" but "hard to sing, awful long." Many people I'd talked to had known little sketches of it, but here was a man belting out what must be the whole of it—and belting it out very well indeed.

The Miramichi Fire

♩ = 108

(H)In or - der to de - stroy their lum - ber

And their coun - try to dis - grace,

He sent a fire ___ in a whirl -wind

In the how - ling wil - der - ness.

1.
This is the truth that I now tell you,
For my eyes in part did see
What had happened to the people
On the banks of the Miramichi.

2.
The eighteenth evening of October,
Eighteen hundred and twenty-five,
Two hundred people fell by fire,
Injured those who did survive.

3.
Oh, some said it was because the people's
Sins did rise like mountains high,
Which did ascend up to the heavens,
He would seek and justify.

4.
In order to destroy their lumber
And their country to disgrace,
He sent a fire in a whirlwind
In the howling wilderness.

5.

It was on the northeast first discovered
Where twelve men there did die;
Then it swept its ways o'er the mountains,
To Newcastle it did fly.

6.

Oh, while the people were all sleeping
Fire seized upon the town.
Though how handsome was the village
It soon tumbled to the ground.

Joe halted here, not sure of where the song went next, but after about fifteen seconds he was off again.

7.

Down it swept to Black River
Where it did burn forty more,
And it swept its way with fury
'Til it reached the briny shore.

8.

Forty-two miles by one hundred
This great fire did extend.
All was done within eight hours,
Not exceeding over ten.

9.

Oh, six young men both smart and active
Were at work on the Northwest;
When they saw the fire coming
To escape they tried their best.

10.

But six miles from where this great camp stood
Those six young men they were found;
And to paint their sad appearance
I can't do with tongue or pen.

11.

As I have spoken of things collected,
Now I will stop and personate,
And to speak of some acquaintance
And to whom I informate.[5]

12.

A lady was driven to the water
Where she stood both wet and cold,
Not resisting her late illness,
She had a babe but three days old.

13.

It burned new ships that we were building
And two more to their anchor lay

---

[5]Other versions have this line as "With whom I was intimate."

Many that did see the fire
Thought it was the Judgment Day.

Joe coughed and hesitated. *"Just shut her off there for a moment now," he said. I did, and for about thirty seconds there wasn't a sound in that room. "O.K." he said.

14.

Oh, sister crying for her brother,
Mother weeping for her son,
And with bitter heartfelt sorrow
Says the father, "I'm all done."

*"I guess that's as far as I can go," he said. I encouraged him simply to go on from where he'd left off. "No," he said, disgustedly shaking his head, "it's no good. I've spotted it." He stood up. "I have to go now. I'll write down the rest of it and send it to you."

It hurt some. I could feel how much he had wanted that singing to be right. A year later, when he sang the song again for me, there were three stanzas he had not sung before. It seems only fair to include them here.

15.
Twelve more men were burnt by fire
In the compass of the town;
Twenty-five more on the water
In a scow upset and drowned.

16.
It killed the wild beast of the forest
And of the rivers many's the fish;
Such another horrid fire
See again I do not wish.

17.
I hear the cries and the screams and the groaning,
See the falling of the tears;
By me it shall not be forgotten
Should I live one hundred years.

The party broke up after Long Joe and his friends left. There was some disappointment, not only that Joe hadn't done better than he had but that another man hadn't turned up who had promised to sing "Peter Emberly." Then Jerry Tremblay had an idea. "Would you like to see the house where Peter Emberly[6] was born?" he asked. "It's only a few miles from here."

I said that would be great. Meanwhile Bobby, Steve, and I went back to

---

[6]This is as good a place as any to mention that while the correct spelling of this name is Amberly (so it appears in the Census), it is almost universally pronounced—and spelled—Emberly.

Edmund's for a little supper, after which the expedition took off down the Shore Road, Jerry and the rest of the Tremblays in his car, Edmund with us.

The house was several miles up the Dock Road from Campbellton— nothing but a shell, its shingles a reddish glow in the evening sun. We walked up the trace of a path leading to it. "Isn't it funny," said Mrs. Tremblay to me and Bobby, "to think that this is the last road that Peter Emberly walked here?"

Both of us were touched to think that this young Island boy, killed three-quarters of a century before in the Miramichi lumberwoods, was still very much alive to people around here, his old home even a shrine of sorts. Some weeks before I had visited his grave. I thought of the last stanza of the ballad:

> And now before I pass away
>   there is one thing more I crave:
> It's that some holy father
>   will come and bless my grave.
> Nearby the city of Boiestown
>   my mouldering bones do lay,
> Awaiting of my Saviour's call
>   on that great judgment day.

And now here I was at his home. I took the requisite pictures and we headed back to Miminegash.

Part way along Jerry waved we should stop. He pointed to a house. "That's where Michael O'Brien lived," he said.

Again, I took the requisite pictures.

A Ceili at the Pendergasts'

It was our final day on P.E.I., and we were in Charlottetown while I did some last-minute newspaper checking in the Legislative Library and made one more unsuccessful attempt to find Gorman's baptismal record, this time at St. Dunstan's Basilica. Above all else, though, I wanted Bobby to meet the Pendergasts. I called and got Mrs. Pendergast, who said it would be fine if we'd stop around after supper, which is what we did.

How was I to know that she and Jim would spend much of the afternoon on the phone arranging a party? But, sure enough, when we walked in there was Judge Duffy and his wife, Mr. and Mrs. Proude, Kenneth Lecky, Austin and Mrs. Trainor, boarder Vic with a lady friend (Amby was predictably absent), the Misses Quinn and McFeeney (new boarders, here for the college summer session), son Reg, Mrs. Pendergast's sister Dorothy Cullen, and a couple of other members of the local Irishry I can't place at this late date.

We bedded four-year-old Steve down in the other room, and it wasn't long before the singing began. Austin Trainor led off, taking over the piano like

No. 12: The old Amberly house on the Dock Road as it appeared when it was visited by the Ives family in August of 1965. *NA P251.*

the professional entertainer he was and giving forth with two fine vaudeville pieces: first "Doherty's Boarding House" and then—especially for me and my family—one about a farmer, "Reuben Haskins by name," just down to the big city "from Skowhegan, Maine." Then I had to get my guitar and sing a couple of Gorman pieces, and, just for the hell of it and considering that the Irish had the hegemony that evening, I also sang "Kevin Barry":

> Another martyr for old Ireland,
> Another murder for the Crown!
> Brutal laws to crush the Irish
> Could not keep their spirits down.

That brought a chuckle from Mr. Proude. "During the war me and a couple of other fellas got singing that in Picadilly Circus one night," he said. "They caught my buddies, but I got away." Then Reg sang a couple, one of them being "The Garden Where the Praties Grow," to Dorothy Cullen's piano accompaniment. Others sang, too, but whenever things slowed down, there was Austin Trainor with a recitation or a song. And over in the corner in his big armchair was Jim, puffing on his pipe, monarch of all he surveyed, asking for this or that song, enjoying.

The party went on until almost midnight. As Bobby and I went out the door—Steve sound asleep on my shoulder—Jim asked when we'd be coming home again. That pleased us both.

Nineteen Fifty-Eight

MY BOOK ON LARRY GORMAN began shaping itself almost as soon as I returned home with the results of my first Island venture. I didn't have the rich harvest of songs I had been led to expect, but I did have several good ones, plus a whole basketful of fragments, and when I added in the material I had gathered in New Brunswick—especially along the Miramichi—and was still gathering in Maine that summer, I knew I had something approaching critical mass. I even felt confident enough to propose a paper on Gorman for the American Folklore Society meetings in Chicago that December (to my infinite wonder, it was accepted), and two other papers of mine had also been accepted for publication in folklore journals, all of which helped me begin to believe that maybe I really *was* more folklorist than litterateur after all. I liked that idea.

By midsummer 1958 I had a rough first draft of the Gorman book and a list of questions—almost as long as the manuscript itself—that I was dying to get back to P.E.I. to try to get answered. But now—by the blessed process of serendipity—there was another lumberwoods songmaker whose long come-all-ye's had been turning up in Maine and New Brunswick, and I wanted to see how well his songs were known on P.E.I. His name was Joe Scott.

I already had a couple of good leads. On an evening in early May I had driven down to Augusta to do my folksongs-with-guitar bit for some ladies club. It was a pretty standard sort of gig for me, but right from the beginning I noticed two men sitting in the last row, not only because they were among the few men present but also because they somehow didn't look like they'd been dragged there by their wives. Sure as hell those guys are from P.E.I., I said to myself, and when I launched into "The Boys of the Island" a few minutes later, I knew I was right. They came up after the program for a shake-hands and a few minutes of talk about the Island—Arthur and Ivan Nisbet. They'd been living in Augusta now for many years, but they still made regular trips back home to West Prince whenever they got the chance.

I had talked a good deal about Joe Scott that night, and even sang his trademark song, "The Plain Golden Band," which prompted them to put together a list of people I ought to see who either knew Scott or could sing the old songs. Heading the list were Angus Enman of Spring Hill and Wesley Smith of Victoria West. "Angus is getting along in years," said Arthur, "but he used to be a great singer. 'Course Wesley's some younger, but he's a pretty good singer too. And both of them knew Joe Scott. I've heard them talk about him."

I said I'd be sure to go see them when I went up again that summer.

Before I made that trip, though, I wanted to try and solve what had been my most frustrating problem in the field the year before: since only a few of the rural homes I visited had electricity, I was extremely limited in how and where I could use my tape recorder. Either I had to get people to move to where there *was* power, or I had to scribble madly and get them to repeat themselves, neither of which was totally satisfactory, considering that I'd already decided it was important to get people's exact words, not my approximation of them. And, of course, when it came to music, I was helpless without the tape recorder (I wasn't to learn musical transcription technique until 1961). Battery-powered equipment was generally unavailable at the time, and what *was* available was far beyond my means. What I finally did was to buy a power converter that allowed me to run the recorder off the car battery; then I could either run a long cable into the house or I could record right there in the car (I discovered, by the way, that a car made a rather good recording studio). The only problem was that the converter was reputed to be very tough on the car battery, estimates being that eight or ten minutes of steady use would drain it completely, and some of Scott's songs were at least that long, and longer.

Saturday, August 16

It wasn't until mid-August that I finally got a week clear to make my way back to West Prince (this time alone), and the first person I went to see was Edmund Doucette up in Miminegash. I had written him that I was planning to come but couldn't be sure just when. He wrote back assuring me that it didn't matter when—just come anytime. He also added that Long Joe was anxious to see me again and would sing anything I wanted to hear this time. No question about it, by now I was more interested in general repertoire questions than I had been before, and there was my new interest in Joe Scott, but my focus was still on Larry Gorman, and once again my time was going to be limited. At any rate, here I was in Miminegash once more, knocking on Edmund's door.

"He's at his barbershop," his wife said. "Go on down." She pointed over toward the dunes. "It's just a little place. You'll find it."

She was right on both counts—a little grey one-room shack—and there was Edmund serving as village barber. The customer was seated in the only chair; the half-dozen others waiting their turn sat on the floor along the wall, and after saying hi to Edmund I joined them. In a way, it was as if I'd never left, except that my arrival had completely dried up the talk I had heard as I approached and replaced it with an air of expectancy. I felt it incumbent on me to say something, so I made a stab. "Edmund, last winter you wrote that you'd seen the Burning Ship once. Was that right off here?"

"Yes," he said, "but that was a long time ago." No one else volunteered.

"I wonder what it is," I said.

"Maybe it's a forerunner," said a man just climbing into the chair.

"What's that?" I asked.

"Before something happens," he said. That was all, and day-to-day talk warmed up some. Edmund took care of his customers, and we went back to his place for a bite of supper, after which we made ready to go over to the Tremblays' again.

The Tremblays were expecting us. Not only had they seen me drive into town but Mrs. Doucette had carried the news as well. I felt very cordially welcomed, not only by the senior Tremblays but by two of the sons, Eddie and Jerry, who had dropped by—along with their wives and several children—to see what the evening might bring.

During supper Edmund and I had talked about what songs he knew and which ones he'd like to sing, and it wasn't long before a circle had formed in the living room, Edmund on one side of it, me on the other, the Webcor pretty much in the middle, and for the next two hours Edmund obliged with one song after another. He'd say what he was going to sing, I'd turn the machine on, he'd sing it, I'd turn the machine off, and there'd be some conversation about it ("That's a good song" . . . "I mind Father used to sing that one " . . . "I didn't know you knew that, Ed," and so on). Then the pattern would repeat itself —all told a pleasant and (as I saw it) productive evening in which I garnered half a dozen songs.[1]

At one point Edmund lit up a cigarette and apparently didn't know what to sing next. I waited as long as my patience would stand it and made a suggestion of my own. Like so many budding folklorists of that era, I was also a folksinger—rolled-up sleeves, levis, guitar, the works—and sometime during the previous winter, Kenny Goldstein landed me a contract with Folkways for a record to be entitled "Folk Songs of Maine."[2] I sent him a list of the songs I wanted to include. Too many long ones, he replied; cut some of them down—it's no crime; add some shorter pieces, and make sure there's at least one Child ballad. At that point in my career I wasn't about to question a man who had edited hundreds of albums, and even though I knew Child ballads were scarce in Maine, I looked about for a suitable one, settling on a New Brunswick version of "Hind Horn" (Child 17) I found in *British Ballads from Maine*.[3] Whatever else that exercise may have accomplished, it planted that

[1] For other songs Edmund sang that evening, see *Twenty-One Folksongs, pp.* 17–25.
[2] *Folk Songs of Maine.* Folkways FH5323 (1959).
[3] Phillips Barry, Fannie Hardy Eckstorm, and Mary Winslow Smyth, *British Ballads From Maine* (New Haven: Yale University Press, 1929), pp.73–75.

ballad firmly in the front of my mind, and I began asking for it, not as "Hind Horn" but by its local title, "The Old Beggar Man." I asked Edmund if he knew it. Yes, he said, and he began.

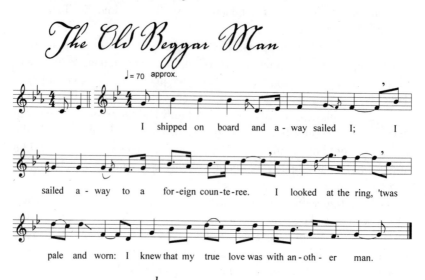

The Old Beggar Man

♩ = 70 approx.

I shipped on board and a - way sailed I; I sailed a - way to a for -eign coun-te-ree. I looked at the ring, 'twas pale and worn: I knew that my true love was with an - oth - er man.

1.
"Where were you born and where were you bred,
In Scotland town in a foreign counteree?"
"In Scotland town where I was born,
'Twas there were a maid and she gave to me a ring."

2.
"If this ring proves bright and clear,
You'll know that I'm true to you my dear,
And if this ring proves pale and worn,
You'll know that your true love is with another man."

3.
I shipped on board and away sailed I;
I sailed away to a foreign counteree.
I looked at the ring, 'twas pale and worn;
I knew that my true love was with another man.

4.
I shipped on board, and back sailed I;
I sailed back to my own counteree.
One day as I was a-riding along,
Whom did I meet but a poor old beggar man.

5.
"What news, what news have you today?
What news have you got for me today?"
"Sad news I've got for you today:
Tomorrow is your true lover's wedding day."

6.

"Come and take my riding suit,
And I will take the beggar's suit."
"The riding suit is not fit for me.
The beggar's suit is not fit for thee."

7.

"Never mind if it's right or wrong."
The beggar's suit he did slip on.
He toddled away at a weary rate;
He laid his sack at yonder gate.

8.

He begged from the parlour, he begged from hall;
He begged from the poorest and the richest of them all.
But as for wine he'd drink none at all,
Unless he'd get it from the bride's own hand.

9.

Down came the bride a-skipping down stairs,
With rings on her fingers and gold in her hair,
And in her hand a glass of wine
To give it to this poor old beggar man.

10.

Out of the glass he drank the wine,
And into the glass he slipped the ring.
"Did you get it by land or on sea,
Or did you take it off a drowned man's hand?"

11.

"I didn't get it on land or on sea.
I didn't take it off a drowned man's hand.
I got it from my true love on our courting day
And given it back to her on her wedding day."

12.

Rings from her fingers she did pull off,
And gold from her hair she did let fall.
"I'll follow my true love wherever he goes.
Although he begs my bread from door to door."

13.

Between the kitchen and the hall,
The beggar's rig he did pull off.
The gold that shone the brightest of them all;
He was the finest young man in the hall.

As Edmund sang, I couldn't help but compare his singing to mine. Same tune, same story in mostly the same words, but mine lacked the steady tension—like a man paying out rope—that Edmund's singing gave it, and that made all the difference.

After another couple of songs and a cup of coffee we all decided it was time to quit, but Edmund wanted to be certain I'd be coming back the next day, so we could go out and visit Long Joe. I said I'd be there for sure.

Sunday, August 17

Saturday had been bright and sunny; Sunday dawned dull and grey, with a chill breeze off the Strait. That, and the fact that Saturday had been a long day, can account for the late start I got that morning.

"Oh, there goes the hearse," said my landlady as she was fixing my breakfast. "Now who could that be?" she mused, as much to herself as to me or her husband in his chair across the kitchen, and she began to run over the possibilities. It couldn't be this one. . . . Maybe that one? No, he was in Summerside Hospital now. . . . How about—no, it wouldn't be coming down this way for her. . . . You don't suppose. . . . Finally she made her determination, and checked it with the telephone operator. She'd been right, of course. "Well, the poor soul's been bedridden·some time now," she told her husband, as she put my eggs on the table. "I guess it's a blessing."

I was fascinated. I had never lived in a community so tight-knit that one could do what she had just done, or, for that matter, where the telephone operator was also the local news broker.

Since I wanted to spend some time with Charlie Gorman, I headed for Burton as soon as I finished my breakfast, but Charlie was not at home when I arrived. "He's not back from Mass yet," said Mrs. Dalton, "but he'll be along soon. Come on in. I'm just fixing dinner."

"How's he been?" I asked, settling into a chair away from the stove.

"Well, he's over eighty, you know, and he's slowed down some this past year, but he's pretty good. He walks everywhere, even to church." She looked out the window. "Oh, there he comes now," she said.

I watched the figure walking up the lane and coming across the farmyard. Yes, he had slowed down. I could see that, but his step was still steady. He stopped to look at my car, then came in.

"Once I saw that Maine license plate I knew it had to be you," he said, "but I was pretty sure anyway, because I remembered you always closed the gate, and most strangers don't think to do that."

I felt truly complimented. Mrs. Dalton said dinner was ready and for me to sit down, which I did, even though I'd just had breakfast.

"Charlie," I said, as the meal came to a close, "remember you sang a song about 'Drive Dull Care Away' last time I was here?"

"Yes," he said. "I was going to sing it at the picnic. It seemed like it would suit the occasion, you know."

"Could I get you to sing that over again?" And I explained about the tape recorder.

"Well, if you'd like me to, yes," he said, "but could we do it tomorrow? I'd like to sort of go over it to get it together first."

I said that would be fine, and I took off for my appointment with Edmund and Long Joe, carefully closing the gate behind me.

I picked up Edmund at his place, and we headed out the St. Louis Road to Long Joe's. He had, of course, been expecting us for some time and greeted me a little more enthusiastically than he had to, but under the circumstances I guess that was understandable. We were ushered into the parlour, at which point I knew I was really company, but as soon as the talk got around to songs, I suggested that since there was no electricity in the house we should move out to my car, so I could use my tape recorder.

Joe sat in the front seat, Edmund in the back, and it wasn't long before a small crowd began to gather around us — not only children but adults as well. "What'll it be, Joe?" I asked, and he launched right into "The Miramichi Fire," doing a fine job of it , but no better than he had done a year ago. I kept the engine off during the recording, and in typical fashion fretted inwardly about the battery.

I needn't have. As soon as he finished I turned the key and was relieved when the car started with only minor protest. Everyone wanted to hear the result, so we opened the windows and I played it back for them. Then Joe said he'd like to try "The Lost Babes of Halifax," remembering, I am sure, his not being able to get through the year before. "Fine," I said, shutting off the engine and turning on the Webcor. "Go to it."

Like most products of the local muse, this ballad tells about "something that really happened." Jane Elizabeth and Margaret Meagher (pronounced "Marr") wandered from their home in Dartmouth, Nova Scotia, and after a massive and widespread search, one Peter Curry found the bodies on April 22, 1844. The ballad has a reputation of being "a tough one" to get through, but Joe did a splendid job of it.

The Lost Babes of Halifax

1.
Good people pay attention to these lines you're going to hear,
And when you will peruse them you can't but shed a tear;
In eighteen hundred and sixty-four on April the 'leventh day,
When those two little children around their home did play.

2.
Their father and their mother both sick in bed did lay,
While those two little children around the doors did play;
'Twas hand in hand together they saw them leave the door,
The eldest was but six years old, the youngest she was four.

♩. = 40

Good peo-ple pay at-ten-tion to these
lines you're going to hear. (Hm) And when you will per-use them you
can't but shed a tear; (Hm) In eight-een hun-dred and
six-ty-four on Ap-ril the 'lev-enth___ day, When
those two lit-tle chil-dren a-round their home did play.

3.
Sarah and Maggie Marr was those two pretty names,
Two fairer creatures never was, no nature seemed to [lays];
'Twas hand in hand together how merry they did play
But mark what followed after, how soon they lost their way.

4.
'Twas in the lonely wilderness they spent a lonesome day,
When night came on they thought of home, their screaming cries gave way;
Those forest gales blew very hard, no stars to show them light,
And beasts of prey they feared by [*day and*] screaming howls at night.

5.
Early the next morning turned out one hundred men
With Teddy Somers and his wife a-searching the lonely glen;
With eyes cast up to heaven and down upon the grove
The cries of those two people was dreadful as their woes.

6.
We searched all that evening, but alas 'twas all in vain,
While those two little children in the forest did remain;
We ofttimes stopped to listen but could not hear a sound,
At four o'clock next evening a little rag we found.

7.
Early the next morning turned out a volun [*valiant*] crew
To search the hills and lonely glen as hunters used to do;
From Halifax to Denmark, from Perth to Portland line.
Turned out one thousand five hundred men for final search to mind.

8.

But Peter Skerry found them at twelve o'clock that day,
On a melancholy mountain lay two little lumps of clay;
The hair was torn from off their heads, their clothes in ribbons torn,
The tender flesh from off their bones by prickle thorns was [gone].

9.

We dare no longer leave them for birds and beasts of prey
But in a decent burial we greeted them with our tears;
We took them to their parents, their mother to behold,
She kissed them o'er one thousand times though they were dead and cold.

10.

Early the next morning they in one coffin lay,
And in the yard of St. Paul's Church their little grave we made.
The rain it fell in torrents and dreadful was the day,
That we conferred their bodies down in the dark cold clay.

11.

Five thousand pounds was offered to the man who did them find,
But Skerry he refused it like a Christian meek and mild;
May God reward him for his care, show him the light of day,
And poor (*power?*] David grant him may ever sing his praise.

Just like his brother, Joe didn't exactly speak his last words when he sang; he simply faded out or, figuratively, turned away from his singing, and when he did I immediately hit the starter. That was a long song by any standard, and once again my enjoyment was marred by my anxiety over the car battery. No problem; the engine kicked right over. Apparently I had a lot to learn about living with my new toy.

We rolled down the windows again and played this one back for people. After it was over, an older woman came along, pushed her way through the kids, and wanted to know what was going on. "Let me hear that," she demanded. I said we'd have to wait until I got the battery charged back up. She frowned, said something in French that panicked everyone, and walked off. I didn't ask for a translation.

"How about one more?" I said to Joe, and Edmund suggested "The Wild Colonial Boy," a prime favourite both in Maine and the Maritimes and well beyond. Joe cleared his throat and went right to it.

The Wild Colonial Boy

1.

'Twas of a wild colonial boy, Jack Dobbin was his name;
He was born in Erin's sunny land in a place called Calais
    [*pron.* Callis], Maine.
He was his father's only pride, his mother's only joy;
How dearly did his parents love the wild colonial boy.

Nineteen Fifty-Eight—77

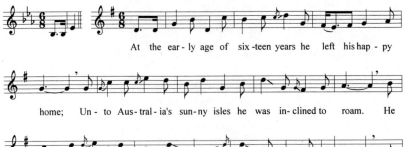

At the ear-ly age of six-teen years he left his hap-py home; Un-to Aus-tral-ia's sun-ny isles he was in-clined to roam. He

robbed the weal-thy squi-ers and their arms he did de-stroy — The

ter-rors of Aus-tral-ia was the wild co-lon-ial boy.

2.

At the early age of sixteen years he left his happy home;
Unto Australia's sunny isles he was inclined to roam.
He robbed the wealthy squi-ers and their arms he did destroy—
The terrors of Australia was the wild colonial boy.

3.

At the early age of eighteen years he began his wild career,
With a heart that feared no danger and a spirit that knew no fear.
He robbed the rich to help the poor, he stabbed Jim MacEvoy—
The terror to Australia was the wild colonial boy.

4.

One morning on the prairie as Jack he rode along,
Listening to the mockingbirds a-singing their lofty song,
Up stepped three mounted troopers, there was Kelly and Fitzroy—
They all turned out to capture the wild colonial boy.

5.

"Surrender now, Jack Dobbin! You see we're three to one.
Surrender now, Jack Dobbin, for you are a plundering son."
Jack drew a pistol from his belt and waved it up on high:
"I'll fight but not surrender!" cried the wild colonial boy.

6.

Jack fired a shot at Kelly, which brought him to the ground,
And as he turned to David he received his fatal wound.
A ball had pierced his proud young heart from the pistol of Fitzroy,
So that's the way they captured the wild colonial boy.

Joe was tired, and, since a light rain had set in, the onlookers dropped off by ones and twos until we were alone. It seemed a good time to quit.

That evening there was a special Mass that just about the whole town attended. It was sort of assumed that I wouldn't be going, and I guess I acted on that assumption. I said there were some things I had to take care of, which wasn't really true, but I sat in Edmund's front room and watched the dark come down over the houses and a lone horse grazing sparse beach grass outside the gate. Little by little the lights came back on. Edmund returned and we went over to the Tremblays', where the circle formed again, and he sang several more songs.

The one that interested me most he called "The Ghostly Fishermen," a song that I as a folksinger had learned from a book and had been singing at gigs for some time, going spookily minor in my accompaniment just as the ghosts climbed over the rail.[4] Edmund let the song do all the work. It's better that way, I decided. No doubt about it, I was learning a thing or two about traditional singing.

The Ghostly Fishermen

♪ = 112

I was tossed a-bout on Geor-gia I went fish-ing down the Bay, Down south in ear-ly win-ter, most an-y-where would pay; I've been in diff-'rent pla-ces on the West-ern Banks and Grand, I've been in her-ring ves-sels that sails from New-found-land

---

[4]William M. Doerflinger, *Shantymen and Shantyboys* (New York: Macmillan, 1951), pp. 181–82.

1.

You may smile if you're a mind to, perhaps you'll lend an ear,
We're men and boys together, well on for fifty years,
Have sailed upon the water in summer's pleasant day,
And through the storms of winter where the howlin' winds do rage.

2.

I was tossed about on Georgia, I went fishing down the Bay,[5]
Down south in early winter, most anywhere would pay;
I've been in diff'rent places, on the Western Banks and Grand,
I've been in herring vessels that sails from Newfoundland.

3.

If they're ice or storms I tell you when things looked rather blue,
But somehow or another was lucky and got through;
I'm not to brag, however—I won't say much, but then,
I ain't as easily frightened as most of other men.

4.

Oh this night as we were sailing, we were off shores a ways,
I'll never shall forget it all in my livelong days;
Twas on those dark night watches I felt a chilling dread
Crept over me as if I heered one calling from the dead.

5.

Right over the rail they climbed her, in silence one by one,
A dozen dripping sailors—just wait till I am done.
Their face was pale and seaworn, shone ghostly through the night,
Each fellow took his station as if he had a right.

6.

They moved about before us, the land was just in sight,
Or rather I should say so, a lighthouse shone its light;
And then those ghostly sailors moved to the rail again,
And vanished in an instant before the sons of men.

7.

We sailed right in the harbour, and every one of the crew
Can tell you the same story, the same as I now do;
The trip before the other, we were on the Georgia then,
Ran down another vessel and sank her and her men.

8.

These were the same poor fellows, I hope God bless their souls,
That our old ship ran under that night on Georgia's shoals;
So now you've heered my story, it's just as I now say,
I do believe in spirits from that time and today.

That was the end of the singing for that night. It had been a great couple of nights for me, but now I had to move on. "Now let's see," said Edmund, and he started ticking off on his fingers the various songs he had sung for me. "That's at least a dozen we've given this man," he said. "Maybe more.

---

[5]"Georgia" refers to Georges Bank, a fishing ground just south of the Gulf of Maine, and the "Bay" is the way local fishermen referred to the Gulf of St. Lawrence.

I'd say that's pretty good."

There was no suggestion in what he was saying that I ought to be grateful — though I was, and said so. In fact, the statement wasn't even delivered to me so much as it was to the others in the circle. It was more a feeling of pride that he — and with him the whole community — had been able to share something with me that we both found valuable. And it was not only the songs, but the singing as well, and the sense of time together both engendered.

The rain had stopped, and driving back to O'Leary that night I was struck by the quality of the dark. Beyond the little patch of dirt road in my headlights, nothing. Black. Then off to the left from time to time a single tiny square of light — soft yellow, or occasionally bright white from a mantle lamp — would drift by and disappear behind me. I remembered a passage in Huizinga's *The Waning of the Middle Ages* where he spoke of how we had lost this sense of true night. I pulled off to the side of the road, turned my lights out, and just sat there for maybe five minutes. Then I went on my way.

Monday, August 18

I was back at Charlie Gorman's, and he and I were sitting in the front seat of my car just outside the gate at the head of the long lane leading down to the Shore Road. I was still concerned about my battery, and my logic was that if I drained the battery I could always jump-start by rolling down the hill. I wasn't much worried about the first song, though, which was "Drive Dull Care Away," but there was no telling what might follow after.

Charlie asked me a grammatical question about a line in what he was about to sing: should it be this way or that way, because he wanted to have it right (he knew I was a teacher). I told him it didn't matter; he should sing it the way he learned it. Which is what he did.

Drive Dull Care Away

1.

Oh why should we at our lot complain or grieve at our distress?
Some think if they could riches gain 'twould be true happiness.
But alas how vain is all their strife, life's cares it will not allay,
And while we're here with our friends so dear we'll drive dull care away.
CHORUS: Away, away, away, away —
              We will drive dull care away!
              And while we're here with our friends so dear
              We'll drive dull care away.

2.

Why should the rich despise the poor, why should the poor repine?
For we will all in a few short years in equal friendship join.
They're both to blame, they're all the same; we're all made of one clay,
And while we're here with our friends so dear we'll drive dull care away.
CHORUS

Nineteen Fifty-Eight—81

♩ = 112

Oh why should we at our lot com-plain or grieve at our distress? Some think if they could rich-es gain 'twould be true hap-pi-
ness. But a-las how vain is all their strife,
life's cares it will not al-lay, And while we're here with our
friends so dear we'll drive dull care a-way. A-way, a-way, a-
way, a-way— We will drive dull care a-way! And
while we're here with our friends so dear we'll drive dull care a-way.
all the same; we're all made of one clay And

3.
The only circumstance in life that ever I could find
To conquer care and temper strife was a contented mind.
With this in store we have much more than all things else will convey,
And while we're here with our friends so dear we'll drive dull care away.
CHORUS

4.
Then let us make the best of life, not rendering it a curse,
But take it as you take a wife, for better or for worse.
Life at its best is but a jest, like a dreary winter's day,
And while we're here with our friends so dear we'll drive dull care away.
CHORUS

The sun had broken through the thin clouds that had been around all day, but only for a few moments. "Great!" I said as I turned the engine on. No problem. I played the song back for him.

"I think that's right," said Charlie. "I think I've got it all there."

"I'm sure you have," I said.

We chatted for a few minutes while I let the battery charge. I remembered there were a couple of empty houses down the road, and, as much to have something to talk about as anything, I asked if there were any haunted houses around.

Charlie considered that for a moment. "No," he said. "Not that I know of. Oh, they say that one time years ago the sexton was cleaning up after Mass in St. Marks over there [we could see it from where we sat] and a strange priest came in and started to say Mass, but when he came to the canon he disappeared. They claim that happened several times, but the sexton didn't say anything because he was afraid it might put him under an obligation. So he told the present priest, who came and watched with him, and when the other priest appeared he approached him and said, 'In the name of the Father, Son and Holy Ghost what are you doing here?' And the other priest thanked him and said he'd taken money for Masses that he never got to say. So the parish priest said to give him the names, and once he'd said all the Masses the other priest was never seen again. Now of course I don't know that for sure, but that's what they say."

Mrs. Dalton stepped out into the yard to call us in to dinner.

As we sat around afterwards, somehow Charlie got onto Ireland and the brutal treatment she had received from her British masters, and in his quiet way he became quite heated. "It's a terrible thing, those years of oppression," he said. "I've got a book upstairs that tells all about it. Perhaps you'd like to see it." And, without waiting for any affirmative from me, he left to fetch it, returning in a few moments with a small green-covered volume, which he handed to me. "That tells all about it," he said.

The binding was loose, and some pages fell out as I opened to the title page: *Ireland's Case*, by Seumas MacManus.[6]

"Oh, Seumas MacManus!" I said. "You know, I met him and heard him lecture once a few years ago while I was teaching out in Illinois."

Charlie looked up. Then he put out his hand. "I want to shake the hand of a man who has met Seumas MacManus," he said, with quiet respect. "He was a great writer."

The talk went on for a while longer. Then I said I had to be going.

---

[6]New York: The Irish Publishing Co., 1918. MacManus (1869–1960) was an Irish author, poet, and playwright who spent much of his life lecturing and otherwise presenting the story of Ireland's struggle for independence to American audiences.

As I went out the door, Charlie shook my hand again. Then he handed me the book. "Here, you should have this. No," he said, brushing aside my demurral, "I've read it many times. You take it now."

I never saw Charlie again. I had already decided to dedicate *Larry Gorman* to Louise Manny, but four years later when the time came to publish it I decided to add his name, too. I wrote to tell him, but the letter was returned. He had died the day before.

But often over the years when I'm searching for something else on my shelves, I come across *Ireland's Case* and take it down. It's a good way to remember a fine gentleman.

The sun kept trying to break through again all afternoon, but the clouds hung around as I revisited people like Mary Cousins and Harry Thompson, mostly to confirm this-or-that detail of something they had told me the year before, but the visit to Harry brought up a new name: Frank O'Holleran. "I don't know why I didn't think of him before," he said, "but he knows some of Gorman's pieces. I don't know that he can *sing* them, but I've heard him word them over, so you ought to see him. His house is handy to Bloomfield Station there."

O'Holleran, a man well into his eighties, I'd say, met me at the door, and the minute I said my name he knew my mission, not only from Harry Thompson, but from Keith Pratt and Mary Cousins as well. The house was very small, and definitely bachelor quarters—unswept linoleum, a sink full of dirty dishes, and a battered kitchen table with three unmatched chairs just about made up the whole of it—but he invited me in and started quietly reciting (Harry was right: he couldn't sing) Gorman pieces before I could even get my notebook unlimbered (of course there was no electricity). I couldn't keep up with him; in fact, I quit and asked if he'd come out to the car so I could use my tape recorder. Sure, he said, but he wanted to go over them sitting at the table first, which was fine by me.

I kept the engine running as he worded over two songs (I never got over my old-maidish anxiety about the battery), the second one being "The Gull Decoy," and since it is a song which did much to spread Gorman's notoriety —some say he was run off the Island for it—and since O'Holleran's text is the most complete I ever collected on the Island—I give it here.

The most common story I've heard is that Gorman was convinced Riley had cheated him out of some wages, but whatever he may have done, that poet dug up all the dirt he could find on him, and (according to some people I've talked to) what he couldn't find he invented. He portrays Riley as an illiterate, superstitious immigrant, cast out from the body of the Church and sponging off his relatives. I'm told the song can still raise hackles along Lot Seven shore, and small wonder!

The Gull Decoy

1.

I'm an Irishman from the County Kerry,
Patrick Riley it is my name.
I was bred and born in that place so merry
And crowned with many great deeds of fame

2.

I took my axe and went to chopping,
Two hundred acres I had procured;
And to the West Point I went a-courting,
I fell in love with young Peggy Steward.

3.

I being so neat, so genteel in acting
And in my head such a piercing eye,
My whole person was so attractive
She fell in love with the Gull Decoy.

4.

Since that time I am much rejected
Sometimes I'm sorry for leaving home.
I have by some been accused of murder
And was expelled from the Church of Rome.

5.

From her Communion I am restricted—
I think of it every time I pass;
From all her rites I'm interdicted,
It's been forty years since I went to Mass.

6.

On Sunday morning to get my breakfast
I go down to my son Pat's;
I sit there 'til I get my dinner
And then I go to my nephew Matt's.

7.

His aged uncle he always honours
The very moment he do me spy;
Goes in the room, takes out the paper
And reads the news for the Gull Decoy.

8.

When I go home I go home delighted,
Fully determined to win my post,
But always careful not to get be-nighted
For in the bush I might meet a ghost.

9.

If it should happen that I should meet one
My heart and conscience would terrify;
I know they're dreadful, I cannot cheat them—
Perhaps they'd murder the Gull Decoy.

Nineteen Fifty-Eight—85

10.
When I go down and begin to whistle
The gulls all 'round me are seen to fly,
And at my feet they come and nestle;
That's why I'm titled the Gull Decoy.

11.
When I'm dead and my friends all round me,
There'll be no tears but a sob and sigh;
But all their tears will be unavailing,
For none can pray for the Gull Decoy.

"You see, he was excommunicated from the Church," he said. "They couldn't bury him in holy ground, "so they buried him down in the field. Oh yes, he was down there; had a little fence around it. It ends up, 'Like a horse they'll bury the Gull Decoy.' That's about all I can think of now, but there's more than that to it."

In fact there's quite a bit more, like verses about him setting a dog on an orphan boy and hounding his brother for marrying a Protestant. But we have enough here to show the kind of character assassination local satire could involve, and few employed it with more zest or skill than Larry Gorman.

Shortly after O'Holleran finished, a car—big, black, and convertible, with Québec plates—drove up and parked nose to mine, and a young man and woman climbed out. "Oh Lord," said Frank, almost under his breath, and got out to greet the woman, a distant relative who had gone to the mainland some years ago. I remember she was wearing a red dress, very high heels, and an oversupply of makeup, and her companion was wearing sandals and carrying a half-empty bottle of vodka by the neck. They raucously insisted we all go inside and have a drink.

"Well, O.K.," said Frank, quietly, "but you'll just have to forgive the appearance of the place. You see," he added, winking at me, "all the new furniture I ordered from Simpson's just hasn't come yet."

I'm not sure they even heard him as they started the bottle around and she asked loud questions about relatives and friends. How's old so-and-so. . . Is Uncle Jim still alive. . .and so on. She asked about one man, and having been told he was fine, "I went out with him some once," she said, "until I found out he was telling people I was nothing but a goddamned tease! Now what do you think of that!" She and the young man laughed loud and long, and Frank and I did our best to join in.

The bottle went around a couple of times more; then the visitors decided they had to be on their way.

The little house seemed awfully quiet after they left. Frank looked at me and shrugged. "Well, that's Montreal for you," he said. "Now I've got another song I think you'd better have." And we went back out to the car, where he recited "Mick Riley."

This song was about the Gull Decoy's son Mick, who, during the off-season, worked as a cobbler. "There was an old saying, 'A mackerel line, a hook, and a pair of Mick Riley's boots and you're a fisherman,'" Joe Tremblay had told me the year before. Unfortunately Mick had done something to incur Gorman's wrath, and the poet responded in his characteristically venemous fashion. "I'm not sure I've got the whole of it," Frank said, "but here's what I know":

Mick Riley

1.
'Twas in the summer season in the year of seventy-six,
'Twas with a crazy cobbler I went to learn some tricks;
To spend the summer fishing along Lot Seven shore.
Where the foaming billows madly leap and breakers loud do roar.

2.
But to my sad misfortune it proved an awful day;
Instead of human beings, they're more like beasts of prey.
They'll cheat you and backbite you and give you lots of chaw—
They'd kill you, skin, and eat you if it wasn't for the law.

3.
It's in the summer season he runs a fishing craft;
It's elegant and pleasing, it's called the *Ocean Lark*.
He goes a-pickarooning, sometimes a prize he gets;
He goes to Richibucto and steals the Frenchmen's nets.

4.
It's in the winter season he runs a cobbler's stall;
He makes a scanty living with his hammer and his awl
For five rude and saucy offspring and a broken-hearted wife
Who's allotted for to spend with him a sad and tortured life.

"And then I forget," he said, "but the last of it goes like this":

And while the life is in him to carry on that game,
Until at length he'll find himself in Hell's eternal flames.

"And I guess that's about all I know," he said. "How about a cup of tea?" I accepted, and we went inside.

Tuesday, August 19
By this time I had pretty well cleaned up most of the questions I had on Gorman—at least until I could get to places in Charlottetown like the Legislative Library. Therefore I decided to look up Angus Enman and talk to him about Joe Scott.[7]

---

[7]The material on Angus Enman has already appeared in very similar form in *Twenty-One Folksongs*, pp. 53–59.

Arthur and Ivan Nisbet had told me exactly where Enman's place was—about a mile down the MacArthur Road—and I found it easily. Angus was just shutting the big barn doors when I drove into the yard about noon. He was a tall, spare man with a craggy face and—in spite of his obvious age—a full head of curly dark hair. I introduced myself and told him who had sent me. "They tell me you spent a lot of time working in the Maine woods," I said.

"Yes," he said ruefully, "and much to my sorrow. I lost the sight of this eye there. Wood chip came back and hit me."

It didn't sound to me as though I had chosen the best of all possible openings, but when I asked about Joe Scott his face lit up. "Yes," he said, "I knew Joe Scott, and do you know how he come to start writing songs?" I said I did not. "Well, let's go inside and sit down and I'll tell you," he said. The story is worth repeating here:

*Well, Joe Scott and a fellow I knew was working in the lumberwoods. He was a Dutchman from River Herbert [River Hebert], Nova Scotia. . .

And Joe was a terrible wicked man. And. . . in them times there was no saws much; we done all with axes, see? We chopped those great big mountain spruce with an axe. And there was a head chopper and a second chopper, and Joe was head chopper. He was the man that led the tree. . . You had to understand leading. If you didn't they'd lodge in a big birch or something . . . Well, Joe hung this tree up. . . and he got right under it and he defied the Lord to fall it on him. And he went on. . . calling the Maker names. And this man said that the limb broke like that [slapping hands] and Joe just got away with his life. He just took his axe and said, "I'm all done in the woods." He never worked another day in the woods. And he went out and started making those songs. And then he'd come in boarding and we all knew him and he had copies, and he made some awful nice songs.

"What songs of Joe's do you still know?" I asked.

"Most I just remember sketches of," he said, "but I think I know all of 'Benjamin Deane,' except for a couple of places I get mixed up on."

"Would you try it for me?" I asked. "Don't worry about getting mixed up."

"Yeah," he said, "I'll try her, but I want to sing it over once before you turn that thing on again."

Most singers consider "Benjamin Deane" a hard song to sing under the best of circumstances. Angus was seventy-eight, and he had not sung for a long, long time, but his voice still had real authority. It was hard and sharp with a lot of head quality in it—a real old woods singer's voice—and while his control of pitch was not as good as it probably had been, he kept on tune very well. Not only had he known Joe Scott, he claimed to have learned the ballad directly from him. He had also known Benjamin Deane. I would have given a great deal to know what was in his mind's eye as he sang.

After he'd sung it through I turned the recorder on, and he sang it again, breaking down in exactly the same places this time that he had in his rehearsal.

Benjamin Deane

1.
Oh my name is Benjamin Dee-un, and my age is forty-one,
I was born in New Brunswick near the city of Saint John;
Nearby the Bay of Fundy where the seagulls loud do call
As they rock with pride the silvery tide as the billows rise and fall.

2.
My parents reared me tenderly, having no other child but me,
Till I became a sporter at the age of twenty-three.

Angus hesitated. *"Now there's where I'm goin' to—"
*"O.K.," I said. "That's all right."
*"Now where do I start in now?"
*"When I arrived in Berlin Falls?'" I prompted.

3.

When I arrived in Berlin Falls some twenty years ago,
The town was then about one half as large as it is now,
And labouring men of every nationality were there,
For work was plenty, wages good, each man could get his share.

4.

The businessmen of Berlin then were making money fast,
And I too thought I would invest before the boom had passed;
A building leased on Mason Street, and into business went,
I ran a fruit and candy store, likewise a restaurant.

5.

My business proved successful, I did the right by all;
I gained the favour of the great, the rich, the poor, and small.
To my surprise before one year had fully rolled its rounds,
In glittering gold I had possessed more than two thousand pounds.

6.

That coming year I wed with one, fairest of the fair;
Her eyes were of the heav'nly blue and light brown was her hair.
Her cheeks were like the dawn of day, her form graceful and fair;
Her smiles were bright as morning light, her step was light as air.

7.

She was brought up by good parents and reared most tenderly,
'Twas little did they ever think she would be slain by me;
The night I gained her promise, her hand to me she gave,
It would have been better far for her had she laid in her grave.

8.

I own I loved this fair young bride, which proved a prudent wife,
'Twas little did I think one day that I would take her life;
But as the years rolled swiftly on upon the wheels of time,
I found the paths of pleasure that led to the fields of crime.

9.

My wife would ofttimes plead in vain my footsteps to retrace;
She told me that the paths I trod led to death and disgrace.
Had I to heed her warning I would not be here now,
And she might yet be living with no brand upon her brow.

Again he looked to me. *"What did you say that other was?"
*"Uh, 'I soon began. . . ,'" I said.

10.

I soon began my wild career caused by the thirst for gold;
The property on Mason Street for a goodly price I sold.
I bought a building on Main Street which cost a handsome sum;
I ran a free-and-easy house and went to selling rum.

11.

My former friends of decent vein my company did shun,
But still I was content to lead the life I had begun;
For gold and silver like a brook came flowing in to me,
By its glitters I was blinded and my danger could not see.

12.

My fair wife she had fled to one whose name I will not write,
Whose character was darker than the blackest hour of night;
To persuade her to return to me it was my whole intent,
And to the house where my wife dwelt, my steps I quickly bent.

13.

I cautiously approached the house and opened the hall door;
I found the way to my wife's room upon the upper floor.
The sight that fell upon my gaze is stamped all on my mind,
For on the bosom of a man my wife's head reclined.

14.

. . . .
I drew a loaded pistol and I aimed it at her breast,
And when she saw the weepon it was loudly she did cry,
"For God's sake do not shoot me, Ben, I am not fit to die."

15.

The bullet pierced her snowy breast, in a moment she was dead.
"My God, Ben, you have shot me," were the last words that she said.
The trigger of me weepon either pulled too hard or slow,
Or else another soul'd a' passed with hers to weal or woe.

16.

The last time that I saw my wife, she lay upon the floor;
Her long and wavy light brown hair was stained with crimson gore.
The sun shone through the window on her cold and lifeless face,
As the officers led me away from that polluted place.

17.

I have two daughters living and they're orphans in a way,
And should you meet them treat them kindly I pray;
Don't chide them for their father's sins, for on them there will rest
A crimson stain long after I am mouldering back to dust.

18.

And now young men a warning take from this sad tale of mine:
Don't sacrifice your honour for bright gold and silver fine.
Let truth and honour be your shield, and you'll be sure to climb
The ladder of success and fame and not be stung by crime.

I wondered about other Joe Scott songs and asked for them by name. Yes, he'd known them; he sang a little bit of "Guy Reed" and recited a stanza of "The Plain Golden Band" at the prodding of his housekeeper. *"I knew all these songs years ago," he said. "but I'm getting out of the habit." I was disappointed, of course, but that disappointment was more than made up for by his vignettes both of Joe and of lumbercamp life in general. *"Joe made his headquarters in Rumford," he said. "It was Rumford Falls at that time, and he used to come up around the camps. See, there was a great circle of camps up around Bemis. That's all tore up I guess now. And then we used to go up back of Andover there and old Blue Mountain, and I was getting around them woods a lot there."

These were evocative names for me; in fact I'd been up in those western Maine hills not more than a week before, and questions were crowding into my head. *"I'm kind of jumping around here," I said, "but did you ever hear the story of the fella who pulled the feathers out of the bird?" He had, and he told it well:

> *Yeah, I heard the boys talking about that up in the woods. Oh, I never heard very much about it, you know. Up there, those moose birds [Canada Jay], you was lunching out, and they'd be thick—they'd be starting, they'd be right there, and they'd come right up on my feet. And there was an old fella setting alongside of me one day, and I pretty near caught one. And he said, "Look," he said, "I could tell you a story about that." He said, "There was a bad fella, a wicked sort of fella, and he got one of the birds." And he said, "He picked the feathers off and let him go—cold of the winter! And," he said, "oh, he passed a remark—oh, he was a wicked sort of fella. He said, 'Let the old son of a bitch that put them on you grow them on again!'" He said, "He woke up in the morning and he was bald-headed as could be." [8]

> I don't know how true that is, but that's what that man told me. I was only a kid then. I went up to the woods when I was young, around sixteen or seventeen, and I was full of curiosity, and them old fellas used to give me pointers, you know. You'd run into some really nice old fellas. I worked with a fella in the woods—he worked fifty-three winters. He was eighty-four. Of course he was just feeding the horses. He said he couldn't stay home in the winter.

Angus was every bit as good a storyteller as he was a singer, but it was the old songs I was especially interested in, and I got the conversation swung back over that way, resulting a few minutes later in "The Dark-Eyed Sailor." It took him a couple of stanzas to settle down on the tune, but after that all went well. The first line of the third stanza should probably be, "Said Willy, 'Lady why roam alone?'" It's something like that in all the other versions I've heard or read, but I leave it as Angus sang it. And while the tune seems to have a basic 5/4 meter, I haven't tried to force everything into it.

---

[8]For more information on this story, see Edward D. Ives. "The Man Who Plucked the Gorby: A Maine Woods Legend." *Journal of American Folklore* 74 (Spring, 1961), pp. 1–8; Bacil F. Kirtley, "On the Origin of the Maine-Maritimes Legend of the Plucked Gorby," *Journal of American Folklore* 87 (1974), pp. 364–65; Edward D. Ives, "'The Man Who Plucked the Gorby': A Maine Woods Legend Debated in Slow Motion," in Abrahams et al. *By Land and By Sea*, pp. 137–40.

The Dark-Eyed Sailor

Parlando rubato ♩ = 108 approx.

"'Tis sev-en long years since he left the land;

A gold ring took from off his hand.

He broke love's to-ken, gave half to me, While the oth-er goes rol-ling,

while the oth-er goes rol-ling In the bot-tom of the sea."

1.
'Tis of a comely maiden fair,
Who was walking out for to take the air.
She met a sailor on her way,
So she paid attention, so she paid attention
To what he might say.

2.
He said, "Lady dear, why roam alone?
The day's now spent, night is coming on."
She answered him while tears down did flow,
"For my dark-eyed sailor, for my dark-eyed sailor
That proved my overthrow."

3.
He says, "[milly] lady, drive him from your mind,
For as good a sailor as him you'll find;
For as love grows old it colder grows,
Like a winter's morning, like a winter's morning
When the fields are clad with snow."

4.
Oh, these harsh words drove Phoebe's fond heart to flame.
She said, "On me you will run no game!"
She drew a dagger and then did sigh,
"For my dark-eyed sailor, for my dark-eyed sailor
A maid I live and die!

5.
"'Tis seven long years since he left the land;
A gold ring took from off his hand.
He broke love's token, gave half to me,

While the other goes rolling, while the other goes rolling
In the bottom of the sea."

6.

Then half the ring did young Willie show,
As she stood a while 'twixt joy and woe,
Saying, "Welcome back! I have land and gold,
For my dark-eyed sailor, for my dark-eyed sailor,
So manfully and bold."

7.

Now in a cottage by the riverside
In unity they do reside.
So maids, be true while your love's away,
For a cloudy morning, for a cloudy morning
Will bring a sunny day.

I asked was there really much singing in the camps. *"Oh great. Ohhh great!" he said. "Well, you know; it wasn't what it is now, singing. Most singers now gotta have a guitar, but then there was no music at all. Saturday night you see, when we'd come into the camp after supper you had to tell a story or sing a song or dance. If you didn't, they'd ding you; they'd put the dried codfish to you."

*"They'd do what?" I said.

*"They had these old dried codfish and if you wouldn't sing or dance or do something . . . they'd take the dried codfish and two or three would throw you down and boy oh boy—"

*"You mean they'd hit you with it?" I said.

*"Hit you! Hard! Yeah! Right on the ass, boy, just as hard as they can swing." He laughed. "You take one of them old Cape Bretoners, great big old Scotchmen; or them Dutchmen, one of them big buggers from River Herbert, Nova Scotia!"

He remembered those nights well. *"If you couldn't sing, you could tell a good story, [or] perhaps you could dance. There'd be a fellow have a fiddle there, see, and give a tune. Old [David] Dyment used to dance, and he was a good song-singer, old David, and he could stepdance pretty good. Oh yes, [somebody] he'd go round: 'Now boy, come on. Do what you're going to do.'"

After singing and telling stories most of the afternoon, Angus apologized for having forgotten so much. Listening to the tapes of that interview almost forty years later, I can see how my semi-checklist approach probably helped to make him feel that way, but hindsight is cheap. As usual, I had special things I was interested in, and, since I only had a few days at my disposal, I wanted to use them as efficiently as I could. Besides, we both enjoyed our time together, and I knew I could always come back again (Unfortunately, as so often happens, I never did).

The wind was picking up, and there were some black clouds looming in the west. For sure, it was fixing to storm, but maybe not for a while, and I wanted to try and see the second person on Arthur and Ivan Nisbet's list: Wesley Smith, who lived in nearby Victoria West. It was late in the afternoon when I left Angus', but since (according to Arthur and Ivan's directions) it was only an easy mile or so to the Smiths', I decided to give it a try. If this turned out to be a bad time, we could at least make plans for the following day.

I found the farm with no trouble at all, and his wife met me at the door. Wesley was working somewhere around the place, she said, but she didn't know where—probably down in the field. I explained my business and told her who'd sent me. A few drops of rain hit the window. "Well," she said, "maybe the rain's brought him in. Probably he's out in the barn. I know he'd like to talk to you. Sit down and I'll go look."

In a few minutes Mrs. Smith returned with her husband, a man in his mid-sixties who had pretty obviously been finishing up the daily barn chores. We talked about Arthur and Ivan for a moment; then I asked about old songs. Well, it had been a long time, he said, and he doubted if he could even get one together now. I played my trump card. "You knew Joe Scott, didn't you?" I asked.

"Yes," he said spiritedly, "and I know two of his songs."

"Will you sing them for me?"

He laughed. "They're awful long. Have you got anything to drink?"

"No," I said, wishing I did, "but will you give them a try?"

"Well," he said doubtfully, "I suppose I could."

Since there was no electricity, we went out to the car so I could run the recorder off the converter. As we settled in, the full storm came across the valley, buffeting the car with wind and rain (I can hear it quite pleasantly on the tapes today). "I think I'll try 'Guy Reed' first," he said. "That's the one I know best." And he launched right into that long ballad that Joe Scott had made over in Maine back in 1898 to commemorate a friend killed when a pile of logs collapsed and crushed him. Like other singers I had heard, Wesley began by humming a bit to get the right pitch, but once he got it he sailed right along in grand style, his voice high and strong, the words clear.

At his request I have added stanza 8 from a later singing.

Guy Reed

♩ = 120

2. The post brought me a let - ter I

has - tened to per - use, 'Twas writ - ten by a

friend of mine but bore me start - ling news, Of

one I knew a fine young man as you would wish to see,

In an in - stant he was hurled in to e - ter - ni - ty.

1.
. . . . . . [hum] I remember one dark and stormy night,
The rain it fell in torrents and the lightning flashed so bright;
The moon and stars above me did not their light reveal,
The dark clouds so gloomy did their welcome light conceal.

2.
The post brought me a letter I hastened to peruse,
'Twas written by a friend of mine but bore me startling news,
Of one I knew a fine young man as you would wish to see,
In an instant he was hurled in to eternity.

3.
He and his companions where the waters loud do roar
Were breaking in a landing on the Androscoggin shore;
They had picked the face on one of them from bottom to the top,
Full thirty feet this landing had one perpendicular drop.

4.
To work this face much longer 'twould be a foolish part,
A jar so slight you see it might this lofty landing start;
There were a few among them did volunteer to go
To roll a log from off the top to start the logs below.

5.
Those logs they quickly started, the landing creaked below,
And on it sped unto the verge but would no farther go;
This young man now approaches the verge of landing high,
While all the crew with pallid cheeks and trembling limbs stood by.

6.
Up went the shout of warning, to warn him of his fate,
And just an instant he did pause, he seemed to hesitate;
He rolled the log just halfway o'er, the landing broke like glass.
And quick as thought he disappeared into that rolling mass.

7.
Those logs they rolled carefully from o'er his mangled form.
The birds were sweetly singing and the sun shone bright and warm;
Strong men knelt down beside him who could not their grief command,
Unbidden tears burst from their eyes and fell into the sand.

8.
[Tenderly they bore him, gently laid him on the green
Beneath a shady tree that grew nearby a purling stream.
The sparkling bubbling waters stealing o'er its sandy bed
Seemed to murmur sweetly, softly, farewell unto the dead.]

9.
His remains were buried by the order of K.P.,
A funeral more attended you would seldom ever see;
The church and yard were crowded with people young and old,
Once more to see that face once fair in death now pale and cold.

10.
His casket was decorated with roses rich and fair,
His pillow too with every hue of flowers bright and rare;
His brothers of the order as they marched two by two,
On the casket they let fall a token of adieu.

11.
This young man's name was Guy Reed, his age was twenty-three,
On September the eighth was killed in the town known as Riley;
In the little town of Byron he sleeps beneath the earth,
He sleeps beside his kindred near the spot that gave him birth.

12.
His mother she died early when he was but a child;
They laid her down to slumber near a forest fair and wild;
His brother and a sister is now sleeping by her side
In the quiet country churchyard near the river's dancing tide.

13.
His poor old feeble father is stricken now with grief,
The joys of earthly pleasures can bring him no relief;
For untold gold or silver, possession, wealth in store,
Sunny skies or music sweet cannot the dead restore.

14.
The cuckoo and the swallow, the sunshine and the rain,
The blackbird and the thrushes in the spring shall come again;
The robin and the swallow from foreign lands will soar,
But they who that in death doth sleep shall ne'er return no more.

No. 13: Guy Reed. *NA P113*. Photo courtesy of Mrs. Wirt Virgin, West Peru, Maine.

15.
Kind friends and loving kindred of him who's dead and gone
To a better land in heaven far away beyond the sun,
The ones that you love dearly you shall ne'er again see more,
'Till you pass through death's dark valley to that bright celestial shore.

In a later interview I asked Wesley if he'd learned that song in Maine. *"No," he said, "I learned that here before I ever went to Maine [*in 1912*]. That's the winter I met Joe. I bought a printed copy from him, and I had it *perfect!*"

Wesley then agreed to sing what he knew of "Howard Carey," which was almost all of it, but he was quite annoyed with himself for forgetting and getting mixed up a couple of times. Almost as if in compensation for these failures he sang two more short songs.[9]

The storm had passed over us. "I guess that's about all I better do," said Wesley. I turned the engine on and put the microphone away. "Would you like some tea?" I said I would, and we went back to the house.

---

[9]These two songs can be found in *Twenty-One Folksongs, pp. 68–72.*

Nineteen Sixty-Three

I DIDN'T GET BACK TO P.E.I. for five years, during which time a great deal had happened. First of all, I had finished up a doctorate in folklore at Indiana University in 1962; back in 1957 and even in 1958 the idea of doing such a thing had not seriously occurred to me. Larry Gorman had been the basis for my dissertation on satirical song and was soon to be published by Indiana University Press. I also had acquired far better equipment than I'd had before: nothing fancy—just a Wollensak 1500 (compact, truly portable, and the folkloristic workhorse for a decade of fieldworkers!) and an Electro-Voice 664 mike—but considerably better than my old Webcor. No question about it, now I was a folklorist for sure!

One thing in particular was the driving force for this field trip: I had a contract with Indiana University's Archives of Folk and Traditional Music (now the Archives of Traditional Music) to put together an LP of traditional singing from Maine and the Maritimes. Never mind that the record itself never got produced; what I was doing was revisiting the best singers I knew in order to get better recordings and more complete representatives of their repertoires.

It was mid-July. I was travelling alone again, and I had just spent better than a week with two of the best singers I knew from New Brunswick— Wilmot MacDonald and Jim Brown.[1] At first I had no firm intention of going out to P.E.I. at all, since my time was limited and I felt I already had what I needed from there, but, looking out from around Richibucto one day after leaving Jim Brown's—well, I knew it was out there in the haze, even if I couldn't see it, and I let myself get homesick. After all, it would be nice to see Edmund Doucette and Wesley Smith again, wouldn't it, and maybe re-record a few songs with my new equipment? And did I have to be in such a tearing rush that I couldn't spare the couple of days the trip would take?

Ineluctably, I was on my way to Cape Tormentine, where I just caught the last ferry.

Sunday, July 14, 1963

As I pulled into his driveway I really wasn't all that sure Wesley would remember me; after all, it had been five years since my last visit, and during

---

[1] For representative samples of their singing, see Edward D. Ives, *Folksongs of New Brunswick* (Fredericton: Goose Lane Editions, 1989), pp. 66–139.

that time I hadn't sent him so much as a Christmas card. But I needn't have worried; he remembered me well and was ready to sit right down and start singing without further delay, but for some reason I can't recall now I had decided to head up to Miminegash and visit Edmund that afternoon, so I made arrangements with Wesley to come back the next day.

So far as I could see, Edmund hadn't changed a bit in five years, but Miminegash had. The Shore Road and the road through town down to the run were both blacktopped, and apparently just about everyone had electricity now. Certainly Edmund did, and I could see in a moment the tremendous difference that made in the quality of life for him and his family—from the refrigerator and electric teakettle in the kitchen to the television set in the living room. It also made a difference in the interview situation. We didn't have to go over to the Tremblays', where he had performed not only for me but for family and close friends; now it was just the two of us, and what was lost in terms of performance for a group was gained in my easy ability to question him about his life and what lay behind the songs while I left the tape recorder running.

As I have already pointed out, I had my agenda. I wanted a better recording of "The Old Beggar Man," and he sang it twice for me, once in the afternoon and once again in the evening after supper (he had had a bad fit of coughing in the afternoon version and wanted to have it right for me). Of course, I also asked him about Joe Scott, and he sang substantial portions of "Howard Carey," "The Plain Golden Band," and "The Norway Bum," but he knew there were parts of them he'd forgotten. *"Oh, I really loved it," he said of "The Norway Bum." "I liked that song. True song, you know. Things like that would happen." Like many other singers I'd talked to, he felt Scott's songs were somehow in a class by themselves.

I was interested in the fact that while there were many Acadian names in Miminegash, and while I was quite sure I could detect some speech patterns that were certainly French, yet the song tradition in the village, according to Edmund, was English.[2]

> . . . *Oh there's places where they don't speak anything else. You take
> along between here and St. Louis [out where Long Joe lived]—all French
> mostly. But they are acquainted with English, but still they hung on to
> their language. Well, I can speak French with anybody but my woman
> can't; she can talk a little all right, but she understands it good. But [my]
> family, there's none can talk it at all and they don't understand it . . .
> because we never speak it here. . . They do get on me, the kids sometimes,

---

[2]Much of the material on the next few pages can also be found in *Twenty-One Folksongs*, pp. 11–13, 31–32.

[that] they'd like to learn it, but I can't get on to it, you know, to talk French in the house.

If he had been brought up French at home, I wondered, where and how did he learn his English:

*Well, we learned it some about the house 'cause there was English neighbours, but mostly in school. The majority [of people around here] is French, and there's not one of them speak French. Oh they're all French people, [except for] three or four families of Irish descent, but they're married in with the French.

*"Do you remember any French songs?" I asked.

*Oh yes, I used to sing them for the kids sometimes. They'd get a great kick out of it. . . . I sung one for Miss Creighton [Dr. Helen Creighton] when she was here that time. That's about the only one probably I know. It's about a sporty guy; he's going along and this girl was in a garden, and he wanted to get acquainted with her. And he took his hat in his hand and he went and he introduced himself, but she had no interest in him. He was dying to make love with her and she refused him, and I guess he was pretty disappointed. And he took his hat under his arm and he bade her good-bye.

It's very seldom you hear a French song [around here]. There was some darned nice ones too— songs made up about fellows killed in the lumberwoods and things like that. . . There was an old lady [and] she used to sing one. . . . It's a terrible nice song, about a fellow by the name of Jerome something. He was killed by a hanging limb that fell on his head. And on his dying bed he tells about when he left home. It was pitiful, it was sad; nice song, awful nice air to it too. [He was] killed here on the Miramichi.

Not only do the foregoing passages give some interesting insights into the local tradition and tastes, but that "here on the Miramichi" is a clue. Edmund had spent many winters as a young man working in the woods along the Miramichi River, and he learned many songs there. Nor was he unique in this way; many young men, both before and after his time, went this same way.

I was asking him about when people used to sing:

*Well, young fellows and girls, that was their only pastime— sing songs like that. No such thing as television, radio, or anything like that. . . .And then a lot of the boys used to go to New Brunswick in the lumberwoods. We'd always look forward for when some of them would come home; they'd learned some of those new songs, you know. [The fellows and girls] would all gather into this one house where this fellow was . . . and he'd sing the song and that's the way they learned them. He'd have to repeat

them until some of the rest would know them, see? . . . And it was
surprising too: you'd hear one of them long songs (you know how long
they are, some of them), well you'd hear them a couple of times and you'd
know them. Now if I heard one of those songs forty or fifty times and I
wouldn't know them. But them times you'd learn so quick!

As Edmund suggests, it had been a long time. The radio and the television
set have had their impact, and the old songs are not much sung anymore.
When he re-sang "The Old Beggar Man" for me, I asked him when was the
last time he sang it.

*"When were you here last?" he asked.

*"Five years ago," I said.

*"That's when," he said.

He sang one more song that evening, one I had never heard before.
Edmund said he learned it from his mother-in-law, and he thought he was
about the only person around who knew it now. He liked the song; so do I.

The Shepherd

♩ = 72 approx.

In Lon - don's fair ci - ty there
lived a rich squire. He had but one
daugh - ter, a beau - ty so fair; She was
cour - ted by a shep - herd of a low -er de -
gree, which caused her mis - for - tune and sad mis - er - y.

I.
In London's fair city there lived a rich squire.
He had but one daughter, a beauty so fair;
She was courted by a shepherd of a lower degree,
Which caused her misfortune and sad misery.

When her father came to hear this his passions grew high
And with a loaded pistol her shepherd he shot;
As he lie a-bleeding his true love passed by,
It's weeping and wailing, most bitterly she cried.

3
"My curse unto riches since my true love is slain,
Through the green fields I'll wander and shun all men's view."
"oh hold your tongue, jewel, my life you can't save
It's wonders you'll see when I'm cold in the clay.

4.
"The flock that I herd, love, my share is but small,

You can take them and herd them to every green plain;
They will be your companions through hail frost and rain."

5.
She picked up his crook, his hat and his [glive],
Like a faithful young shepherd through the valleys did glide;
It's when that they seen her, around her they came,
It's [reeting] and bleating her love to remain.

6.
"I might have been happy in my father's right home,
But it's been the cause of my sorrow downfall;
Through the green fields I'll wander 'til death ends all pain,
I will mourn for my shepherd 'til the day I will die."

Monday, July 15

I spent the night very comfortably on Edmund's couch. At breakfast he wondered if I'd drive him over to the doctor's in Alberton. Nothing serious, he claimed, but he'd just been feeling kind of tired these last couple of weeks. I said sure, and evidently the doctor reassured him all was well. On the way home we stopped in to see Long Joe, who had just gotten out of the hospital after appendicitis. He wasn't in any shape to do any singing, but his first hospital experience had been quite an adventure. He was laughing at himself. "That morning the doctor came in and said, 'Well, Joe, it's time now for your enema,' and I said, 'By God, that's a good thing because I'm really hungry!'"

Edmund asked me to leave him there at Long Joe's, saying he'd get a ride home later, so I headed off for Wesley Smith's.

Wesley was all ready to get started and met me at the car, assuming we'd be recording there as we had done before, but since he now had the electricity we went inside and, after a drink at the kitchen table (a pint was standard equipment for me now), I set things up in the parlour.

We spent a considerable amount of time just talking, not only about Joe Scott but also about where he learned songs and where he sang them. Born in 1892, Wesley started travelling over to the Maine woods when he was about twenty, and he worked there off and on for about twenty years, mostly over around Rangeley. In fact, it was during his first year there that he met Scott, *"over in Wildwood there across the lake from Oquossoc." At the last of it, though, he went up into the Cuxabexis region, which the Great Northern Paper Co. was just opening up. *"Ed Enman—he was a neighbour boy here— he took charge for the Northern and pretty near all the PI's from around here, that's where they'd head for." And, of course, he learned a lot of his songs in the woods. *"If I heard a song twice," he said, "I could learn it all."

Then we got to singing. There's not much to be said about this first song. I had never heard it before, but it was one that Wesley—putting on just a trace of a brogue in places—clearly enjoyed singing.

Pat Murphy

♩. = 53

2. Me name 'tis Pat Mur -phy, a   far- mer am I;   I
cour -ted a lass and I   felt ra - ther shy. She   bid me come in for a
min -ute or two. "Well be dam - ned," says I, "I don't care if I do."

1.
Well, you asked me to sing you a bit of a song;
Well, it's not very short, nor it's not very long.
You asked me to sing you of something that's true.
Well be dam-ned, says I, I don't care if I do.

2.
Me name 'tis Pat Murphy, a farmer am I;
I courted a lass and I felt rather shy.
She bid me come in for a minute or two.
"Well be dam-ned," says I, "I don't care if I do."

3.
We entered her kitchen, 'twas cozy and bright,
And a fine hearty supper I put out of sight.
She said, "Have a drop of that old mountain dew."
"Well be dam-ned," says I, "I don't care if I do."

4.

So after I'd finished I picked up me hat.
Says Peggy, "Me darlin', don't leave me like that.
Just give me a kiss as all fond lovers do."
"Well be dam-ned," says I, "I don't care if I do."

5.

So we hugged and we kissed in true lovers' delight,
'Til she up and she asked me to make her me wife.
She says, "I've a coo [cow] and an acre or two."
"Well be dam-ned," says I, "I don't care if I do."

6.

So early next mornin' to the church to get wed;
The priest stood for an instant with a book and he said,
"If you will take Peggy, and Peggy'll take you?"
"Well be dam-ned," says I, "I don't care if I do."

7.

So now we are married, and happy are we;
Not a chick, not a child for to bless her or me.
She says, "Wait a while, and we may have a few."
"Well be dam-ned," says I, "I don't care if I do."

While the next ballad, "The Silvery Tide," seems to be best known in northern tradition (particularly in the Northeast), it has also been found in Tennessee and Missouri. British variants are reported from both Scotland and England. The tune Wesley uses for the ballad is not one I have seen for it elsewhere. His shifting of the heroine's name from Molly to Polly and back to Molly again is accidental. The first stanza's opening musical phrase is unique; all succeeding stanzas begin like stanza 2, as given below.

The Silvery Tide

1.

There was a come-lye maiden lived down by the seaside,
She was come-lye and handsome, she was called the village pride.
There was but one sea captain whose Molly's heart did gain,
And it's true she proved to Hen-e-ry whilst on the raging main.

2.

Young Henry being long absent, a nobleman there came
A-courting pretty Molly but she refused the same;
"Your vows are vain for o'er the main there is but one," she cried,
"So now begone, I love but one; he's on the silvery tide."

3.

This nobleman in a passion flew and unto her did say,
"To cause your separation I will take your life away.
I'll watch you late and early 'til all alone," he cried.
"Then I'll send your body floating out on the silvery tide."

♩. = 52

There was a come-lye mai-den lived down by the sea-side; She was com-e-lye and hand-some, she was called the vil-lage pride. There was but one sea cap-tain whose Mol-ly's heart did gain, And it's true she proved to Hen-e-ry whilst on the ra-ging main. 2. Young Hen-ry be-ing long ab-sent, a no-ble-man there came A-...

4.

This nobleman went walking one day to take the air;
Down by the rolling ocean he espied this maiden fair.
Now says this cruel villain, "Consent to be my bride,
Or I'll send your body floating out on the silvery tide."

5.

"Oh no," says pretty Molly, "my vows I ne'er shall break.
'Tis Henry I love dearly, I will die for his sweet sake."
With a handkerchief he bound her hands, then threw her o'er the side,
And screaming she went floating out on the silvery tide.

6.

It was not a great while after young Henry arrived from sea,
Expecting to live happy and name their wedding day;
"Your own true love is murdered," her aged parents cried,
"Or has proven her own destruction down on the silvery tide."

7.

That night in his bed chamber, young Henry could find no rest;
The thoughts of pretty Molly disturbed his aching breast.
He dreamed that he went walking down by the ocean side,
And his own true love sat weeping on the banks of the silvery tide.

8.
Young Henry arose from his chamber for to search the sea banks o'er;
'Til four o'clock next morning he roamed from shore to shore;
At four o'clock next morning pretty Molly's corpse did find,
That to and fro went floating out on the silvery tide.

9.
He knew it to be his own true love by a gold ring on her hand,
And when he untied the handkerchief it brought him to a stand;
The name of her base murderer was there before his eyes,
Who had put an end to Molly out on the silvery tide.

10.
This nobleman was taken, the gallows was his doom
For murdering pretty Molly all in her youthful bloom;
Young Henry was so dejected that he wandered 'til he died.
And his last word it was "Molly," who died on the silvery tide.

I don't know that I ever saw a man get more fun out of singing a song
than Wesley got out of this next one. "It's just a foolish thing," he said. "Maybe
you ought not to put it on the machine." But we went ahead and recorded it
anyhow, and while it was obvious that he was having great difficulty keeping
a straight face while he was singing, he only broke out laughing once. Wesley
didn't have a title for it, but I've always called it "Cheese and Marrowbones."

Cheese and Marrowbones

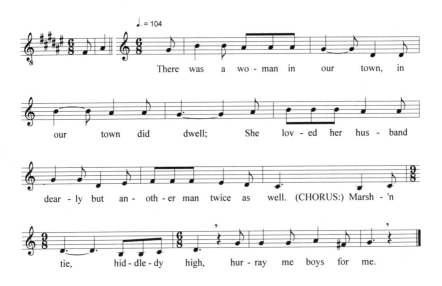

♩. = 104

There was a wo-man in our town, in
our town did dwell; She lov-ed her hus-band
dear-ly but an-oth-er man twice as well. (CHORUS:) Marsh-'n
tie, hid-dle-dy high, hur-ray me boys for me.

1.

There was a woman in our town, in our town did dwell;
She loved her husband dearly but another man twice as well.
CHORUS: Marsh'n tie, hiddledy high, hurray me boys for me.

2.

She went to the doctor to see if she could find,
To see if she could find something for to make her old man blind. [laughter]
CHORUS

3.

"Just feed him on cheese and marrowbone and feed it to him all,
And he will get so gosh darned blind he'll not see you at all."
CHORUS

4.

She fed him on cheese and marrowbone and fed it to him all,
And he did get so gosh darned blind he couldn't see her at all.
CHORUS

5.

One day the old man said to her, "I'm tired of this life.
I think I'll go and drown myself, and that will end all strife."
CHORUS

6.

They walked along and they talked along 'til they came to the river's brim;
The old man said to her, "My dear, I wish you'd push me in."
CHORUS

7.

She ran back some paces and ran to shush him in;
The old man stepped to one side and she went tumbling in.
CHORUS

8.

She screamed and she hollered, she cried and she bawled.
The old man said, "I'd help you dear, but I can't see you at all."
CHORUS

9.

She swam around, she swam around 'til she came to the river's brim;
The old man grabbed a cedar pole and shoved her farther in.
CHORUS

10.

So now my song is ended, and I can sing no more,
But wasn't she a gosh-darned fool she didn't swim ashore?
CHORUS

How long had it been since he'd done much singing, I asked? *"[It'd] be quite a number of years," he said. "You know, the radio and the television they've taken this. You never hear any of them old songs now around here . . . . Years ago, you know, you'd just meet in places and anybody could sing, why, you'd have all these old songs . . . . But it's different altogether now. . . . Before the radio. . . that's all the entertainment you had."

I wondered about more recent years. Surely there'd be some singing at a party, I suggested. He shook his head. *"Not in late years," he said. Then he shifted his mind. "Oh well," he added, "I said 'not in late years,' but I was down to a birthday party at my sister's—she's eighty this year—and they wanted me to sing. I sung that song I just sang you. . . . They wanted it. And that other one, too ["Pat Murphy"]. So that's about all the singing I've done in late years, old songs."

The final song of the day he called "Last Winter Was A Hard One." Its more official title is "When McGuiness Gets A Job," and, in its grim lighthearted way, it deals with four related problems: unemployment, immigration, politicians, and booze. According to folksong scholar Norman Cazden, the song goes back to about 1880. Wesley learned it in the Maine woods in the 'teens or early 1920s. The "three-cornered box," by the way, is a hod, and "mason's clerk" is a fancy name for a hod carrier.

Last Winter Was a Hard One

1.
Last winter was a hard one, Mrs. Reilly did you say?
Sure it is meself that's known it for many's the long day.
For your old man's not the only one that stood beside the wall,
For my old man McGuiness, sure he had no job at all.
The politicians promised him work upon the boulevard,
Working with a pick and shovel, shovelling dirt upon the cars.
Six months ago they promised him that work he'd surely get,
But believe me, my good woman, they're promising that yet!
CHORUS: But it's cheer up, Mrs. Reilly, don't give away to the blues.
Soon you and I will cut a shine in bonnets and new shoes.
For meself I'm done a-sighing. No more I'll sigh nor sob,
But I'll wait 'til times get better and McGuiness gets a job.

2.
Springtime now is coming—sure there'll be lots of work.
McGuiness he'll go to his trade; sure he's a mason's clerk.
You should see him climb the ladder as nimble as a fox;
Sure he's the lad can handle that old three-cornered box.
The boss he's always shouting, "Hi there, don't you stop!
Keep your eyes turned upward, Pat, and let no mortar drop."
But my old man is careful. Sure nothing he lets fall,
And Divil a word he has to say to your old man at all.
CHORUS

3.
The Eye-talians, Divil bless them! Why don't they stay at home?
For we've enough of our own sort to ate up all our own.
They swarm like bees in summer, from foreign lands they stray;
The contractors they have thousands at forty cents a day.
They work along the railroad shovelling snow and slush,
But one thing in their favour: Eye-talians never get lush.
They always take their money home, they drink no gin and wine,
And that is more than I can say of your old man and mine.
CHORUS

♩. = 66

Spring -time now is com-ing-- sure there'll be lots of work. Mc-Guin-ess he'll go to his trade; sure he's a ma-son's clerk. You should see him climb the lad-der as nim-ble as a fox; Sure he's the lad can han-dle that old three-cor-nered box. The boss he's al-ways shout-ing, "Hi there, don't you stop! Keep your eyes turned up-ward, Pat, and let no mor-tar drop." But my old man is care-ful. Sure, noth-ing he lets fall, And Di-vil a word he has to say to your old man at all. CH: But it's cheer up, Mrs.___ Reil-ly, don't give a-way to the blues. Soon you and I will cut a shine in bon-nets and new shoes. For me-self I'm done a-sigh-ing. No more I'll sigh nor sob, But I'll wait 'til times get bet-ter and Mc-Guin-ness gets a job. The Eye-tal...

And that was that for one afternoon. We had a final drink, and I headed for the ferry, having made arrangements to visit an old friend—another fine singer—in New Brunswick the next day.

I'd had a pleasant and profitable two days' sojourn, I told myself, as I drove along the road to Borden, especially because I'd renewed acquaintances with two strong singers and I had promised both myself and them that we'd see each other again (a promise, as it turns out, that for once I was to keep).

I was glad I'd looked out from Richibucto forty-eight hours ago.

Nineteen Sixty-Five

TWO YEARS HAD GONE BY, and my focus had shifted again. Not so much shifted, though, as sharpened. With my book on Larry Gorman behind me (it had been published the year before), I was now hard at work gathering material for a study of Joe Scott. It had been my good fortune to receive both a sabbatical and a Guggenheim Fellowship, which would allow me to spend full time at this task. My objective for the coming months was both to talk to people who had known Scott and to gather as many versions of his songs as I could find.

Since the sabbatical wouldn't start until September 1, I had been teaching folklore at the University of New Brunswick all summer, where I'd spent most of my off hours reading through late nineteenth-century Woodstock newspapers (Scott had been born and had grown up in Lower Woodstock) to see what I might chance on that was relevant to him, and I'd found enough to have made it well worth my while. Now my family—Bobby, sons Steve and Nathaniel, and daughter Sarah—and I were back on Prince Edward Island for a couple of weeks camping and general knocking around, and of course part of my knocking around would be visiting Island people who had written me in response to letters I'd published in the local papers. Since once again most of those responses had come from West Prince, we had pitched our tents at Jacques Cartier Provincial Park and settled in for a spell of swimming, kite flying, and gabbing with our campsite neighbours. It was what family camping should be, even to the nocturnal raids of a pair of amiable and unhurried skunks.

What follows, then, in this chapter are the highlights of two weeks' fieldwork sandwiched in between some wonderful days on the beach. Ultimately that fieldwork would lead me to the other end of the Island, but as usual most of my time was to be spent on the west end, and that is where this account begins.

Tuesday, August 24

I'd been spending several days chasing down people who had either written to me or been recommended by others. No songs, really—not whole ones anyway—but I had just finished a marvellous interview over in Howlan with John Dignan, who had known Scott over in the Maine woods up around Magalloway Plantation. *"He was selling these songs," he said, "I believe ten cents apiece. I think I got possibly three or four of them."

It was always exciting to listen to someone who'd actually seen and talked with Joe, and Mr. Dignan's soft and halting voice—like a man speaking from a dream—somehow made it even more exciting. I was on a high when I left there and just wanted to drive around for a while, but I was also hungry and managed to make my way slowly over toward Campbellton, where I was pretty sure I could count on something at the Cousins'. I hadn't seen Mary Elbridge for several years, but we'd written back and forth some, and after all, it *was* very nearly teatime.

I was right all around. Everyone was just sitting down to the table, so Mary immediately set a place for me between son John—home from Prince of Wales College and fishing with his father for the summer—and one of the daughters (I can't remember which), and I gratefully set into the fresh mackerel, all the time enjoying Mary's wonderful talk about things past and passing.

At one point I steered the conversation onto the poet Dan Riley. She had first told me about him back in 1957, when she sang two of his songs, and that winter, when I wrote her with some question about the Burning Ship, she mentioned in her reply that there was another one she'd sing for me next time I came by. Yes, she said, that was the one they always called "The O'Halloran Road Song," and she recited it for me there at the table.

It was just a short piece, and I knew I should go right out to the car, get my equipment, and have her go over it again, but somehow I didn't want to inject the tape recorder into that pleasant conversational ambience. I'd wait for a decent while, I decided, until we'd moved into the parlour, and then I could ask again. Unfortunately, once we had moved, other company arrived—old neighbours who'd moved away and were back for a brief visit— and it seemed best for me to move on. I knew where the song was, I told myself, and there'd be a time to get it.

I wanted Mary to meet my family; she had become far more than just an "informant" to me, and I knew she and Bobby would hit it off famously. I asked if we could stop by Sunday afternoon on our way down to Cavendish, our next campsite stop. "That'd be fine," Mary said. "We'll all be here."

I said my good-byes and reached to unhook the screen door.

"Don't you think you better leave by the same door you came in by?" said Mary.

That stopped me. I didn't know what she was talking about. "You think I'd better?" I asked in honest puzzlement.

"Well," she said, "that's an old superstition, and I'm half Irish, so maybe you *had* better."

"Right!" I said, heading for the kitchen door. "See you Sunday."

Thursday, August 26

Reg Porter had been born in Tignish, but he was now going to college in Montreal, where he had become very interested in folklore. He had written me from Montreal earlier in the year about a folklife project he was interested in setting up, and at the end of my answering letter I had said that since I'd be in Tignish in late August why didn't we get together then. He was agreeable, adding that he knew several people I ought to see. Now here I was in his grandmother's kitchen having a second breakfast with him while we discussed who we ought to go see first.

"One person you've got to see is my great aunt, Malvina Doucette," he said. "When I heard her singing 'Howard Carey' around the house the other day, I told her about you being here, and she's been practicing it ever since to make sure she's got it together right. She's right next door. We can stop in after breakfast."

Unfortunately, Mrs. Doucette had gone berry-picking for the day. "That's O.K.," Reg said. "We'll catch her later this afternoon." We climbed into my VW bus to go see several other people, none of whom were at home. It looked like it was going to be one of those "water haul" days, but Reg thought of someone else. "Frank Buote's moving to Montreal soon," he said, "so it's pretty likely he'll be home packing up. Come on. It's not far from here. And I've heard him sing 'The Norway Bum.'" We headed down the road.

"This isn't the most approved fieldwork method," I said, as we drove along.[1] "I come booming into town, see a few people who have written me, follow up some of their leads, and then go booming off home again after a few days. Actually, it's more of a raid than a systematic collecting method, but when you're looking for something as specific as I am, it works pretty well, and besides," I added in self-defense, "compared to some collector-raiders I know, I'm just thorough as hell. How much further out this road does this guy live now?"

"That's his place up there on the left," Reg said, pointing to a small, quite new house. We pulled into the drive.

Buote (that's pronounced Bee-YOT) was home, a vigorous dark-haired man of about sixty, and the house was what one might expect under the circumstances: a confusion of trunks and packing cases. We all sat down on a selection of upturned crates, and Reg told Frank what I was after. "And one of the songs he's interested in," he concluded, "is 'The Norway Bum' and I remembered hearing you sing it once or twice, so here we are."

"Yes," said Frank, "I used to sing that one alright, but I don't know, it's been so long now."

---

[1]The material on the interviews with Buote and Emile Arsenault is taken from my *Joe Scott*, pp. 282–87.

"Well," I asked, "could I get you to try it anyhow?"

He thought for a minute. "Sure," he said. "Why not? I guess I still know it."

I set up the tape recorder, and he started in.

Reg had said he had a strong voice, and he was right. It completely filled that little house. He went on in grand style until he came to the fifth stanza, where he faltered and then quit. "Nope," he said disgustedly, "I can't think of it. That's all I know of it." We talked for a few minutes and had a cup of coffee. Frank was obviously disappointed with himself. "But wait," he said. "If you want to get that song, I'll tell you who *does* know it, and that's Emile Arsenault."

I looked over at Reg. "Do you think we could get *him* to sing it for me?" I asked.

Reg and Frank looked at each other consideringly. "Hard to say," said Reg, "but he just might at that. I think it's worth a try anyhow, so let's go. Want to come, Frank?"

Frank said he did, and we headed off.

Following Reg's directions, we soon arrived at a big weathered farmhouse set well back from the road in a district of Tignish called Ascension. "There's his sister coming now," Frank said, as a generous grey-haired woman of about seventy came to the kitchen door. "Hello, Clotilda." They talked for a few minutes, and then Frank asked for Emile and explained our mission.

She thought for a minute. "He's lying down," she said. "Went into his room about an hour ago. I don't know what he'd say. And, you know, he's almost seventy now, and he hasn't been too smart these last few days—kind of tired all the time." There was a long pause in which she seemed to be weighing her brother's nap against the fact that it was too bad to turn away callers. "Well," she said at last, "it won't hurt to ask. Come on in and I'll get him up."

We all went into the kitchen, a big dark room with the feel of afternoon about it. Clotilda went through a door behind the stove, and we could hear her talking to her brother. In a few minutes she came out, smiling dubiously, and sat down by the stove. Then Emile came in.

He was a short man, a little stooped, his hair and mustache still brown, and everything about him from his shuffling, slippered walk to his tousled hair showed a man who had just come out of a deep sleep. He grunted hello to Frank, looked blankly at me, nodded at Reg, and sat down near the window on the far side of the room.

Frank mentioned about old songs and asked specifically about "The Norway Bum." Emile took no notice. He hadn't been feeling well, he said; couldn't sleep nights and then tired all day. Frank commiserated and asked again about old songs. Emile shook his head. "No," he said gruffly, looking at me and then at the floor, "damn it all, I'm not singing no songs today. My singing days are over and that's that, so you might just as well forget it! I'm not singing no songs for anyone!"

It sounded pretty final to me. I didn't see much hope in the uncomfortable silence that followed, and perhaps the only thing to do was to make an awkward good-bye and be on our way. I was just about to do that (I hardly blamed Emile his annoyance anyhow), when Reg started talking to him in French. I couldn't get it all, but in what I did catch he was saying something about old songs and how not many people remembered them anymore and that was too bad. Emile nodded. This man (meaning me), Reg continued, was a professor from Maine and he wanted to preserve these songs and make a record of them with his machine so they would not be forgotten. Emile nodded again, his whole aspect softening a little. Frank chimed in too, telling about how he'd forgotten the words to "The Norway Bum" but remembered that he (Emile) knew it, so here we were. Emile continued nodding thoughtfully, looking around at us. "*Oué*," he said. Then it was quiet again.

"I used to be a pretty good singer," he said after a bit. "I knew a hell of a lot of songs." Then he looked at me. "What was that song you wanted?" he said.

"'The Norway Bum,'" I said.

"Well," said Emile, "you better go get your machine."

I went out to the car and brought in the big Roberts I had. We set it up, I made my usual announcement on the tape, and told Emile to go ahead.

He cleared his throat. *"It's a hard song to sing," he said. "I have no wind to—jumping old Judas! Well—." He cleared his throat again and sang.

Parlando rubato ♪ = 100 approx.

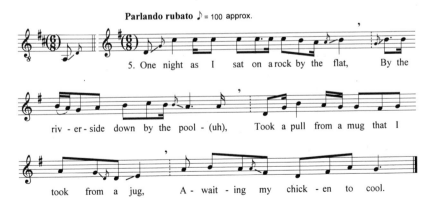

5. One night as I sat on a rock by the flat, By the riv - er - side down by the pool - (uh), Took a pull from a mug that I took from a jug, A - wait - ing my chick - en to cool.

1.

You may think by my dress I would rob a bird's nest
Or do anything that is bad;
I am sure if you do you will not make a miss,
You will hit the nail fair on the head.

2.

You may think by my togs they are all I have got,
If you do you will sure make a miss;
In this dirty old sack I just threw from my back,
I've another far nicer than this.

3.

Although I'm a rake and a dirty old fake,
I'm used to the world and its ways;
Although I'm a bum and addicted to rum,
I'm a man that has seen better days.

Emile paused for a minute. *"Now what do I say next?" he said. Then he remembered.

4.

Give me one glass of rye, for I am so dry,
'Twould help a poor fellow along;
I will dance you a reel, an old fashioned reel,
I'll sing you an old-fashioned song.

5.

One night as I sat on a rock by the flat,
By the riverside down by the pool,
Took a pull from a mug that I took from a jug,
Awaiting my chicken to cool.

6.

After eating my fill with a hearty good will
And watching the sparks in their flight,
A vision arose before my blur-red eyes
All in the dark shadows of night.

7.

I saw my dear home by the ocean's white foam,
Way down by those valleys and hills;
The foresty wild that I roamed when a child,
Way down by the rippling rills.

8.

The church bells they rang and the birds sweetly sang,
In the meadow and down in the dell;
I listened with joy as I did when a boy
To the chimes of the old village bells.

9.

How I once was a lad to make mother's heart glad,
I was once what they called fair of face;
But I loved a fair lass far beneath my own class
To my father and mother's disgrace.

My father in his anger drove me from his door,
My mother in grief pined away;
Her cries of despair still ring in my ears,
They will ring on for many a day.

11.

But my story's not told, nor it's not told for gold,
We were married and settled in life;
Three years passed away like a bright summer day,
How dearly I loved my young wife.

12.

One night while away a patient to see,
My ears caught a terrible sound;
'Twas the firebell borne on the evening breeze,
Old Norway was fast burning down.

13.

I rushed to my home through the terrified town
To find my own buildings on fire;
I stood there aghast for there, there alas,
All peace and happiness expired.

14.

I saw my dear wife in a window so high,
Who with accent so terrible and wild,
"Oh my God," she would cry, "Oh my God in the sky,
Save me and my dear little child."

15.

But the flames did hold high between child, wife, and I,
Oh merciful God, what a sight!
With her child in her arms she fell back in the flames,
'Twas the last time I saw her that night.

16.

So it's now for my part with a sad broken heart
To drown sorrow I plunged into rum;
Now my days they are passed, and my joys they are cast,
And now I am only a bum.

I was impressed. Emile's voice was no longer strong or sure, but it fit the song and the room very well. *"How in hell would you remember all that?" said Frank with admiration.

Emile seemed pleased. *"I learned that song forty years ago or more," he said. He couldn't remember who he learned it from, but he knew he didn't bring that one home from the woods. *"I learned that in this part of the country."

*"Would you like to hear that back?" I asked. He said he would, so we heard it all again. Then, in my single-minded way I bored ahead, asking about Joe Scott. The name meant nothing to him, but he recognized several of his songs when I asked for them by name and even sang a stanza of "Howard

No. 14: *Left to right:* Frank Buote, Émile Arsenault, Reg Porter, Clotilda
Arsenault, and two neighbour children. NA P233.
Photo taken August 16, 1965.

Carey" at my request. "Benjamin Deane?" He nodded. *"That's a song I'd always liked to learn, and I never did learn it. Yes, I liked that song."

*"Do you like 'The Norway Bum'?" I asked.

*"Oh," he said deprecatingly, "I wouldn't say I like it. I liked it one time. Years ago I thought it was a good song, but like I said just now perhaps it might have been ten years since I sung that song. I think of it once in a while, but I don't ever sing it."

*"How about 'Guy Reed'?"

*"No," he said, as if he was getting a little tired of this line of talk. "The only time I ever heard anybody singing 'Guy Reed,'" he added after a long pause, "I was working in the potato fields on a farm down on the Maine/New Brunswick line by Aroostook Junction. I worked there for a fella by the name of Hallock, Charlie Hallock. He used to sing that song, this 'Guy Reed.'"

Since it had finally sunk in that I wasn't going to learn any more about Joe Scott and his songs from this man, I moved on. *" Could you give us another song?" I asked.

*"I might give you another one, just one more. I'll sing you one of Jimmy [deRoma's?] songs, 'The Old Arm Chair.' You heard that," he said, mostly to Frank, who agreed he had. That used to be one of Jimmy's songs. 'Twas Jimmy I heard it from, learned it."

I'd never known just what to call songs like this. "Folk" didn't quite seem correct; perhaps "popular song" or "parlour song"would be all right, but the people I collected songs from didn't seem to be worried about a distinction. Certainly Emile wasn't. It was just another song for him. "Why make a distinction when the folk makes none?" Phillips Barry had asked many years before, and I decided it would be best to leave it at that.

The Old Arm Chair

I.

My grandmother she at the age of eighty-three
One day in May was taken ill and died.
Now that she was dead, the will of course was read,
By a lawyer as we all stood by his side.
To my brother it was found she had willed a thousand pound,
The same unto my sister, I declare.
But when it came to me, the lawyer says, "I see
She has willed to you her old arm chair."
CHORUS: How they tittered and how they chaffed,
                How my brother and sister laughed
                When they heard the lawyer declare
                Granny only left to me an old arm chair.

♩ = 92

My grand-moth-er she at the age of eight-y-three One day in May was tak-en ill and died. Now that she was dead, the will of course was read, By a law-yer as we all stood by his side. To my broth-er it was found she had willed a thou-sand pound, The same un-to my sis-ter, I de-clare. But when it came to me, the law-yer says, "I see She has willed to you her old arm chair."

CHORUS: How they tit-tered and how they chaffed, How my broth-er and sis-ter laughed When they heard the law-yer de-clare Gran-ny on-ly left to me an old arm chair.

2.

I thought it hardly fair, still I said I didn't care;
In the evening I took the chair away.
My brother at me laughed, the lawyer at me chaffed,
And he said, "It will be useful, John, some day.
When you settle down to life, take some sweet one for your wife,
You'll find it very handy, I declare.
In the cold winter night when the fire's burning bright
You can sit there to your old arm chair."

3.

What the lawyer said was true, for in a year or two
Strange to say I settled down in married life.
I first the girl did court, and then the ring I bought—
Took her to the church and then she was my wife.

Now the dear girl and me are as happy as can be,
And when my work is over I declare
I [had abroad could] roam but each night I stay at home,
I'd be seated in my old arm chair.

4.

One night the chair fell down. As I picked it up I found
The seat had fallen out upon the floor;
And there before my eyes I saw to my surprise
A lot of notes—ten thousand pounds or more!
When my brother heard of this, the poor fellow, I confess,
Went nearly wild with rage and tore his hair,
But I only laughed at him, and I said unto him, "Jim,
Don't you wish you had the old arm chair?"
CHORUS: No more did titter, no more did chaff,
          No more did my brother and sister laugh,
          When they heard the lawyer declare,
          "Granny only left to you her old arm chair."

The conversation got back to "Benjamin Deane" and how he wanted to learn it from a friend, Jim Perry, now dead. *"I'd see him once or twice every week, and I asked him a couple or three times or more for to sing 'The *Flying Cloud*' for me—no, not 'The *Flying Cloud*' but 'Benjamin Deane'—and he said he didn't think he could put it together. He didn't sing it anyway. He could sing it one time. I'll tell you another old fella used to sing that: old Linus Christopher. Perhaps he could even sing it now if you give him a couple of drinks. He might try to sing it. He was a hell of a good singer at one time, Linus, but he's old. Christ, he must be eighty-four or five! I heard him sing that song fifty years ago at a wedding."

It had been a good session, for sure, but it was time to quit, and Reg and Frank—now almost as hot on the trail as I was—decided we ought to go see Linus Christopher. We all went outside so I could take a couple of pictures. "I'm glad you came," Emile said to me. "Come back again, and maybe I'll remember some more."

Clotilda was smiling broadly on all of us.

"Linus' place isn't far," Reg said. "He used to have a house out on the Western Road, but he got burned out a couple of years ago and now he's got this little place back from the road up here. Just one room, really. But it's all he needs, I guess."

I turned in where my two guides told me, and an elderly man came out the door as if he'd been expecting us, which, in fact, he had. It seems the blacksmith had been by carrying the news that I was around looking for old songs and wondering if I'd been there yet. So Linus was ready to roll! In fact, he started right in on a song. "Wait!" said Frank. "Wait until he gets his machine!"

Linus waited, and, as soon as I brought in my UHER (there was no electricity), he got right to work with "Brennan on the Moor," a widely known outlaw ballad very much like Long Joe Doucette's "Wild Colonial Boy."

Brennan on the Moor

One day up-on the East high-way as Bren-nan he sat down, He met the Mayor of Cash-eer a mile out-side the town. The Mayor he knew his fea-tures. "I think, young man," says he, "If your name is Wil-ly Bren-nan you must come a-long with me." CHORUS: Bren-nan on the moor, Bren-nan on the moor, Bold and un-daun-ted stood young Bren-nan on the moor.

1.
Oh, it's of a famous Irishman the truth to you I'll tell;
His name was Willy Brennan and in Ireland he did dwell.
It was on the Calgary Mountains he began his wild career,
For many a wealthy gentleman before him stood with fear.
CHORUS: Brennan on the moor, Brennan on the moor,
                 Bold and undaunted stood young Brennan on the moor.

2.
Oh, a brace of loaded pistols he carried each night and day;
He never robbed a poor man upon the King's Highway.
And what he had taken from the rich, like Curbans and Black Bess,
He always did divide it with the widow in distress.
CHORUS

3.

One day upon the East Highway as Brennan he sat down,
He met the Mayor of Casheer a mile outside the town.
The Mayor he knew his features. "I think, young man," says he,
"If your name is Willy Brennan you must come along with me."
CHORUS

4.

Oh, Brennan's wife she being in town provisions for to buy,
It's when she saw her Willy she began to weep and cry.
He says, "Give me that blunderbuss." As soon as Willy spoke,
She handed him a blunderbuss from underneath her cloak.
CHORUS

5.

It is with this loaded blunderbuss, the truth I will unfold,
He made the mayor to tremble and he robbed him of his gold.
Five hundred pounds he offered for his apprehension there,
And Brennan with horse and saddle to the mountains did appear.
CHORUS

6.

One day he robbed a peddler by the name of Jeweler Bond;
They traveled on together 'til the day began to dawn.
The peddler seeing his money gone, likewise his watch and chain,
He at once encountered Brennan and he robbed him back again.
CHORUS

7.

Oh, Brennan saw his comrade was as good a man as he;
He took him on the highway his companion for to be.
The peddler being true hearted he threw his pack away,
And he proved a loyal comrade until his dying day.
CHORUS

8.

In the county of Proprarie in the place they call Promoor,
Brennan and his comrade was made to suffer sore.
Oh, they laid him on the ferns that grew thick upon the field;
Nine wounds he received before that he did yield.
(*Spoken*): Brennan on the moor.

Christopher sang in a very relaxed and pleasant manner, placing the song just about where his speaking voice lay, with no attempt to "get it up high" like some of the woods singers I have heard. And it was clear he took great pleasure in his singing. Once he got through with "Brennan on the Moor," though, I started in on him about Scott and his songs. "Emile said he thought you knew 'Benjamin Deane,'" I said. "Is that right?"

*"No," he said, "I never knew it. If I did, I won't tell you no lies. I'll do all I can to help a man. Now 'Frozen Charlotte' was another pretty good one. You ever heard that one?"

*"Yes, I have," I said, not really wanting to hear it again at the moment. It was a good old song alright, but it was long, long, long, and definitely not

No. 15: Linus Christopher, Tignish, NA P261. *Photo taken August 26, 1965*

part of my present agenda. However, he wanted to sing it, and that was that, but he only got about five stanzas into it. *"I forget," he said. "I'm sorry." I recommenced about Scott's songs. "Howard Carey?" He recognized the name. *"I don't know it," he said. "I often heard it, but I never learned it. It's an awful long song. It goes like this." And he sang the first line. *"That Grand Falls is handy to where you live in Maine," he said. "I worked up there."

I named other songs. Yes, he'd heard them, but didn't know them. *"Would it be all right if I sung 'The Crockery Ware'?" he asked. "You needn't record it," he added almost shyly.

*"Oh, I'd love to record it," I said, having no idea what song he was talking about.

*"Well, it's a kind of a Sunday song," he said, puzzling me even more, "but there's not a bad word in it. It's about a fella went to see a girl and how they come out, but there's not a smutty word in it. I wouldn't sing it if it was smutty. I'm not a saint, but I'm not a devil either. Record away, then."

He started to sing, but broke off. *"Oh by gosh, give me a sup of that," he said, pointing to the pint of whisky I'd brought along. He tipped it up and handed it back to me. *"You'll pay for your songs yet, boy!" he said.

*"Well, I'm game," I said, laughing.

*"I only took a sup," he said. "It kind of clears me throat." And began singing again.

The Crockery Ware

1.
Oh, a Swansea lass as I hear tell,
A Swansea lass I knew right well,

"Don't smile now," he said.

I asked to her one question right,
If I could stay with her one night.
CHORUS: To me right down fon the didden I gee oh,
          Me right down fon the didden I gee oh.

2.
Oh, this pretty fair maid she did consent;
Straightway up to bed she went.
She placed a chair on the middle of the floor,
And onto it put some crockery ware.
CHORUS

3.
Oh, the young man got up in the middle of the night,
All for to embrace his heart's delight.
He knocked his knee against the chair,
And all fell down of the crockery ware.
CHORUS

♩ = 118

Oh, this pret-ty fair maid she did con-sent;
Straight-way up to bed she went. She placed a chair on the
mid-dle of the floor, And on-to it put some crock-ery ware. CHORUS: To me
right down fon the did-den I gee oh, Me right down fon the did-den I gee oh.

4.
Oh, the young girl got up in a terrible fright,
Half splitting her joints with the joke she made.
Oh, she says, "Young man, now don't you fear;
You got to pay Mother for the crockery ware."
CHORUS

5.
Oh, the bill was called without any more delay;
It was the same I had to pay.
Five shillings for the darned old chair,
And five pound ten for the crockery ware.
CHORUS

6.
So come all young men when you go to spark,
Be aware of rambling in the dark.
Beware of every step you steer,
And try and keep clear of the crockery ware.

All of us burst out laughing. *"That's wonderful!" I said.

*"It's fifty-some years since I sung that," he said, pleased with its reception. But since it became obvious that was all the singing there was going to be, we passed the whisky around one more time, and Reg, Frank, and I made our departure.

As a kind of footnote, it's worth pointing out that, in both this song and the previous one, Christopher omitted the chorus for the last stanza, and, rather than speaking just the final word or two in the manner of so many traditional singers, he spoke the entire last line.

We dropped Frank off at his place and returned to Reg's grandmother's to find Mrs. Doucette there ready and eager to sing "Howard Carey" for me.

"She's been practicing it ever since she got back from berry-picking," said Mrs. Gaudet, and to help herself along she had written down the first words of each stanza on a little card. I got the machine set up, and she was off, referring to the card when she needed to and singing in what in this part of the world I had come to call Acadian *complainte* style: high, hard-edged, slow, parlando rubato, melismatic. It is interesting that of all the singers in this book, she and Edmund Doucette show this style most clearly. Joe Scott's great ballad was in good and caring hands.

Howard Carey

I rose up from my rest-ing place, as the dew drops bright rose fair Had bid the ro-ses a fond a-dieu, we watched them dis-ap-pear. One by one did fade a-way be-neath the sun's bright ray; The time has come when I must leave, I could no long-er stay.

1.
My name is Howard Currie, in Grand Fall I was born
In a pleasant little cottage near the banks of the Saint John.
My parents [they have been] poor, could not maintain us all,
For I had to leave my native home, for our little farm was small.

2.
The day I left my happy home they took me by the hand,
Saying, "Don't forget your parents, lad, when in a foreign land."
My mother led me to a seat beneath a willow tree,
With quivering lips bade me set down for she wished to talk to me.

3.
"You see yonder that hillside where the grass is growing green,
Where the lilies and the violets and the wild rose can be seen.
Those flowers are magnificent and attractive to the eyes,
But still remember there is snakes beneath those colour lies.

4.

"When you are tempted to do wrong, have courage to say no,
For many a good boy has gone wrong in starting young, you know.
Shun bad company, my boy, and of strong drink refrain;
Don't patronize those gamble halls, look on them with disdain."

5.

I rose up from my resting place, as the dew drops bright rose fair
Had bid the roses a fond adieu, we watched them disappear.
One by one did fade away, beneath the sun's bright ray;
The time has come when I must leave, I could no longer stay.

6.

I kissed my mother's dear tender face, bid her a long farewell;
My feelings at that moment no mortal tongue could tell.
My brothers and my sisters in a group stood by the door;
I waved my hand and left them by that cottage by the shore.

7.

Since then I've travelled through the east and through the south also;
I travelled through the western lands where the lofty redrose grow.
But my mother's warning did [heeled] away, like that silly fly
Got tangled in her silken web, and now I am doomed to die.

8.

Today I'm lying in a room near the town of Rumford Falls;
My feverish eyes are [wovering] around upon its whitewashed walls;
The agony I undergo I can't no longer [inure];
My limbs are weak and painful, I am dying slow but sure.

9.

My money it has longly fled, my friends they are but few;
I will snatch this tender thread of life, and I'll bid this world adieu.
I will tie this cord unto the hinge upon my chamber door;
There's room enough for me to hang beneath it and the floor.

10.

Farewell to Earth and all things gay, home and friends adieu;
Farewell unto the girl I love, may God watch over you.
No more we'll rove in groves so green, where the flower did bloom as gay.
What signifies that mortal man when slumbering in the clay?

11.

At twelve o'clock John Darken came to see his charge once more;
He found his body hanging [*from a hinge*] upon the door.
He cut him down and spread the news as many a cheek grew pale,
And filled with wonders many a heart for to hear that mournful tale.
Adieu.

Mrs. Doucette had grown up in Palmer Road and claimed to have learned all the songs she knew in her early teens. That raised three interesting points for me. First of all, Palmer Road was and still is a decidedly French community, and, as I have already pointed out, Mrs. Doucette's singing style clearly had a French cast. Naturally enough, most of the songs she knew were in French. *"Where we were brought up French was our language," she said, "and my mother didn't speak too good English. It was all French."

*"Then how come you learned this English song," I asked, "especially one that you say was long and difficult?"

She laughed. *"Well, it was kind of a novelty for us to learn it," she said. "Didn't make any difference what it was as long as it was a song that was English. We were fascinated by an English song. Those that could learn it first thought it was something, you know. Didn't make much difference what it was, as long as it was English. It was just to be a little popular. If we knew an English song we really thought we were something, especially if it was long like that."

When she was about eighteen she went away to the States to work. *"I was down there for about fourteen years," she said. "Then came back, married, and we went away another five or six years and raised children, and I wasn't interested in songs at all. Only for him," she said, pointing at Reg. "He got after us last week over this."

Which leads me to the second point. A few days before, Reg had recorded her singing of "Howard Carey," remarking to her that this professor from the States would be interested in hearing it, too. I was able to compare the two singings and found that the first time around she had completely forgotten the second line of stanza four. In the version she sang for me, she filled that gap in with a line entirely of her own invention. At least nothing like it occurs in any other version I've heard, and I've heard a great many. As I've said, Mrs. Doucette had been rehearsing the ballad for several days, and, since obviously she was determined to "have it right" when she sang it for me, she had to do something about that missing line. What she did was to invent one that would fit, and it fit so well that I never noticed it until I came to write this book—one more splendid example of why folklorists should gather multiple versions, even from the same singer, and why they shouldn't throw anything away!

Finally, while Joe Scott's original ballad was nineteen double-stanzas long—and most performances where the singer claims to "have the whole of it" run to at least fifteen or sixteen—Mrs. Doucette's version gets all the essentials into eleven, and not only does her version in no way feel incomplete, it *isn't* incomplete. It makes no difference at all that it "leaves out" close to half of what Joe Scott had in his "original." What she sang—and sang very well—was whole, and that's all there is to it.

Friday, August 27

Jacques Cartier Campground is a lovely spot, but today, with a cold wind off the sea driving the rain under the tent fly, all of us quickly decided we needed joys less soggy than those board games you're always supposed to bring along for just such occasions. Therefore, in the interest of sheer self-preservation, we took a trip into town, town in this case being Alberton. Bobby headed for the laundromat with all the cheer she could manage under the circumstances, taking our daughter Sarah with her. I bought the boys off with a couple of bucks, turning them loose in the local equivalent of a five-and-ten, while I treated myself to a haircut and the concomitant privilege of thumbing through several ancient magazines. It beat hell out of Parcheesi in a leaky tent.

The rain had let up when I emerged shorn about an hour later, and since Bobby was still busy in the laundromat I went down the street to check on the boys. All being well there, I went back to wait by the car, only to find an elderly man studying my license plate.

"What part of Maine?" he asked.

"Near Bangor," I said.

"Oh, Bangor," he said, nodding. "I know Bangor well. Used to race my horses there sometimes." And the conversation took off . . . . Did I know so-and-so? Was the old Exchange Hotel still there? . . . And then the inevitable: "What brings you to Alberton?"

Sort of to test the waters, I mentioned Larry Gorman, and he brightened right up, reciting bits of several songs, including a stanza of "Michael O'Brien."

"How about Joe Scott?" I asked. "Ever hear of him?"

He said he had not. "He was sort of like Gorman," I said. "He made up songs, but his were long come-all-ye's, like 'Howard Carey.'"

"Oh, 'Howard Carey,'" he said. "'My name is Howard Carey, in Grand Falls I was born.'" And he went on, wording off a couple of stanzas. "I used to sing that," he said.

I was excited. "Do you think you still could" I asked.

"Oh, gosh," he chuckled, "it's been so long. I'd have to get it together."

"Lookit," I said. "We're camping out at Jacques Cartier Campground, and I've got to take the family back out there. That'll give you some time. Then when I come back I can record what you know of it. It's pretty important to me to get those songs the way different people remember them."

He was agreeable. "The name's McAlduff. Frank McAlduff," he said, and gave me directions to his house.

I got the family home in good order, fixed myself half a sandwich, and headed back to Alberton.

I found Frank out in his workshop, a room filled with woodworking tools. The walls were covered with framed photographs of trotters and pacers, and we looked at them together for some minutes. "You know, I'm sorry," he said after a while, but I just can't seem to get 'Howard Carey' together at all. I feel bad bringing you all the way back out here on a night like this for nothing, but it's no good. I just can't do it. Look, though," he added after a long pause, "maybe we ought to go see Mrs. Ben Smith because she knows a lot of old songs like that. Used to, anyway. Come on and have some supper, and we'll go see her afterwards."

I was disappointed, and somehow I wasn't hopeful about the evening's prospect. Maybe it was the weather, which had turned from rain to patchy drizzle and fog, but I was hungry and managed to take my frustrations out on the generous table Mrs. McAlduff had spread.

Twenty minutes later Frank and I were on our way to visit Mrs. Smith. "She's over eighty," Frank explained as we drove along, "and Ben himself is over ninety. Come to think of it, he knew Larry Gorman, but I doubt that he can tell you much now. She's the one, though. I've heard her sing. Here, pull in that drive on the left."

It was a big grey-shingled house just out from the centre of town, badly in need of repairs, a couple of rotting planks laid down for a walkway to the kitchen door. An old woman, motionless and dishevelled, was looking out the window. If I had wanted an image to express that chill monochrome evening, that shawled figure would have been it.

Frank knocked, and then we walked in to a kitchen—dark, unswept, and overheated—that was in its way the counterpart of the house's exterior. "Hello Laura," he said to the woman, who, it turned out, was in a wheelchair. She looked up but didn't recognize him until he got closer. Then she smiled. "Why Frank! Hello. What brings you here?" Introductions all around followed, as Frank explained our mission and Mrs. Smith bustled around in a friendly way to get us all a cup of tea.

"Didn't you know Larry Gorman?" Frank said to the old man in the rocker next to the stove.

"I met him once over in Bangor," the old man replied, "but I didn't know him." Then he got up and tottered out of the room. He was back and forth several times during our visit, paying us almost no attention at all.

I started to ask Mrs. Smith about old songs and was disappointed to find that she knew none of the Scott ballads I was interested in. She knew "The Millman and Tuplin Song" though, and recited the whole of it. "He never did it, you know," she said. "Another man made a death-bed confession. I knew his name once, but I forget now. Have you heard 'The Schooner *Gracie Parker*'?" she asked.

A song by that name had been in the back of my mind ever since Tom MacLeod of Baring, Maine, mentioned it back in 1957 as "a good one" that the Prince Edward Island boys used to sing a lot. "Do you know it?" I asked.

"Oh yes," she said, and recited it off quietly.

"Do you remember the air to that?" I asked, and finding that she did I said I'd like to record it and went out to the car to get the Roberts.

She sang it beautifully, as if it mattered. And, as I was to find out, it did matter.

(I have added the first stanza from a manuscript version I have).

The Schooner Gracie Parker

On the thir-teen of De-cem-ber in the fall of nine-ty-three, The schoo-ner *Gra-cie M. Par-ker* from this port was put to sea With a hea-vy load of lum-ber to Saint-Pi-erre she was bound. Lit-tle were they thought 'twould be their lot on those drear-y isles to drown.

1.

On the thirteenth of December in the fall of ninety-three,
The schooner *Gracie M. Parker* from this port was put to sea
With a heavy load of lumber to Saint-Pierre [*pron.* PEEyur] she was bound.
Little were they thought 'twould be their lot on those dreary isles to drown.

2.

The wind blew from the northwest, and it blew a heavy gale,
When the schooner [insending] heavily with her closely reefed down sail.
But when she struck that sudden rock, and with a dismal sound,
The seas roared high, no help was nigh, and all on board was drowned.

3.

'Twas early the next morning a man by chance did stray
Down along the sea beach where two dead bodies lay;
And further on the prow was found, the [educated][2] wreck
Of the schooner *Gracie Parker* that sailed from Cascumpec.

---

[2]Mrs. Smith said "educated" quite clearly. Several manuscript versions in my possession have "indicated," which is probably what was intended.

4.

The crew was seven in number, only two on land was found.
They were no one left for to tell the tale how the vessel run aground,
But we suppose by what we hear it must have happened so,
By laying-to, pray, wait for day when she struck that sudden rock.

5

They were Captain Farrell and his brother Will, the mate was Doherty;
Frank McAlduff and Fred Matthews, all married men were they.
The cook was Johnny Oliver, supercargo was Doiron [*pron.* DYron] —
I have numberated all her crew while in this simple song.

6.

Their widows and poor orphans they're with us here to weep,
While the bodies of them they loved so dear is slumbering in the deep.
Over them the seabirds loud do cry and the stormy winds do weep;
The thunder, too, can loudly roar but can never wake their sleep.

She let her voice drop at the end, and the kitchen was very quiet for a moment. *"I thank you very much," I said softly, and, as much to break the silence as anything, I asked if she knew who wrote the song.

*"Yes sir," she said. "I don't know who the man was, but he was a Frenchman from Tignish. He was an Arsenault, but I can't tell you any more."

*"Do you remember the wreck itself?" I asked.

*"Oh! We were down that morning!" she said. "See, Tom Gray's my cousin, first cousin of mine. He wanted to go cook. And Uncle Tom [*his father*] said, 'Go, boy! You couldn't boil potatoes without burning them.' And his sister Josephine and I went down with him. That's the first time I ever was down there [*at Alberton Wharf*] and the *Gracie M. Parker*, they just had things on their shoulders carrying the lumber. And when he got down there to hire, Johnny Oliver got on ahead of poor Tom, so he didn't get drowned."

*"Did you know many of the people named in the song?" I asked.

*"We knew every one of the crowd!" she said. "We knew every one except Mr. Doiron. He was the supercargo. His wife was the music teacher. She was a Miss Gaudet [*pron.* GOODy], and poor little Joshua wasn't born 'til long after his father was drowned. There's not many of [*those families*] here now," she added rather wistfully, "but Ed Oliver was here the other day to see me. He was just ten years old when the *Gracie Parker* was wrecked. We knew them all so well." With that she wheeled off to the other end of the kitchen on some errand of her own. That was all the singing there was going to be, and Frank and I made our exit.

"That Frank McAlduff in the song was my uncle," said Frank on the way home. "I was named for him."

Saturday, August 28

It didn't look like much of a day, certainly no better than yesterday, what with the sun in and out and the rain coming and going, but as usual Bobby shooed me from our campsite and told me to get to my work. Twelve-year-old Steve decided to come with me; he liked it that on the back roads I sometimes let him steer.

There were a number of people I wanted to look up, people who had written me or been recommended to me along the way, but mostly I wanted to see Wesley Smith again, and we stopped at his place about noon just in time to catch the whole family climbing into the car to go over to Tyne Valley for the Oyster Festival Parade. They'd all been over the previous night for the fiddling and stepdancing contests. "Damn, I wish I'd known about that," I said. "We'd have loved to come down for it."

"Oh, it was great," said Wesley. "But look, we won't be long. We should be back about four. Come on back, 'cause there's a couple of songs I want to sing for you. Stay for supper too, why not?" I said that would be fine, and Steve and I went on our way.

We were back as promised, and, after sitting around in the kitchen for a while, Steve went out to the car and brought in the Roberts, and we set up in the parlour. Wesley pulled a little blue notebook out of his pocket in which, it turned out, he'd a list of what songs he'd sung for me and what songs he hadn't. "This is the one I wrote you about," he said, putting the notebook away. "It's called "The Sheriff's Sale.'"

I had never heard it before, but it sounded like many another nineteenth-century parlour songs—"The Black Sheep," for instance—and for sure this was a genre Wesley favoured. Notice that there are two tunes involved here: tune I is the basic one, but tune II is sung for stanzas 3 and 6, as if they were a refrain, and I have set the words to those two stanzas in as a reminder.

The Sheriff's Sale

1.

There's an old rustic cottage stood down by the square,
And for ninety-odd years that old cottage stood there,
Surrounded by trees was a fence that was worn—
'Twas the home of my forefathers. There I was born.

2.

'Til misfortune o'ertook us, and a tale soon did tell;
The Sheriff came in our old home for to sell.
It was then I did weep and our mother did moan,
As we begged him in vain for to spare the old home.

I ♪ = 108 approx.

Then Bro-ther left home to find some-thing to do, But where he had gone to not an-y-one knew. So I toiled late and ear-ly to keep down the debts, and oft-times I hear my-self plead-ing as yet:

II

Spare the old home! Please spare it I pray! Don't turn out Moth-er so fee-ble and grey, And my dear lov-ing sis-ter so weak and so frail--

Auc-tion-eer, Auc-tion-eer, won't you please stop that sale?

3.
Spare the old home! Please spare it I pray!
Don't turn out Mother so feeble and grey,
And my dear loving sister so weak and so frail—
Auctioneer, Auctioneer, won't you please stop that sale?

4.
You never could find much a happier lot
Than our little family that dwelt in that cot;
There was Father and Mother, Sister, Brother, and I,
'Til sickness come o'er us and Father did die

5.
Then Brother left home to find something to do,
But where he had gone to not anyone knew.
So I toiled late and early to keep down the debts,
And ofttimes I hear myself pleading as yet:

6.
Spare the old home! Please spare it I pray!
Don't turn out Mother so feeble and grey,
And my dear loving sister so weak and so frail—
Auctioneer, Auctioneer, won't you please stop that sale?

7.

In vain did I plead without any avail;
The auctioneer continued to cry out the sale.
When a voice from amongst us was a man quite unknown;
He paid down his money and purchased our home.

8.

Then Mother and Sister with hearts sad and worn
Prepared to depart from their old cottage door.
When this stranger spoke saying, "Your sorrows are done.
I have purchased your home for I am your own son."

9.

Love and rejoicing was there on that day,
When Brother embraced my dear mother so grey.
With a welcome from me and my sister so frail —
That put an end to the old sheriff's sale.

After this we talked for quite a while about Joe Scott, and he sang me "John Ladner" the way he remembered it. Then he checked his little notebook. *"This is a dream song," he said, slipping the book back in his pocket, and he launched into the following song, which I had always known of as "Erin's Green Shore." Daniel O'Connor is, of course, the great Irish politician Daniel O'Connell (1775–1847), known as "The Liberator" for his leadership in the struggle for Irish independence. The symbolism of the "damsel" needs no underlining, I'm sure.

Erin's Green Shore

♪ = 84

Her cheeks were like two bloom - ing ro - ses, Her teeth were the i - vor-y white, And her two spark-ling eyes shone like dia - monds Or like stars on a clear fros - ty night.

1.

One evening of late as I rambled
By the banks of a clear pearly stream,
I sat down in a bunch of primroses
And soon I fell into a dream.

2.
I dreamed I espied a fair damsel;
Her equal I ne'er saw before.
And she sighed for the rights of her country;
She had rambled from Erin's green shore.

3.
Her cheeks were like two blooming roses,
Her teeth were the ivory white,
And her two sparkling eyes shone like diamonds
Or like stars on a clear frosty night.

4.
Her dress was the neatest attire,
And green was the mantle she wore,
Embroidered with roses and shamrocks,
She had rambled from Erin's green shore.

5.
I boldly addressed this fair damsel,
Saying, "My jewel, come and tell me your name,
For I know in this country you're a stranger,
Or I would not have asked you the same."

6.
"I'm the daughter of Daniel O'Connor;
From Ireland I've lately sailed o'er.
I came here for to wait on my brother,
Who has wandered from Erin's green shore."

7.
From my fancy of earth I awakened,
And I found it was only a dream.
My pretty fair damsel fled from me.
How I long for to slumber again.

8.
May the heavens above be her guardian,
For I know I shan't see her anymore.
May the sun in its brilliance shine on her,
As she rambles round Erin's green shore.

*"That's a fine song," I said. "My Lord—"

*"I had it a little too high," he said, "for me anyway." He was right about that. "That's as old as—a lot older than I am, I guess. Likely come over from Ireland." He was right about that, too.

We broke for some supper at this point, and since Wesley's son had gone down to the shore the day before and gathered half a bushel of clams in less than an hour, that was the main course, and we made a considerable dent in that bushel. Unfortunately son Steve had not yet learned about clams, and he devoted his attention to a batch of Mrs. Smith's fresh doughnuts, getting through half a dozen and asking if there were any more. "My God, I never see anybody go after doughnuts that way before!" said Wesley, and everybody laughed as Steve polished off two more. "Next time you come, Steve," said Wesley, "we'll make sure to have a barrel of them on hand."

After supper we went back in the parlour for a few more songs. Some he had sung for me before but I wanted to hear again, like Joe Scott's "Howard Carey"; others were new ones from his little notebook, like "Sally Monroe."

It's a strange story: James Dixon falls in love with Sally Monroe, but her parents say no. His employment forces him to travel to distant lands, but he sends a letter by a friend who doesn't deliver it and, worse yet, misrepresents him to her mother. Still, by chance he meets Sally and convinces her to run away with him, which she does. The ship they leave on sinks, she is drowned, and he mourns not only for her but for her aged parents who are now left alone. It's a ballad that doesn't show up very often, and many of the versions I know of tell the story in a fragmented or confused form. Wesley's is no exception.

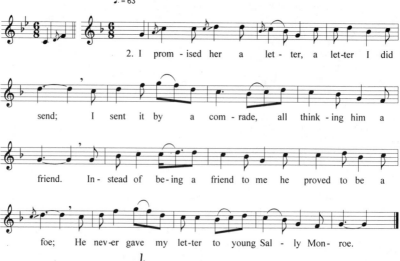

Sally Monroe

♩. = 63

                2. I prom - ised her a let - ter, a let-ter I did

send; I sent it by a com - rade, all think - ing him a

friend. In - stead of be - ing a friend to me he proved to be a

foe; He nev -er gave my let-ter to young Sal - ly Mon- roe.

1.
My name is Jimmy Dickson, a blacksmith by trade;
'Twas in the town of Erin that I was born and reared.
From there down to Belfast to working I did go;
It's there I fell in love with young Sally Monroe.

2.
I promised her a letter, a letter I did send;
I sent it by a comrade, all thinking him a friend.
Instead of being a friend to me he proved to be a foe;
He never gave my letter to young Sally Monroe.

3.

He gave it to her mother for to be aware of me.
"He has a wife and family in his own country."
"If that's what you tell me, my lad, it is so.
He never shall enjoy my young Sally Monroe."

4.

As I walked out one evening upon yon sandy shore,
It's there that I espied her, the lass that I adore.
I asked her if she would consent along with me to go,
Providing I'd prove loyal to young Sally Monroe.

5.

We sailed down the river in a sweet and pleasant gale,
Leaving all our friends behind us to weep and to wail.
A dark cloud came over about six o'clock,
And all in an instant our ship she struck a rock.

6.

Three hundred and twenty passengers were all down below,
And one among that number was Sally Monroe.

7.

'Twas through no ill intentions I stole her away,
Which causes me to mourn until my dying day.
'Twas through no ill intentions that ever I done so,
Which causes me to mourn for young Sally Monroe.

It was getting late. In the usual sense of that word, I'd "collected" a half-dozen or more songs, but from my perspective at the time our talk about Joe Scott was what really mattered. Most of it repeated what he'd told me in previous years, but it was important to hear it again. He also sang a far better version of "Howard Carey" than he had sung seven years before, one of the best I'd heard from anyone. All told it had been a wonderful afternoon, but it was time to quit.

On the way home I let Steve steer the whole length of the old MacArthur Road.

Sunday, August 29

A beautiful sunny day at last! We broke camp at Jacques Cartier in the morning, planning to set up that night at Cavendish, since I had a number of people near there I wanted to see. However, I had planned to stop in and introduce my family to Mary Cousins over in Campbellton, so we took the Dock Road across the Island. That would allow us to stop at the old Peter Emberly place on the way.

The old house was about the same as it had been in 1957, just a little more fallen in. We walked up the path, shooing sheep out of the way and panicking several who were inside when we got there. As we walked back, I watched a

No. 16: Wesley Smith, Victoria West. NA P267. *Photo taken August 28, 1965*

man who had been raking hay in the field across the road get off his tractor and come over to look at our license plate.

"Maine, eh?" he said when we got back. "Whereabouts in Maine?" It was a familiar question, and I had a pretty good idea what would follow my answer.

"I don't suppose you ever get over to Rumford, do you?" he asked.

"Yes," I said truthfully, "and I'll be over there again sometime next month."

"Do you know any McKennas there?"

"Sure," I said. "As a matter of fact, there's an Omer McKenna I'm planning to look up."

The man was quite excited. "Why, he's my uncle," he said. "Haven't seen him for years. I guess he's getting kind of old now, but you tell him Ronald's all right and so's the family and we say hello."

I said I would. It's the kind of message I've carried often. Never anything much more than hello, but just enough to show that the Maine-Downhome ties are still there.

The Cousins family had just finished Sunday dinner when we arrived, but of course there was still plenty for the Iveses, and we set into it while Mary and the girls did up the dishes and the talk flowed. Wonderful talk, as always! Mostly it was Mary who carried it forward—moving easily, weaving past and present, family and community into a solid fabric that made you wonder on reflection why you didn't call it art—while son John and the girls added comment and correction. Elbridge, stone deaf as he was, looked on contentedly. I remembered Harry Thompson telling me that one time he and Elbridge had to drive to Boston and bet Mary ten dollars she couldn't keep talking the whole way. They lost, of course, but I doubt that they ever expected to win that one, or even wanted to.

We made one more brief stop, this time at St. Mark's churchyard to pay our respects to Charlie Gorman.

Arriving at Cavendish just about dark, we discovered we had neither matches nor salt. We managed to scare up some of both from neighbouring campsites, but still we went to bed grumpy.

Monday, August 30

The morning dawned cold and continued grumpy, with a rain that turned to hail almost as soon as we stepped outside to start breakfast, driving us back under cover. It was then I noticed my Harris Tweed jacket lying on a stump where I'd left it the night before. We certainly hadn't had much luck with the weather these past few days, and when I suggested a trip to Charlottetown everyone agreed it was a great idea.

I dropped my jacket off at a dry cleaners, and we moseyed around town for a couple of hours. I had made arrangements to see one John Morrison, who lived way out the Mt. Edward Road, but since I had to wait until he got home from work, we stopped in to Pendergasts' for tea. Then Bobby dropped me off at Morrisons', where she and the kids would pick me up about eight.

John Morrison was about fifty-five and had grown up in Conway, Lot Eleven, where his father ran a lobster-packing factory. As a boy he had spent a great deal of time along the shore with the fishermen and the men who worked in the factory, and in time he worked there himself, sleeping in the shanties along with the other men. *"Shanties, that's what we called them," he said. "They were just small, rough buildings with board bunks in them and burlap bags sewed together and filled with straw. And you'd flatten them down when you were done sleeping on them for two months! When you opened them, the straw would just fall down like chaff. It was all broken up. Some fleas in them if you wanted to look for them. Around the shore there's lots of fleas.

*"These were the shacks we slept in at night," he continued, " and on a stormy day, when the fishermen couldn't fish, they'd be all laying around the bunks. We'd have everything done up in the factory. The lobsters would be all cooked and canned, and we'd be just in there having a day of rest. And, oh, there'd be fellas stepdancing and playing the mouth organ, singing."

*"Any violin?" I asked.

*"Not too much violin, because it was too easy to get broken around there. Oh, they'd play the jew's harp or the mouth organ. And I remember a fella who used to take a circular saw that was fairly thin. And he used to put his thumb in the hole where it went on the mandrel, and he'd get it up to his head and he'd play a tune with his knuckles on the side of that saw, ringing— the saw kind of ringing."

But the main thing he recalled was the singing, the shanty songs, as he called them, and he had just sung me one, a pretty good version of "John Ladner." Then he recalled a local song. It was about *"these fellas from Alberton," he said. "There was supposed to be a fight at some kind of a dance and a fella was killed." That's all he could remember about it, but it brought to mind another one:

> *And there was another song made up a good many long years ago,
> where there was a schooner come into Alberton Harbor, and they had a
> young fella tied by the two thumbs on one of the cross-arms. He was a
> stowaway. In one part of the song it said after nine days,
>
> When I nine days had left him, back to him I then did go,
> I said, "My kind and loving master, one kind favour to me show."
>
> He was tied by the two thumbs for nine days without water or food, and
> he pleaded with him for to give him a morsel that the dogs wouldn't eat.
> But when they came into Alberton Harbor and they seen him hanging

by the thumbs, the people went out and they told the Captain just as quick
as he could to cut him down. They'd of killed him, shot him there.

I was puzzled. It sounded like it *could* be an old come-all-ye, though I knew of nothing even remotely like it, and I said so. But three decades later, during a dull afternoon's serendipitous reading, I was to stumble on "The Cabin Boy," the story of one Captain James who sadistically starved his servant to death.[3] John Morrison's memory had been on the money.

Bobby and the family came for me about eight, bringing with them my now beautifully restored jacket, and we returned to our campsite at Cavendish.

Tuesday, August 31

Overnight the weather had turned round—still windy, but a beautiful blue morning auguring well for anyone who wanted to spend time on the beach while I went about my business. However, Steve decided he'd rather come with me, and I was always glad of his company.

We set out to find John O'Connor of Hope River. Back in February he'd sent me interesting handwritten copies of two Scott ballads, and when I asked if he'd sing them over for me when I came up in the summer he said he'd be glad to. Well, here I was, but it turned out our first job was to find Hope River, and, while the map made that look easy, we evidently missed it because we soon found ourselves in Stanley Bridge. I asked directions, and the next thing I knew we were in St. Ann, which meant that while we now had Hope River nicely bracketed, we'd obviously driven right through it twice! Once again I asked for help, only this time I said who I was looking for. "Oh, Jack? Sure thing," our new guide said, and, following *his* directions, we soon found ourselves where we ought to be.

Mr. and Mrs. O'Connor enthusiastically welcomed us into the big kitchen, one wall of which he had just finished plastering that morning. Since they'd been out west for some years the old family home had fallen into disrepair, and they had spent most of the summer fixing it up again. He'd wondered when I was coming and had pretty well given up on me by this time, but he was ready to sing those songs, if that's what I wanted. I said it was, and he excused himself briefly, coming back without his overalls and in clean shirt and pants. Steve meanwhile had gone out to the van and brought in the Roberts and the mike and stand.

Mr. O'Connor had a strong voice, and he sang "Howard Carey" and "The Boys of the Island" in a very straightforward, no-nonsense manner. At some point I asked him how he'd go about learning a song. It would get in his head, he said:

---

[3]See the Notes for more information on this ballad.

No. 17: John O'Connor, Hope River, and Stephen Ives. *NA P268.*
Photo taken August 31, 1965.

*I'd hear a man singing a song tonight, and I'd listen pretty attentively, and I'd like it, you know. Well then, the next day it would be going through my head and I'd be getting different words of it, perhaps two or three lines out of a verse, and I'd be humming it all the time, you see. And I'd say to myself, "Gosh, I must go again and hear that fella." Well, I'd get in touch with him or go to his place, and I'd hear him again. And I'd have the most of it the next, second time. Oh, about the third time [I'd have it all].

He said he'd learned many of his songs while working over in the Miramichi lumberwoods. I asked if that was where he'd learned "The Plain Golden Band" (that was one of the two he'd sent me in February). No, he said, he learned that right around here from a man named Gabe Warren back about 1925, but of course he'd heard it often enough over there. I could well believe that; I'd already found close to two dozen versions of it in New Brunswick, but on the Island I'd only found a few, all of them fragmentary. O'Connor thought he knew the whole of it and agreed to give it a try.

Of all Joe Scott's ballads, this is the one most closely identified with him. Even people who didn't know the song itself would often tell me that it was about Joe's own life—that this Lizzie had jilted him and it broke his heart. And, as it turns out, the story is essentially true. Joe and Lizzie Morse, a beautiful young woman from near Andover, Maine, got engaged in the fall of 1893, just before he went into the woods for the winter. They even filed intentions of marriage, but the marriage itself never took place, and a year later she married another woodsman, Sam Leonard, a long-time friend of Joe's. No doubt about it, the event was the central trauma of Joe's life. He never really recovered from it.

O'Connor himself didn't know the story, but here is the song as he sang it for Steve and me.

The Plain Golden Band

1.

I'm thinking tonight of the days that are gone,
When the sun glimmered over the hilltop at morn,
And the dewdrops from Heaven like diamonds did glow,
A-kissing the roses in the valley below.

2.

By the clear purling waters so mild and so blue
There came a low whisper, "To you I'll be true."
Now flowers bloom brightly upon the dark shore
When I parted from Lizzie, the girl I adore.

♩. = 50 approx.

1. I'm think-ing to-night of the days that are gone, When the

sun glim-mered o-ver the hill-top at morn, And the dew-drops from Heav-en like

dia-monds did glow, A-kiss-ing the ro-ses in the val-ley be-low.

3.
She was lovely and fair as the roses in June;
She looked like some goddess or some gracious queen.
She was fair as the lily that bloomed by the shore;
She's the pride of this valley, the girl I adore.

4.
Oh the day that we parted I ne'er shall forget;
I fancy I see those sad tears falling yet.
My poor heart was broke and with sorrow did sting
When she drew from her finger that plain golden ring.

5.
Saying, "Take back this ring that I fain would retain,
For the wearing of it only causes me pain.
Our vows are all broke that we made on the strand,
So take back, I pray you, the plain golden band."

6.
"Retain the engagement ring, darling," I cried.
"You know that you promised that you'd be my bride.
My love it is true—it shall never grow cold.
Retain, I beseech you, this plain band of gold."

7.
"My darling, I know that your love it is true;
I know that you love me and that I loved you.
You know I deceived you that night on the strand
When you placed on my finger the plain golden band.

8.
"One bright starry night when the moon it shone bright;
All nature seemed gay in its pale mellow light.
It was there a dark stranger crept over the moor
As I strayed from my cottage to roam on the shore.

9.
"A young man approached me, and him I well knew;
He told me false stories, false stories of you.
He vowed that he loved me and offered his hand.
I there placed a stain on the plain golden band."

10.

"Retain our engagement, my darling I pray,
E'er you lay me to sleep in my cold silent grave,
With those fond cherished letters in my own right hand,
And on my cold bosom lay the plain golden band."

11.

In the cool shady forest so far, far away,
Where the deer loves to ramble and the child loves to stray,
While nature looks gay and the scene's wild and grand,
You'll there find the author of "The Plain Golden Band."

We talked a little more about the lumberwoods and how there were good
singers there, but, he added, there were a couple of good singers "right around
here, too." One song he'd learned from a neighbour he called "My Seventy-
Six Geared Wheel," which tells of a man's trip via bicycle from his home in
Wellington to where his fiancée lived in Rustico:

My Seventy-Six Geared Wheel

♩. = 120

Oh, I long for the sol - id roads in the mer - ry month of June. When the birds are sing - ing gai - ly, all na - ture seems in tune. Va - ca - tion is my hap - pi - est time, how jol - ly I will feel A - rid - ing down to Rus - ti - co on my sev - en - ty - six geared wheel.

1.

Oh, I long for the solid roads in the merry month of June,
When the birds are singing gaily, all nature seems in tune.
Vacation is my happiest time, how jolly I will feel
A-riding down to Rustico on my seventy-six geared wheel.

2.

All the birds are singing pleasant songs to cheer me on my way;
They seem to bid me hurry up on the bright and sunny day.
But brighter are the objects that fill my heart with zeal,
As I eagerly push forward on my seventy-six geared wheel.

3.

I started in the morning, and in an hour's ride
I've spun into the little town of pretty Summerside.
I'll take a couple of glasses that makes my head reel
And the road gets strangely smoother on my seventy-six geared wheel.

4.

Then on I go like Gallagher, my very level best;
The next place that I pass through they call it Travellers Rest.
Then Kensington comes next in view, and you bet I'll happy feel
Arriving at this mighty speed on my seventy-six geared wheel.

5.

I'll just drop in to Lane's Hotel, and there I'll rest a while
Before I start for Margate, a distance of three miles.
And pleasanter thoughts come in my mind as I onward gently steal
'Til I arrive at Clifton on my seventy-six geared wheel.

6.

And Stanley Bridge comes next in view, and a pretty place it is,
And when I cross the railroad track you bet I let her whiz.
Then taking straight a southeast course by Simpson's and McNeill's,
'Til I arrive at the garden gate on my seventy-six geared wheel.

7.

And opening up the large front gate, and inward I do score,
Up the marble pathway unto the large front door;
And smiling Mary gently stands, you bet I'll happy feel
As I alight into her arms from my seventy-six geared wheel.

*"That's great," I said enthusiastically and asked what he knew about it.

*"There was a man over here by the name of Ambrose Cosgrove made that," he said. "The story was he lived at Wellington, the other side of Summerside, and he had a girl down here in Rustico at the [*Cavendish*] Capes. Her name was Mary Fleming, and he used to ride down on his bicycle, do you see, to see her, and this was the story he made himself. He was a schoolteacher."

But what in the world was a "seventy-six geared wheel?" The word "wheel" itself is no problem, being simply an older locution for bicycle (that's what my mother always called mine, for instance), but "seventy-six geared"? After some assiduous digging, the best I can come up with is that since, in the late nineteenth century, gear-driven bikes were swiftly taking over from the older ungeared models (like the famous penny-farthing), and since "seventy-six" is probably a then-current way of referring to a bike's power (a derivation involving gear-ratio and wheel size, perhaps), Mr. Cosgrove is saying that he's riding the last word in bikes.

If we trace out his route, we can see he'd be grateful for that. From Wellington he'd have taken the Western Road as far as Miscouche, where he'd pick up the St. Eleanors Road. Then—rather than taking the shortcut directly across to Travellers Rest, he'd continue on the St. Eleanors Road through Summerside. That added about four miles to his trip, but as a cyclist it would have been worth it to travel the better road. From Travellers Rest he had a straight shot through Kensington, Margate, Clifton, and New London to Stanley Bridge. From there he would have had to do some back-roading to get onto the Cavendish Road (there were, by the way, Simpsons and McNeills along there) and then onto the Back Cape Road and ultimately to the garden gate and smiling Mary herself—all told, a distance of some forty miles, and not all of it first-class highway.

Wednesday, September 1

Another cold morning, the coldest yet! In fact there was a heavy frost that was only just beginning to melt in the now bright sunlight. We all stood close to the table, and until our woodfire came up we all shivered around the little Coleman stove that was starting our breakfast. "When are we going home?" asked Steve, giving a voice to what was in everyone's mind.

"Well, I've just got this one more man I ought to see, but he's way down to the east. He sent me a good version of 'Howard Carey,' and I really ought to get his tune. If it wasn't for that we could start right now."

The kids were enthusiastic about the idea, and even I was beginning to wonder if I needed the one more tune all that much when compared to a hot bath and a real bed. "No," Bobby said, "you better go see him. Otherwise I'll have to listen to you whining all winter wondering why you didn't."

That settled the matter, but we decided to break our present camp and take our chances on where we'd stay that night, perhaps someplace down east. And there was always the chance this man wouldn't be home, and we could make a mad dash for a late ferry anyhow.

The man in question was Joseph Walsh, and all I knew was that he lived in Morell, down near St. Peters Bay, better than fifty miles from where we were at the moment. But I figured I could always ask at the Post Office as I had reliably done in the past elsewhere.

Unfortunately, I had forgotten about the general Maritimes custom of having shops and businesses close on Wednesday afternoons, so naturally when we arrived in Morell everything—including the Post Office—was buttoned up tight. Seldom have I seen a town so deserted, but at length I spotted an elderly man puttering around in his yard and asked him where in Morell I could find one Joseph Walsh.

"He doesn't live in Morell," he answered. "He's out in Morell Rear." He

No. 18: A barrack—a moveable roof designed to protect hay from rain and snow. At one time these structures were quite common in eastern Kings County, though not much found elsewhere on the Island. The present photo was taken in 1969 in St. Charles. *NAPhoto* 753.

pointed down a side road with his hedge clippers. "You go about three miles out that way and turn right. Joe's will be the first place on your left. Can't miss it," he assured me.

It was a huge house, well back from the road in a small grove of trees. There was no sign of life as we drove into the yard, but I stopped around to the kitchen door. A young girl answered my knock, and I explained who I was and what I wanted.

"Well, he's out in the fields right now," she said, "but why don't you just drive out there? I know he'd be glad to see you. Just take the road around behind the house."

I demurred a bit, saying I hated to interrupt a man at his work (and, truth to tell, I was still thinking about that late afternoon ferry), but she assured me that he wouldn't mind at all. We drove out through the field along a lane bordered by a row of splendid birches, and after passing through a gate and a hedgerow we saw Mr. Walsh driving a horse-drawn reaper. He saw us at the same time and, leaving the horses to munch on some of the sheaves, he came over toward us — a tall, weathered man dressed in overalls, denim jacket (what in Maine is called a frock coat), a wool cap, with the dirt of a good day's work on him.[4]

I identified myself, and he recognized me immediately. His ready smile and welcoming manner put us all at ease right away. "Remember you sent me a version of 'Howard Carey'?" I said. "Would you sing me over a bit of it, just to give me the tune?"

"Yes," he said confidently and obligingly, and he set right in. "Wait!" I yelped, and he waited patiently while I got out the UHER. Then he leaned up against the gatepost and sang the whole ballad, his voice a clear and gentle tenor that was a pleasure to listen to. He didn't speak the final words the way so many older singers did; he simply let his voice fade out.

"Fine!" I said.

He smiled. *"There's a little section in there that I got in wrong," he said, and he corrected it fror me. We talked for a little while about the song. I wondered had he learned it here on P.E.I. or in the woods of Maine. *"I learned that here," he said. "I learned that from a fella by the name of Tom Keefe. He's dead now, killed in a car accident. He worked on the railroad and when he was going on his vacation him and his brother-in-law got into a car and the train he had been reporting for ten years hit them at the crossing."

We both grimaced and shook our heads. There didn't seem to be anything much to say. We walked back over to the car, and I asked him about Larry Gorman.

---

[4]Most of this story is taken from *Lawrence Doyle*, pp. xv–xviii.

"I'd heard of him," he said, "but I never knew the man and I never heard any of his songs. But we had a man down here who used to make up songs. His name was Larry Doyle."

I jumped at the name. I'd heard of Doyle while I was writing my book on Gorman as a rival candidate for the authorship of "Prince Edward Isle, Adieu." "Do you know any of his songs?" I asked eagerly.

"Oh yes," he said. "There was one he made about a bear that some fellas shot down at Grand River one time." And he sang a couple of bits of it.

"Could you sing the whole song for me, so I could record it?" I asked.

"Larry Doyle had a good many songs," he said, "and there's one I know better than that. I'd have to think that Bear Song over a little bit for to get it all together. I know it all, but—you know—this other one I know better."

"Fine," I said, checking the tape recorder. "Go ahead with it."

And he did.

Fogan MacAleer

1.
There lived in bonny Scotland a man named MacAleer,
And plenty means and ways he had of land and working gear.
Yet he had the queerest notions, they were like perpetual motion
Or like waves that rock the ocean, don't you know what I mean?

2.
He liked the men his neighbours and the boys both one and all,
But he could not bear the capers of the women great or small;
Not a woman could he bear then, sure the girls they would scare him—
How they schemed and tried to snare him, don't you know what I mean?

3.
Oh Fogan was his christened name and Fogan was in need
Of a mare to match his sandy mane of equal strength and speed;
Yes he knew where one was handy that would suit him like a dandy,
So he'd go to blacksmith Sandy, don't you know what I mean?

4.
"Oh well now," says Fogan, " come listen unto me,
I'm looking for a mare to buy and I have come to thee;
Lauchlan Ban he has the very mare and only for the women there
I'd go and ask his terms, don't you know what I mean?"

5.
"Oh well now," says Sandy, "I will do the best I can,
I will see the women safe away and then see Lauchlan Ban;
You can call there at your pleasure, tonight if you have leisure,
For the mare she is a treasure, don't you know what I mean?"

6.
So Fogan he went home then a contented happy man,
And that evening he went over to see neighbour Lauchlan Ban;
The old man was kind and civil while upstairs the women sniveled
For the blacksmith played the devil, don't you know what I mean?

♩. = 112

There lived in Bon - ny Scot - e-land a man named Mac - A-
leer And plen - ty means and ways he had of land and wor - king
gear. Yet he had the queer - est no - tions they were like per - pet - u - al
mo - tion Or like waves that rock the o -cean, don't you know what I mean?

4. (2nd half)

Lauch - lan Ban he has the ver - y mare and on - ly for the
wo - men there I'd go and ask his terms, don't you know what I mean?"

[7. 3rd phrase on]

Oh I like her breed and col-our, she is ev - er - y -thing that's nice, I will
wa - ter, brush, and bed her, keep her in in stor - my weath -er, And in
day - time out on teth - er, don't you know what I mean?

[10. omit 1st phrase]

[12. like 4, plus these two phrases]

And so things turned out con - trar - y, not the mare he got but
Ma - ry, But he got the mare with Ma - ry, don't you know what I mean?

No. 19: Joseph Walsh, Morell Rear. NA P253. *Photo taken September 1, 1965, just minutes after he sang "Fogan MacAleer."*

"Oh well now," says Fogan, "my business I need not tell,
For Sandy has already told how I like her very well;
Oh I like her breed and colour, she is everything that's nice,
I will water, brush and bed her, keep her in in stormy weather,
And in daytime out on tether, don't you know what I mean?"

8.

"In the name of God," says Lauchlan, "what's come over you at all?
For we never intend selling her like cattle in the fall;
She has plenty things to fit her and has something to take with her
But 'tis we will sorely miss her, don't you know what I mean?"

9.

Then, "I do not want your presents," said Fogan MacAleer,
"I can pay the money down for her and find her working gear;
If you keep her in the stable, it is now I will be able
For to pay you on the table, don't you know what I mean?"

10.

"We don't keep her in the stable but upstairs she's snug and dry;
I will call her down this minute, since the two of you are in it
'Tis yourselves that should begin it, don't you know what I mean?"

11.

Then he hollered out for Mary while poor Fogan stood amazed,
With the beads of sweat upon his brow on Lauchlan Ban he gazed;
But he had no time for thinking, it was done as quick as winking
And poor Fogan's heart was sinking, don't you know what I mean?

12.

When Mary stepped into the room her father this did say:
"I suppose your mother told you what brought Sandy here today."
Then Mary blushed a rosy red and Fogan raised his drooping head,
His bashfulness was over, don't you know what I mean?
And so things turned out contrary, not the mare he got but Mary,
But he got the mare with Mary, don't you know what I mean?

We all burst out laughing: Mr. Walsh, Bobby, me, even the kids in the back seat. *"That is *wonderful*," I said, when I caught my breath.

*"Never heard that one before?" he asked, obviously pleased.

*"Never," I said. "Larry Doyle made that up?"

*"That was Larry Doyle," he said. "That was a story an agent, a traveling salesman told him about this old fella in Scotland. I learned that about fifty years ago."

Mrs. Walsh came along. She had been out in the next field looking for blueberries. We talked for a few minutes, and while I didn't want to keep Mr. Walsh from his work any longer, I passionately wanted to hear some more of his singing. *"Listen," I said, "supposing we were to stop back this evening. Could we get you to sing some more for us?"

*"Yes, yes," he said, seeming to be just as pleased with the whole encounter as we were. "Let's see," he considered, "this is Wednesday evening. We're not

going anywhere, there's nothing going on. Come back any time. Seven or half past, if it suits you. Any time, quarter to eight or whatever time suits you. We'll be here then until ten o'clock or so."

"So much for trying to catch an evening ferry," I said as we drove away. "I hope you don't mind too much."

"My God, no!" said Bobby. "What a wonderful man!" The three kids kept any opinions to themselves, but they were marvelously quiet and well-behaved during the evening of songs that followed our return to the big Walsh kitchen at seven-thirty.

Joe sang ten songs, the "Bear Song" and nine others. What follow are among my favourites, leading off with "The Irish Jubilee," a folksong tour-de-force if there ever was one, which in itself probably explains why it doesn't turn up very often in collections. Actually there's a whole genre of these Irish—or Irish-American—songs describing the whoopee and excess at imaginary christenings, weddings, wakes, and other celebratory occasions, but so far as I know this is the only one celebrating an election.

Notice that there are two tunes, which I have labeled A and B, and I have set the half-stanzas sung to the A tune in Roman type, those sung to the B tune in italic.

The Irish Jubilee

1.
A short time ago, boys, an Irishman named Dougherty
Was elected to the Senate by a very large majority.
He felt so elated that he sent for Dana Cassidy,
Who owned a big barroom of a very large capacity.

2.
"Now," he says to Cassidy, "Go down to the brewery
For a thousand kegs of lager ale and give it to the poor.
Go down to the butcher shop and order up a ton of meat;
Be sure that all the boys and girls have had enough to drink and eat.

3.
"For since I am elected, I mean to show my gratitude
By giving the finest supper that was ever given in this latitude.
Send out the invitations in twenty different languages,
And be sure to tell them to bring their own sandwiches.

4.
"Tell them that the music will be furnished by O'Rafferty
And assisted on the bagpipes by Felix McClafferty.
And anyone that wants to come, remember I'll foot up the tin
And anyone that doesn't come, be sure and do not let them in."

♩. = 130

A short time a-go, boys, an I-rish-man named Dough-er-ty Was e-lec-ted to the Se-nate by a ve-ry large ma-jor-i-ty. He felt so e-la-ted that he sent for Da-na Cas-si-dy, Who owned a big bar-room of a ve-ry large ca-pa-ci-ty. 2. "Now," he says to Cas-si-dy, "Go down to the brew-er-y For a thou-sand kegs of la-ger ale and give it to the poor. Go down to the butch-er shop and or-der up a ton of meat; Be sure that all the boys and girls have had e-nough to drink and eat."

5.
Cassidy at once sent out the invitations—
Everyone that came was a credit to his nation.
Some of those that came, boys, forgot their invitations,
While others as they came brought all their near relations.

6.
Some came on bicycles because they had no fare to pay,
Others didn't come at all, made up their minds to stay away.
Two by three they came marching through the dining hall—
Old men, young men, and girls that were not men at all.
Blind men, deaf men, men who had their teeth in pawn,
Single men, double men, and men with their glasses on.

7.

Sure in less than a minute every seat was taken,
Front room, [mash] room were packed to suffocation.
Says Cassidy to the Manager, "Try and fill the chair,"
So we all sat down and looked at the bill of fare.

8.

There was pigs head, goldfish, mockingbirds, and ostriches,
Ice cream, cold cream, vaseline, and sausages.
There was roast beef, baked beef, roast rib was here and there,
Roast ribs, spareribs, and ribs that we could not spare.

9.

There was fried liver, baked liver, Carter's Little Liver Pills;
Everyone was wondering who was going to foot the bill.
There was whitefish, bluefish, fish-hooks, and partridges,
Fishballs, snowballs, cannonballs, and cartridges.

10.

For dessert we had ice picks, toothpicks, all that you could cluck about,
Cat chops, hurry up, deer meat and sauerkraut.
There was reindeer, snow deer, deer meat, and antelope—
The women ate so much that the men said they can't elope.

11.

When the supper was over we all went out to have a dance;
Donald got drunk and thought he was the Queen of France.
There was the finest lot of dancers that ever you set your eyes upon—
Men that couldn't dance at all were dancing with their glasses on.

12.

The music and the dancing could be heard for miles around;
Gallagher was in the air, his feet were not upon the ground.
When the dance was over, Cassidy then told us
For to join our hands together and sing this good old chorus:

[To the tune of "Auld Lang Syne"]
"Should auld acquaintance be forgot wherever we may be,
Think of the good old time we had at the Irish Jubilee."

Joe hadn't sung that song for some time. *"Oh, I suppose there's odd things
I leave out of it," he said modestly, but clearly he was pleased that he had
remembered it as well as he did. He loved to sing, and we moved on to another
song. *"'The Hell-Bound Train,'" he said. "Did you ever hear it?"

Somehow I was surprised to have him mention a song which I had always
associated with the south and west. *"No, I haven't," I lied, "and I'd like to
hear it, too."

*"There's a moral in it," he said. "Oh, it's kind of grim alright, but there's
a moral in it. Well, if you're ready, I'll—"

I said I was, and he began.

The Hell-Bound Train

♩. = 90

Tom Gray lay down on the bar-room floor, Hav-ing drunk so much he could drink no more; He fell a-sleep with a trou-bled brain To dream that he rode on the Hell-Bound Train.

1.
Tom Gray lay down on the barroom floor,
Having drunk so much he could drink no more;
He fell asleep with a troubled brain
To dream that he rode on the Hell-Bound Train.

2.
The engine with blood was red and damp
And dismally lit with a brimstone lamp;
An imp for fuel was shoveling bones,
And the furnace roared with a thousand groans.

3.
The boiler was filled with lager beer,
And the Devil himself was the engineer;
The passengers made such a motley crew—
Church member, atheist, gentile, and Jew.

4.
Rich men in broadcloth, beggars in rags,
Handsome young ladies and withered hags;
Black men, red men, yellow, and white
Chained together—a horrible sight.

5.
Faster and faster the engine flew,
Wilder and wilder the country grew;
Louder and louder the thunder crashed,
Brighter and brighter the lightning flashed.

6.
And all the passengers shrieked with pain
And begged the Devil to stop the train;
But he capered about and danced with glee
And laughed and joked at their misery.

7.

"My faithful friends you have done my work,
And the Devil can never a payday shirk;
You have bullied the weak and robbed the poor,
And the hungry brother you've turned from your door.

8.

"You have gathered up gold with a canker rust
And given full vent to your hellish lusts;
You have drank and rioted and murdered and lied
And mocked at God in your hellish pride.

9.

"You have paid full fare, so I carry you through,
For it's only right that you get your due;
For every labourer is worth his hire,
So I'll land you safe in my lake of fire.

10.

"Where my fiery imps will torment you forever,
And all in vain you sigh for your Saviour."
When Tom awoke with an awful cry,
His clothes soaked wet and his hair standing high.

11.

And he prayed as he never prayed before
To be saved from Hell and the Devil's power,
And his crying and praying was not in vain,
For he nevermore rode on the Hell-Bound Train.

Since, as I said, I always thought of that song as southern or western, I wondered where he had learned it. "Around here?" I asked.

*"No," he said, "I didn't learn that around here. I learned that from a fella by the name of Fred Kennedy over in Nova Scotia. One winter I was working in the woods over there. He was the only one I ever knew or heard with the song. I've been around camps [in Nova Scotia, New Brunswick, and Maine] where. . . there was some nice singers—some good singers in the camps betimes. They had some very nice songs, too. Some of them weren't so nice. I never learned none of those. Well," he added thoughtfully, "very few."

Since this didn't seem like the time to follow that up, I moved on. *"Did you do much singing in the camps yourself?" I asked.

*"Oh yes," he said, "I always sang. Especially when we were up in [Katahdin] Iron Works [in Maine]. Bunch of the fellas there—what was their names? Lancasters. There was Levi, Billy, and Harold, and they were awful fellas to sing, and there wasn't many in the camp that year could sing either! I was only about eighteen, and they used to keep me at it all the time. Every night. I didn't mind singing then, but my voice is not—you know, it's fading. But I love to sing. I love to sing! Oh, sing anywhere!"

I was always eager for songs about the lumberwoods. *"Do you know any woods songs?" I asked him, fully expecting "The Jam on Gerry's Rock" or maybe "Jack Haggerty."

*"There's one I used to know," he said, "and I guess I still do." And he went right to it.

Come lis - ten to my sto - ry, the truth I'll tell to

you; It is a- bout a team - ster in Jack Mac - Don - ald's crew.

1.
Come listen to my story
  the truth I'll tell to you;
It is about a teamster
  in Jack MacDonald's crew.

2.
[It fell unto a married man,
  Leslie Stubbs by name,
Who came into the lumberwoods
  his family to maintain.]

3.
Our crew it was a merry one
  of eighteen men or more;
Our winter's work had scarce begun
  when Death had darked our door.

4.
We were talking after supper when
  one of the teamsters said,
"I hear young Stubbs complaining of
  a pain that's in his head."

5.
The night passed on and morning came,
  the sickness it grew worse;
We moved him from the lower bunk
  into the upper berth.

6.
And when we went to breakfast
  we dared not leave him alone;
We wrapped him up in his blankets warm
  all for to take him home.

No. 20: Earl Stubbs, the ill-fated teamster in "The Teamster in Jack MacDonald's Crew." The photo was taken in 1900, probably at the time of his marriage. NA P3683. *Courtesy of Mrs. Hartley Anderson, Stubbs' daughter, Sherman Mills, Maine.*

7.

Jack MacDonald and Tom Proctor
  Took a pair of trotty bays,
And before the stars had ceased to shine
  they were miles upon their way.

8.

They took him to his little home
  in the town of Sherman Mills,
And to break the news unto his wife
  it did require great skill.

9.

They sent for Dr. Harris while
  his wife and family cried.
But to rescue him from Death's cold grasp
  It was in vain they tried.

10.

Here's to MacDonald and his crew,
  our blessing do we give;
And may their troubles they be few
  and happy may they live.

11.

And when Death comes knocking at our door
  and we are called to go,
Let us pray that we will meet our Lord,
  let His mercy on us show.

*"I haven't thought of that song for years," said Joe afterward, a little amazed at what he had just done, "but it's still there, you know." He didn't know much about the song—neither who Stubbs or any of the others were, nor where Sherman Mills was. He seems to have learned the song largely because an old friend of his had a hand in making it up. Years later I spent some time checking the details and found them to be essentially correct: one Earl Stubbs, aged 28, having contracted spinal meningitis in a lumbercamp, died at his home in Sherman Mills, Maine, January 23, 1908, and Dr. Francis Harris had signed the death certificate. But for Joe it was just a song—its own reality—written by a friend and telling about a way of life he had known well.

A few minutes later Joe thought of another piece he hadn't sung in a while. *"It's supposed to be sung by a man and a woman," he said. "My father and mother used to sing it. They were both very nice singers."

The Wee Cup of Tay

1.

As Jack from the market came the other day,
His wife she sat drinking her wee cup of tay.
He up with his foot, gave the table a kick,
Saying, "You and your taypot may go to Old Nick!"
Laddy tin dee I ay, laddy tin dee i ay.

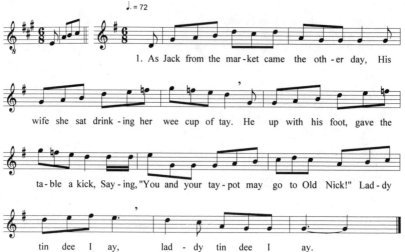

♩. = 72

1. As Jack from the mar-ket came the oth-er day, His
wife she sat drink-ing her wee cup of tay. He up with his foot, gave the
ta-ble a kick, Say-ing, "You and your tay-pot may go to Old Nick!" Lad-dy
tin dee I ay, lad-dy tin dee I ay.

2.
"I say quit your folly! I'll have you be civil.
I'll comfort my body—you go to the Divil!
For that's all the comfort I have night or day
Is to cheer up my heart with a wee cup of tay."
Laddy tin. etc.

3.
"Oh, you can go out with your bonnet and veil
And three rows of flounces around your gown tail.
Your gay Spanish boots and your apron so black.
Whilst I must work hard, not a shirt to my back."
Laddy tin, etc.

4.
"What money you spend in whisky and beer
Would buy you a new suit of clothes once a year,
And still you're exclaiming at me night and day
For taking my slim cake and wee cup of tay."
Laddy tin, etc.

5.
"You impertinent jade, take care what you say;
You're bound by the laws of the land to obey.
And while I am able, I vow and declare
I'll never allow you the britches to wear."
Laddy tin, etc.

6.
"I'm bound by the laws of the land to obey,
And while you me [nourish] I will you obey.
I'm the flesh of your bone which you cannot disjoin;
Therefore by the law half the britches are mine."
Laddy tin, etc.

7.

"You say you're the flesh of my bone? It's a fib,
For a woman is made of an old crooked rib.
She's crossed in the grain and she's just like a mule,
And you might as well try a wild ass for to tame."
Laddy tin, etc.

Joe paused here, not quite sure what it was came next. "Your jesting. . . ,"
whispered his wife, and he was off again.

8.

"Your jesting and jibing I care not a fig,
For what could you expect but a grunt from a pig?
Poor Nebuchadnezzar he had to eat grass,
And you are no better, you poor silly ass!"
Laddy tin, etc.

9.

Come all my good fellows, take warning I pray:
Don't rail at the women for taking their tay.
For if you would rail them from the head to the toe,
They would have the last word or if not the last blow.
Laddy tin, etc.

As I've already pointed out, Joe didn't follow the traditional practice of
dropping to a speaking voice for the last word or two. Like Edmund Doucette,
he'd just let his voice trail away, but sometimes—as with the present song—
he'd slowly raise his hand in a sort of farewell gesture. It made a nice ending.

*"That's a *wonderful* song," I said.

*"Did you never hear that one before?" he said. I said that I hadn't, and
in all the years since I have found it in only one other printed collection,
and for the life of me I can't remember what that was.

At some point Bobby had bedded down the two younger children out in
the bus, but Steve—wide-eyed and bolt upright on a kitchen chair—would
have none of that, even refusing the suggestion of a nearby couch. We all
knew it was getting late, but no one, least of all Joe, wanted to quit yet. I asked
about sea songs. Yes, he knew a few, he said, and offered to sing "The Drunken
Captain."

The story line is clear enough. A Gloucester fishing schooner on its way
home—probably from the Bay Chaleur, though New England fishermen
frequently spoke of the entire Gulf of St. Lawrence as "The Bay"—puts in to
one of the small harbours along the Strait of Canso for the night. Next
morning the drunken captain orders all sails set for a rousing trip home. Even
with the wind coming out of the northeast—an ominous sign—there is no
serious problem until he comes to the open ocean beyond Chedabucto Bay,
where he hits heavy weather but refuses to take in any sail. The situation gets
desperate, the crew mutinies, and everyone gets home safely.

The Drunken Captain

♩ = 80

In Can-so Strait our ves-sel lay; We had just re-turned
in from out the Bay. Our ves-sel was built both stout and strong,
And to Glos-ses - ter she did be - long.

1.
In Canso Strait our vessel lay;
We had just returned in from out the Bay.
Our vessel was built both stout and strong,
And to Glos-ses-ter she did belong.

2.
Our anchor weighed and our sails were peaked,
As the gentle breeze swept o'er the deep.
We were homeward bound and all ready for sea,
While our drunken captain got on a spree.

3.
At the dawn of day on the deck he came
With a bloodshot eye and a dizzy brain.
He staggered round and those words did say:
"Get your anchor weighed, boys, and fill away."

4.
We filled away at his command;
We had all sails set when we left the land.
We left Sand Point far in our lee,
As we sailed out the Bay on a head-beat sea.

5.
The night grew dark, and the dark clouds lowered,
And the billows on the ocean roared.
As our vessel through the sea did dash,
And the blue waves on our deck did wash.

6.
We kindly asked him to shorten sail,
Or he'd run us under in the heavy gale;
But he cursed and he swore as the wind did blow,
Saying, "I'll show you now how my ship can go!"

7.

There came a squall from the angry sky,
As our vessel sank and she did not rise,
'Til the jib gave away with the heavy strain;
Then she rose and came head to wind again.

8.

We kindly asked him if he would comply,
But he staggered round and made this reply:
"I am captain here, and I will not fail
For to shoot the first man who slacks a sail!"

9.

Then up spoke one of our gallant crew,
Saying, "You're only one, and we're twenty-two.
We will shorten sail and to sea we'll go,
And if you resist you'll be tied below."

10.

We shortened sail as we steady steered,
And soon the broken ledges cleared,
And it's off the Capes we are sailing now,
And she rides a white foam before her bow.

11.

We were homeward bound as the billows roared,
And we made Thank God when we reached the shore,
But never again do I wish to sail
With a drunken captain in a heavy gale.

Mrs. Walsh had started the kettle boiling, and when she started to put together a lunch Bobby got up to help her. The night was winding down, but Joe kept on singing. "Do you know 'The *Flying Cloud*,'" I asked.

*"Yes," he said, with a patient smile. "I know it all right, but I never much cared for it. I just learned it because people were always asking for it, but it was never a favourite of mine. I'll sing it, though, if you want me to."

Mrs. Walsh said tea was ready, and we all pulled up to the long table. It was a pleasant time among new friends in an old house. Joe had been born in this house, and so had his father, his grandfather having come here from the Old Country. Joe showed us the original deed just before we left to drive back to Charlottetown, where we luckily found a cabin for the night.

Nineteen Sixty-Eight

I DIDN'T DO ANY MORE WORK ON P.E.I. for over two years, but I made up for it by several months of intensive fieldwork in Maine, New Hampshire, and New Brunswick, followed by more months of trying to bring together all I'd learned about Joe Scott—and through him about traditional songmaking—into the book I knew was there. The schedule I had laid out for the folks at the Guggenheim Foundation called for a completed manuscript by the fall of 1967, but they were both too well-mannered to demand—and far too experienced to expect—such promptitude. Things dragged on as my sabbatical ended and a full academic schedule took over again, but I kept plugging away on my writing as time permitted. And even as it didn't.

But the harder I worked the less satisfied I was with how it was coming along. It wasn't a matter of losing faith; I knew where I was going and how to get there, but—no doubt about it—I was spinning my wheels. Salvation came—as salvation so often does— serendipitously, in the form of an invitation to deliver a lecture at Prince of Wales College in Charlottetown in the spring of 1968. Coming as it did during the University of Maine's spring break, I decided to spend a week seeing what I could find out about Lawrence Doyle, and not surprisingly Bobby decided to come with me.

Once again, my time was very limited, and once again I would use it on some very specific things. Naturally I wanted to see Joe Walsh again, since he was the one who really got me started that wonderful September day back in 1965 when he sang three of Doyle's songs and went over bits of several others, but once again I put a letter in the Charlottetown *Guardian* asking for information. The result was that by the time we were ready to leave I had leads from something like three dozen people. Always, though, such leads winnow themselves down by a kind of self-triage, but just as always one person leads to another as fieldwork moves along. At any rate, it looked like we would have a pleasantly busy week ahead of us.

We arrived in Charlottetown late Saturday and settled into the quarters Prince of Wales had generously provided for us. We spent most of Sunday, a beautiful cold day, visiting several people around town who had written me— lots of talk but no songs—and then spent the late afternoon pleasantly with our old friends the Pendergasts. But since all my leads from the letters were from Kings County, we planned to drive down there and get to work early Monday morning.

Monday, April 1

It was a miserable day, cold and on the edge of sleet, and we were in Phonsey Whitty's kitchen in Farmington, gratefully snugged up to his stove and talking about his Great Uncle Lawrence. Earlier we had been talking with his older sister, Mary John MacIsaac, and Phonsey had just gone over rather apologetically what few fragments of Doyle's songs he happened to remember. "That's about all I know," he said, "but Leo Gorman knows all those songs. He's the man you want to see, him and maybe old Art Cahill."

"Do they live near here?" I asked.

"Not far," he said. "Just over in Groshaut—well, they call it St. Charles now. I can take you over there. I'm not doing anything this afternoon."

"Great," I said, and we were soon on our way.

Phonsey was welcomed warmly by the Gormans, almost as if they hadn't seen him for years (which, all things considered, was quite possible), and almost before we knew it we were all old friends. Both Leo and his wife had seen my letter in *The Guardian* and had meant to write but just never got around to it. How was I doing? Did I have "The Picnic at Groshaut?" He sang me what he knew of it. "That happened right down here at the church," he said proudly, and the conversation turned to "what really happened," followed by Leo singing fragments of several other Doyle songs. He was rather disappointed that he couldn't remember more, but it was decided we really ought to get hold of Art Cahill, who lived just up the road, or John D. Gorman, Leo's brother, who lived the next farm down. The choice fell on Cahill, but before we left to call on him Leo got started on a song he felt he knew all the way through, "Saville the Brave Man."

In all likelihood, this song refers to the setting-out of lines of lobster traps on the opening day of the season in late April. In spite of the fact that the outlook was for stormy weather, Saville and his partner got out on the banks early to stake out their particular patch of ocean. Once they arrived, they had to wait for sunrise before running their lines, and that's when the storm hit them. *"That happened for sure," said Leo. "It was in the days of sailboats. There were no motors then. Storm came up just at sunrise as they got out to the fishing grounds."

Saville The Brave Man

1.

Come list while I tell you a tale of the ocean,
A story that one time was told unto me;
When Saville the brave man, while other men trembled,
Defied the fierce wind and the wild raging sea.

♩. = 60 approx.

2. It was on the morn - ing of the twen - tieth of Ap - ril, A morn - ing that each man must run out his lines; But when they had looked at the clouds to the west - ward, It was plain to be seen that it would not be fine.

2.

It was on the morning of the twentieth of April,
A morning that each man must run out his lines;
But when they had looked at the clouds to the westward,
It was plain to be seen that it would not be fine.

3.

But Saville he started in spite of all warnings,
For which he received a most courteous thanks;
And soon the old *Alma* she plied the wild billows,
Arriving at last on the fishermen's banks.

4.

And he with MacKenzie, his mate and his partner,
Sat down for to wait for the hour they must run;
When a fierce gale of wind and a wild raging snowstorm,
Swept over the ocean with the rise of the sun.

5.

Saville doffed his sou'wester, throwed it down in the cuddy,
While MacKenzie stood near him with bailer in hand;
Now reefing her snugly and weighing their anchor,
They hauled by the wind and stood in for the land.

6.

They looked out from Cape Spry with pitying glances,
They thought that no power could that old *Alma* save;
They thought as they watched them dash on o'er the billows,
These young men would soon fill a watery grave.

7.

But Saville looked [out and such a cleft] the wild billows
While the wintery wind tossed his long curly hair;
And MacKenzie stood near him looking brave and determined,
His face seemed as if it was loaded with care.

No. 21: Leo Gorman, St. Charles. NA P764. *Photo taken April 2, 1968.*

8.
They knew not the spirit of those worthy seamen,
Who was always determined to do or to die;
But soon they were in where the water was smoother,
And landed them safe on the shore at Cape Spry.

That brought to mind parts of another song, which he went over for us. Then we climbed in the bus—Leo, Phonsey, Bobby, and me—and went off to see if Art Cahill could be cajoled into coming down and singing a few songs. "He'll be glad to come, I know," said Phonsey, but before we stopped they had me drive about a mile up the road so that I could see St. Charles Church, on whose grounds the famous "Picnic at Groshaut" had taken place. Then when we came back by Cahill's Leo told me to wait on the paved road while he slipped up the lane to the house. Cahill came to the door, they talked for a moment, and I saw him nod yes, whereupon he went inside to get his coat and boots.[1]

Back at Leo's, he sat in a straight chair next to the stove, cup of tea in hand, a tall, erect, rawboned man who would only confess to being "over eighty." He sang his songs slowly in a high throaty tenor, and all of us in that bright friendly kitchen listened—Leo, his wife, daughter Susan (home on holidays from Montreal), Phonsey, Bobby, and me—the wood fire in the stove sweet smelling and crackling, Susan knitting, Leo smiling and singing along quietly where he knew the words and goodmanning encouragingly from time to time. Art had been at the picnic himself. He sang with his eyes closed, or so it appeared. What was he seeing as he sang, I wondered? Outside the window I watched the cold soft rain come down.

This is one of those local songs you have to know something about ahead of time before it makes much sense, and the singing of it will almost always lead to comment on what really happened. In brief, then, outdoor "tea parties" or picnics were common Island fund-raising events a hundred years ago, and great effort went into the preparations. There were booths for games, rides for children, and women set up tables where they politely hawked their specialties (floating island, chocolate cake, whatever), while over it all was the constant sound of fiddle and pipe—sometimes even a band or two. Strong drink was ritually forbidden, but it could usually be found, if not on the grounds at least conveniently close by off them. Father Walker felt he could solve *that* problem by providing plenty of cider, and he managed to purchase a supply at a bargain rate.

The great day dawned lowery, but preparations went ahead until the rain

---

[1] This same story is told in *Lawrence Doyle*, p. 19.

came and forced postponement until the next day. But those who were there thought it too bad not to have a glass of cider before going home, so they broached a keg, only to discover that a wonderful mistake had been made: Father Walker's bargain turned out to be hard cider! Soon the rain moved off, people began arriving, and it wasn't long before the good Father had a real donnybrook on his hands. After it was all over and everyone had been sent home, he carefully and heavily watered what remained in the kegs, and the next day everything was sober and uneventful.

And now for the song itself. It should be noted that Cahill used the tune for stanza 1 only once again—for stanza 7. For all others he used the tune for stanza 2.

The Picnic at Groshaut

♩. = 96

1. Oh come lis-ten to my song for it won't de-lay you long, 'Bout what hap-pened here a month or two a-go; And I'm doubt-ful if my rhyme will do jus-tice to the time That was held up-on the tea-grounds at Gros-haut. 2. The mor-ning dawned up-on us and the rain came down in tor-rents And the ta-bles set so neat-ly in a row; And the lad-ies all pre-pared to do busi-ness on the square And to make the tea a cred-it to Gros-haut.

1.

Oh come listen to my song for it won't delay you long,
'Bout what happened here a month or two ago;
And I'm doubtful if my rhyme will do justice to the time
That was held upon the tea-grounds at Groshaut.

2.

The morning dawned upon us and the rain came down in torrents
And the tables set so neatly in a row;
And the ladies all prepared to do business on the square
And to make the tea a credit to Groshaut.

3.

Another day we'll borrow, let the tea come off tomorrow
And it's merry altogether we will go;
And the violin sweetly droned and the cider barrel groaned
Just the day before the tea was at Groshaut.

4.

About noon it turned out fine and the sun began to shine,
What was done was for the best you all well know;
If it wasn't a success, 'twas a frolic nonetheless
And 'twas time to have a picnic at Groshaut.

5.

There was scuffles through the crowd and the noise was rather loud,
'Twas from jolting one another to and fro;
And old men with foreheads bare threw their dusters in the air
Wanting someone for to fight them at Groshaut.

6.

The boys and girls were dancing and the older ones a-prancing
While the cider in their goblets did o'erflow;
And they stepped so high and light like a hen would in the night,
'Twas a funny time that evening at Groshaut.

7.

It may rise the price of shirts but there's no one badly hurt,
And I hope there's no ill feelings to bestow;
There were picnics held before a little nearer to the shore
And they might be called twin brothers to Groshaut.

8.

See how Noah was respected, in the Ark he was elected
And from grapes he caused the richest wine to flow;
When he made the wine, you see, he got as drunk as drunk could be,
Just as drunk as any man was at Groshaut.

9.

Perhaps it was a shame but there's no one for to blame,
'Twas nothing but an accident, you know;
'Twas continued the next day but the spirit died away
And the cider turned to water at Groshaiut.

10.

So now the tea is over and the boys again are sober
And they'll always taste the cider for to know;
If it's hard, they'll take it light, if it's soft they'll leave it quite,
But they'll not forget the tea was at Groshaut.

Some years later I sang this song for a group in Rumford, Maine, figuring there would be at least a scattering of PIs in the audience. I was right, and several of them came up to talk with me afterwards. One man recalled that his father had been at the church concert where Doyle first sang this song, and of course Father Walker was there, too. "When the song was over, everyone waited to see how he'd taken it, and he said, 'Now Lawrence, would you sing it again!' And he did." Indeed, only a complete sourpuss could possibly have objected to a song as good-natured as this one.

Everyone in that kitchen enjoyed Art's performance and clearly wanted to hear more. *"Now, would you be heard on the 'Millman Murder Trial'?" asked Leo. "I was trying to hum it here, and I couldn't do it."

*"I used to know that," said Art. "I don't know whether I could go over it yet or not. There was a part of it I used to get stuck on." He paused. " You know some of it, do you, Leo?"

*"I've been working on it here," he said, "but there's part of another verse I can't get.

Art agreed to give it a try.

The Millman Murder Trial

♩. = 84 approx.

They talked a while of mat - ters that were
fore - most to their view; This trust - ing maid seemed
not a- fraid to walk some dis - tance too. Un - til they came to a
lone - ly spot well suit - ed to the deed; With
crav - ing heart did well his part, the vil - lian did the deed.

1.
It's of a lovely country girl most innocent and fair;
Content and free she used to be without one thought or care.
Just budding into womanhood, that pure and holy state
That God ordained should be sustained in purity complete.

2.
Alas, how often do we find down by some life's stream,
[Kind some] gentle maid by being betrayed away from virtue's side —

Art faltered, unable to come up with the missing couplet. *"As evening shadows gently glide," suggested Leo, and Art carried on.

3.
As evening shadows gently fell o'er streams and o'er hills,
Poor Mary went on purpose bent their meeting to fulfill;
For Millman on that evening was waiting for her here,
With murderous heart to do his part and end the girl's career.

4.
They talked a while of matters that were foremost to their view;
This trusting maid seemed not afraid to walk some distance too.
Until they came to a lonely spot well suited to the deed;
With craving heart did well his part, the villain did the deed.

5.
He quickly took her in his arms and hastened to the shore,
And soon eloped within a boat prepared by him before.
A rope he fastened round her waist, fixed to the end a stone;
One gentle splash and like a flash the murderer was alone.

6.
Alone? Oh no! One seeing eye was watching from on high,
For God is just and the murderer must from his dread vengeance fly;
The brand of Cain is on his brow, no peace again he'll find,
Until upon the gallows he expatiates his crime.

7.
The river is searched and the body found, now Millman hold your own,
The best made plans of mice and men are ofttimes overthrown;
The very means that we supply to ward suspicion [*pron.* sus-pi-she-un]
Her in the end would surely tend to cut your young life short.

8.
The arrest soon followed after, [*long pause*] the trial I will not trace;
In spite of able counsellors the prisoner lost his case;
For the jury found him guilty and no one can deny,
For justice grim was served to him, he's now condemned to die.

9.
Now parents mind, a warning take, no matter what's in view,
For you know you must guard well in trust what God has given you;
A strict account you'll have to give when called before the throne
To answer for your children's sins as well as for your own.

*"That's it," said Art, a little dubiously, when he had finished. "It's kind of jumbled up, but there it is." The fact is I hadn't much wanted to hear it. It was getting late, and Bobby and I had made plans to spend the evening with Joe and Winnie Walsh in Morell Rear about twenty miles away, and after all I had Mary Cousins' singing of it from ten years before, but Leo was quite insistent that I hear it. Of course, it turned out to be an entirely different song from Mary's—another example of how one should take one's chances and go with the flow!

And it looked like the flow was about to continue even further, because just as we were fixing to leave again, Leo's bachelor brothers—Ambrose and John D.—came in. I think Mrs. Gorman had called them earlier, but however it was, everyone wanted John D. to sing Doyle's "The Bay Bridge," which he did. After that, we managed to make our excuses and leave, arranging to come back the following afternoon.

We dropped Phonsey off at his place in Farmington and made our way hurriedly to the Walshes'. Since Joe had told me over the phone that his long lane was hub-deep mud in places, we parked out on the hard road and walked in for a pleasant evening of talk and song, plus a very welcome lunch, since we'd had no supper. No new songs this time, but several good singings of ones he'd sung three years before.

Tuesday, April 2

We were back at Leo's by about one. John D. hadn't arrived yet, but Leo patiently sang over a couple of Doyle pieces I'd accidentally erased while changing tapes the day before. *"Not many songs getting threw together these days like olden times," he reflected. "Them old men, they were wonderful old fellas."

*"Yes, all those things are all forgotten now since radio and television," Mrs. Gorman added. "Back then people'd come on a visit there'd likely be singing. Now they watch TV."

*"Oh, there was an old fella one time," said Leo. "Hughie, from St. George. Had a girl in here in Selkirk. Hughie Lauchlan MacDonald. He used to drink, but anyways I don't know how it come, but he made a song about himself like, you know, some of it was a story and some of it was true. He was a good poet, but he didn't make as many as Larry Doyle. He made up one about the girl, too, but I couldn't remember any of that one. I remember the one he made about the grey mare, though."

*"Would you sing it?" I asked.

*"Hard to get the air of that one," said Mrs. Gorman

*"Yes," agreed Leo, "but I can just—as the fella said, I can just give you the words and *holler* at them! Anyhow, he got a little bit drunk in Georgetown

across here. He had the mare at it nearly all night." And with that he began
to sing.

Aside from needing to know that the "large roomy stable" in stanza 2 is
no stable at all and that the "glass bottle" in stanza 5 is an insulator, "The
Crazy Grey Mare" tells a pretty straight story of a wild drunk, first from the
point of view of the drunk and then from that of a horse who makes Balaam's
Ass sound like Calvin Coolidge.

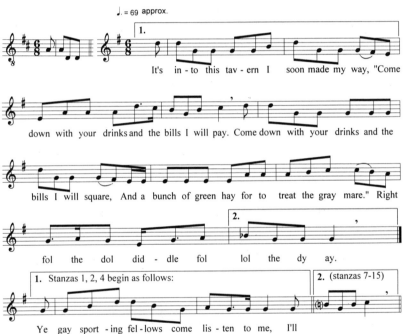

It's in-to this tav-ern I soon made my way, "Come
down with your drinks and the bills I will pay. Come down with your drinks and the
bills I will square, And a bunch of green hay for to treat the gray mare." Right
fol the dol did-dle fol lol the dy ay.

1. Stanzas 1, 2, 4 begin as follows: **2.** (stanzas 7-15)

Ye gay sport-ing fel-lows come lis-ten to me, I'll

I.

Ye gay sporting fellows come listen to me,
I'll give you a sketch of my terrible spree;
It being my encounter with the Georgestown train,
I may not be in humour when I meet you again.
Right fol the dol diddle fol lol the dy ay.

2.

On a hard frosty morning I started away,
I called to a tavern was near the highway,
Where the wild Irish whiskey was sold by the small,
And a large roomy stable without side, roof, nor wall.
Right fol, etc.

3.

It's into this tavern I soon made my way,
"Come down with your drinks and the bills I will pay.
Come down with your drinks and the bills I will square,
And a bunch of green hay for to treat the grey mare."
Right fol, etc.

4.

On the hard frosty roads I have started again,
And what should appear but the Georgestown train?
And from it my mare took a terrible fright,
I was threw from the sleigh in the air like a kite.
Right fol, etc.

5.

No doubt you will smile but for me 'twas no joke,
I was landed on top of a telegraph pole;
I knew there was news by the ring of the wire,
I found a glass bottle some fellow hid there.
Right fol, etc.

6.

I crawled down the pole, I felt very queer,
I looked up and down but where was the mare?
"The treacherous old villyan she's crushed by the train,
I'll never lay eyes on that devil again."
Right fol, etc.

7.

I went down through the city as fair as a die,
And a large brigantine at the wharf there did lie;
They were hoisting up lumber and they told me there,
I'd get a good job if I had the grey mare.
Right fol, etc.

8.

So I turned on my heel and upstreet again,
I was bound for to punish the hands on the train;
"Now I'll make them pay, or else it is clear,
I'll get a good price for the sleigh and the mare."
Right fol, etc.

9.

I was passing that tavern right nearby the square,
At a post quite contented there stood the grey mare;
I walked up beside her, put my hand on her head,
Saying, "You treacherous old villyan I thought you were dead."
Right fol, etc.

10.

She put back her ears, made a claw for the post,
Saying, "That can't be you, it must be your ghost.
I killed you down there, and I'll bet fifty pounds
That's some red-headed fellow belongs to this town."
Right fol, etc.

11.

"To the very first yankee that will cross over the main,
I'll sell you for greenbacks and I'll ride on the train."
"That's all very fine, sir, what you do say,
But what will you do with the harness and sleigh?
Now the night is so dark and the roads are so clear,
Now take my advice and hang on to the mare.
Right fol, etc.

12.

"It's when you are sober, I very well know,
You feed me so good and you drive me so slow;
But when you are tipsy I pay for it all,
You'll drive like the Devil and feed none at all.
Right fol, etc.

13.

"And you'll never imagine how weary I feel,
I'm all over ice from my head to the heel;
Do you mind where you tied me last night in the cold,
And the rest of my story is easily told.
Right fol, etc.

14.

"Now please will you look in the box in the sleigh,
It's there you will find some oats and some hay;
For the sake of old friendship please give that to me,
And forgive the grey mare when you're over your spree."
Right fol, etc.

15.

Now you gay reckless fellows take warning by me,
If you have the misfortune to go on a spree;
If you have a wild horse keep a hold on the rein,
And keep a look-out for the Georgestown train.
Right fol, etc.

Shortly after this, John D. arrived, and Leo was at him about "The Millman Trial" almost before he had his coat off, but John D. simply couldn't start it. *"Can't seem to hit on the first line of it," he said. Then, after a long pause, he turned to Leo. "You don't know that first line?"

*"That's what I'm trying to find out," said Leo. "No, I don't remember it."

After considerable discussion of what that line might be, they both gave it up, and John D. decided to get on firmer ground. Whether or not it was a coincidence is anybody's guess, but he came up with a pair of songs about the fighting Irish. First came the widely known saga of that colourful nineteenth-century pugilist, John J. Morrissey. Immigrant boy, street brawler, heavyweight champion of the world, friend of such luminaries as Cornelius Vanderbilt, Morrissey was beloved of Irish everywhere, and when he died in 1878, fifteen thousand people followed his coffin to the cemetery.

While John Heenan ("the Benicia Boy") is described in the song as his second, in real life he and Morrissey were bitter rivals; in fact, Morrissey gained the American heavyweight title only after defeating Heenan in 1858. But there is no record of a fight between Morrissey and anyone with a name remotely resembling "Ned the blackman" from Melbourne or anywhere else.

Morrissey and the Black

2. At six in the mor-ning the fight did be-hold. There were thou-sands as-sem-bled with sil-ver and gold, And twen-ty to one was the cry on Black Ned That Mor-ris-sey the I-rish boy would be killed dead.

1.
Ye true Irish heroes come listen to me;
I'll sing you the praises of John Morrissey,
Who's lately been challenged for five thousand pounds
To fight Ned the black man from Melboro town.

2.
At six in the morning the fight did behold.
There were thousands assembled with silver and gold,
And twenty to one was the cry on Black Ned
That Morrissey the Irish boy would be killed dead.

3.
At six in the morning the fight did begin;
They stripped to the belts and jumped into the ring.
"Come lay off your belt, boy," the black man did say.
"Your life I will take in the ring on this day."

4.
Bold Morrissey jumped into the ring like a bear,
Saying, "Here stands the bones of an Irishman here,
Who's never been conquered by white, black, or brown,
Well known to his country with Irish all round."

5.
The first round being over, the Irish would cry,
"Three cheers for the country that's bred you, my boy,
And never for bribery your country disown—
This day we have bet all we're worth on your bones."

6.

The fourth, fifth, and sixth round and up to the tenth,
Bold Morrissey received several blows on the belt.
And up to the fourteenth was severely knocked down;
Morrissey bled from his ears while he lay on the ground.

7.

Refreshed by John Heenan, his second surprise,
Bold Morrissey jumped into the ring like a lion.
From the fourteenth and fifteenth to the twenty-fourth round,
Every blow the black man got he would come to the ground.

8.

The twenty-fifth round it was fought in great style;
Bold Morrissey jumped into the ring like a lion,
And into Black Ned with a mightiful stroke
He laid him cold dead with three ribs of his broke.

9.

The fight now is over and Morrissey has won,
And the Irish all cheer him while leaving the ring.
Such cheering and shouting never 'fore has been seen
As there was on that day for old Erin the Green.

10.

Here's a health to bold Morrissey, a great man of fame;
He's conquered all bruisers all over the main.
He's a true Irish hero that never was put down;
He belongs to Tipperary in Tempermore town.

John D.'s second song moves the scene of conflict from the bare-knuckles prize ring to the deck of a Western Ocean packet ship out of Liverpool bound for New York.

Bold McCarthy

1.

Come all ye true-bred Irishmen, a story I will tell
Concerning bold McCarthy who in Liverpool did dwell.
Down by the western docks one day McCarthy chanced to stray,
And on board of a western packet ship he stowed himself away.

2.

As we pulled down the river, my boys, to New York we were bound,
This Irish lad he came on board to leave his native ground.
This Irish lad he came on board to leave his native shore
On board of a western packet ship, the *City of Baltimore.*

3.

'Twas early every morning the mate he called us to;
'Twas early every morning the sailors was put through.
Saying, "Where is that Irish stowaway, it's me he'll stand before.
He'll rue the day he stowed away on the *City of Baltimore.*"

No. 22: John D. Gorman, St. Charles. *NA P757. Photo taken April 2,*
1968.

♩. = 76

Come all ye true-bred I-rish-men, a sto-ry I will tell Con-cer-ning bold Mc-Car-thy who in Liv-er-pool did dwell. Down by the wes-tern docks one day Mc-Car-thy chanced to stray, And on board of a wes-tern pack-et ship he stowed him-self a-way.

4.
"I'm here," said bold McCarthy. "What do you want of me?"
"Oh, what in the mischief brought you here? What made you stow away?
If you're a man of courage bold, it's me you'll stand before.
I'll fight you fair all on the deck, the *City of Baltimore*."

5.
The mate he being a cowardly lad before him would not stand,
And with an iron b'laying pin at McCarthy then he ran.
McCarthy being a strong young man soon laid him in his gore,
Saying, "I'll fight you fair all on the deck of the *City of Baltimore*."

6.
Our second mate and boatsman came to their mate's relief,
But McCarthy with a capstan bar soon caused them to retreat,
And when his Irish blood did boil like a lion he did roar,
Saying, "I'll fight you both all on the deck of the *City of Baltimore*."

7.
Our captain was a Scotchman, MacDonald was his name,
And when he saw what McCarthy had done, straight forward then he came.
He took McCarthy by the hand, saying, "Do not fight any more,
And I'll make you first mate on the ship, the *City of Baltimore*."

*"How was that?" John D. asked me.

*"Oh," I said enthusiastically, "that was fine, yeah!"

*"Not very fine, no," he said, laughing and shaking his head, but he knew better. He had of course begun this little session with the almost ritual disclaimer that he hadn't sung for a long time and wasn't sure he could get through it, but he knew his song and sang with confidence and clarity, coming down strong on the beat. It was clear he loved to sing.

*"Good for you, John D.," goodmanned Leo. "Altogether wonderful." And he spoke for all of us.

But our day wasn't over yet. There were still several people I wanted to check in on—people who'd been recommended to me by others, and we spent a long and tiring afternoon searching them out. None of them was able to add much to what I already knew, and the last one we'd stopped in on was just about a textbook case of what it's like to be old, poor, and alone, not only on P.E.I. but anywhere. The fire was out; I offered to rebuild it, but no, he was going to bed anyway. An old man in a tattered sweater, waiting…

It was dark when we got back on the paved road. We were both tired, but Bobby seemed especially quiet. I knew that what I wanted more than anything was to drive straight back to Charlottetown, have a good dinner and go to bed, and I guessed she felt the same way, but there was one more call I wanted to make. Several people had spoken to us about John Miller, who lived right on the main road in Morell and who was supposed to have "a whole book of Lawrence Doyle's songs all printed out." I was skeptical, because I had chased similar "books" of both Joe Scott's and Larry Gorman's songs all over Maine and the Maritimes with notable unsuccess, but I knew I had to check this lead out. Mercifully we would discover the book didn't exist, and we could head for the city.

"I really ought to find this John Miller and see about the book he's supposed to have," I said. "It won't take long, I'm sure."

There was no answer. "You O.K?" I said, turning toward her. She said nothing, but in the lights of an oncoming car I could see tears on her cheek, and I knew pretty well why. "Aww hell," I said as sympathetically as I could, "we'll just go on by. Maybe tomorrow—"

"No," she said. "I'll be O.K. Just give me a couple of minutes. It was that last place."

"Yeah, I know," I said. "You sure you'll—"

"Yes," she said convincingly. "I'm fine, really."

We found Miller's house and pulled into the yard.[2] There was a light on in the garage and someone was moving around inside, so we knocked there first. A tall, slight man in a mackinaw came to the door, a man with a slow shy smile and blue eyes and the gentlest voice I had ever heard. Yes, he was John Miller, and I was the man put that letter in the paper, was I? How was I making out? I said I was doing just great, and then I mentioned the book he was supposed to have. He looked puzzled. "A book of Lawrence Doyle's songs? No, I don't have one," he said. "I've got an old book of Irish songs, but that's all."

---

[2] I tell the same story in *Lawrence Doyle*, pp. 121–22.

I was relieved. The way looked clear for Charlottetown. "Well, I just thought I'd stop by and ask," I said, edging toward the door. "You just never can tell and I thought I'd better check, but we'll be on our way now."

We were out the door on our way to the car, when he called quietly after us. "Have you got all his songs?"

"No, not all," I said, "but we're making out pretty well."

"Have you got 'When Johnny Went Plowing for Kearon'?"

I stopped dead. "No, not the whole of it. Do you know it?

"Yes"

"Will you sing it for us?"

"Yes."

We went in the house and sat in the kitchen. There were nine children from a boy of high school age to a baby in Mrs. Miller's arms. The smaller children were in and out, and there was never less than one child in Miller's lap, yet all was quiet and peaceful as we recorded five songs.

Here is the Kearon song as he sang it that evening—a story of a greenhorn's plowing mishap and how his boss decided to show him how it's done, only to wind up worse off than his pupil.

When Johnny Went Plowing For Kearon

♩. = 54

With a step like a ma-jor Kear-on walked to the plow. "I'll take her my-self or you'll mur-der the team." He light-ened it up, but the plow being a brute, It laid in a-gain and took hold of a root. La de ten de i day, la de ten de i dale.

No. 23: John Miller and his wife, Morell. NA P765.
Photo taken April 4, 1969.

1.

Oh, as Johnny went plowing for Kearon one day,
The land it was hard and the field it being lea;
In the month of November the weather was cold
And Kearon himself for to plow was too old.
La de ten de i day, la de ten de i dale.

2.

Johnny went to the plow and he took charge of the team,
Not being used to the engine (*pron.* "en-jyne") it went to the beam.
"Oh, begorra," says Johnny, "if Kearon comes now!"
And large drops of sweat fell from Johnny's broad brow.
La de ten, etc.

3.

Johnny picked up an idea he'd leave all and run,
But looking around he saw Kearon had come. .
"Oh, Johnny, dear Johnny, take courage and try,
And in a strange place don't be any way shy."
La de ten, etc.

4.

With a step like a major Kearon walked to the plow.
"I'll take her myself or you'll murder the team."
He lightened it up, but the plow being a brute,
It laid in again and took hold of a root.
La de ten, etc.

5.

[*tune for following: phrases C and D*]
Kearon cursed and he swore and he looked at the sun,
And poor Johnny he thought his last hour had come.
La de ten, etc.

6.

So Kearon went to give Johnny a bit of an advice,
Telling him how the land could be treated very nice:
"While rising a hill you must bend your backbone
And shut your eyes tight when you're striking a stone."
La de ten, etc.

7.

So Johnny gave ear to what Kearon did say;
He plowed all along for the whole of that day.
The sod it was wide but the plowing was done,
And poor Johnny would laugh when he'd look at the sun.
La de ten, etc.

The whole episode is a good example of how not to do fieldwork; the singer (who wanted nothing) was more anxious to sing than the fieldworker (who wanted his supper) was anxious to collect. But John Miller's quiet generosity saved the day.

And eventually we got our supper.

Thursday, April 4

Among the letters I'd received back in Maine was an especially enthusiastic one from Vivian Banks of Annandale, saying that not only did her husband remember pieces of several Doyle songs, but, better yet, his father remembered the man himself, so why didn't I stop around when I was on the Island? I said we'd be there, and now here we were.

It was a small house right next to the road, with a big barn back a ways. A couple of hens were loose in the yard, picking around in the omnipresent spring mud, and a mid-size dog woofed us but kept enough distance so I decided to risk it. I was about halfway to the door when a woman about my age stepped out on the porch. "Marie!" she yelled at the dog. "Get away!"

The dog withdrew. "You've got to watch her," the woman said. "She'll get around behind you otherwise. You must be Professor Ives. Come on in."

"And you must be Vivian Banks," I said, motioning to Bobby to come along.

"The kitchen's a mess," she said. "The freezer broke down last night, and this man's trying to see if it's worth repairing."

"It ain't," the man said. "You could get a new one for what it'd cost."

Mrs. Banks grimaced. "Well," she said. "Might as well sit down and have a cup of tea until Reggie gets here." Which is what we all had just started to do when he came in from the barn and was given the bad news.

He laughed fatalistically. "No way out of it, I guess," he said.

The repairman packed up his tools. "I can have the new one in here tomorrow morning," he said, coiling up his trouble light. "Just keep this one closed up 'til then and you probably won't lose anything."

"O.K." Mr. Banks said. "I'll pay you tomorrow."

And that was that. We had a shake-hands, and very soon the conversation got around to Lawrence Doyle and his songs. "Well, you don't want to be talking to me," said Reggie. "Vivian, give Pop a call."

The room began to fill up, as various Banks children ranging from teen-age down to maybe seven put in appearances and were in and out all afternoon. A neighbour, Wilbur Wood, dropped in and stayed. And about a half-hour later eighty-eight-year-old John Banks appeared, at which point I broke out the UHER.

He had known Doyle well, he said, some seventy-five years ago. *"He had no family, but he adopted a boy. A great singer this young fella was, but poor old Lawrence wasn't much of a singer."

*"He *wasn't*?"

*"No," he said, "he wasn't much of any. But he could make the songs! Oh, he could make 'em. No trouble in the world. Made lots of them."

What followed for the next hour or so was a wonderful mix of the old man trying hard to go over this song and that of Doyle's while his son and daughter-in-law and even Wilbur Wood prompted and urged him on. *"There's lots more," he said at one point, "but I never thought there'd be anybody interested in it at all. I learned them some seventy-five years ago, and they're getting badly mixed up now." He wanted very much to remember, though.

At one point the conversation shifted over to the yarns of a local storyteller, and Reggie told the following:

*His nickname was Crubeen[3] MacDonald. Anyway he had no grain for his hens that winter. They were poor people, so he went to the mill and he got sawdust, and he fed the hens sawdust all winter. In the following spring the old ladies at that time used to set the hens with so many eggs under them to hatch out chickens, so when hers come out they were all the beautifullest bunch of woodpeckers you ever seen!

So another time he went shooting; he was a great man with a gun. 'Course right down below his own place there was ducks in the river there. . . and that day he had poor luck. Everything he fired at he missed. When he was coming home, what did he see but a black fox. And a black fox at that time was quite rare and worth a lot of money. So he had no shot — he had all kinds of powder but no shot. So he filled up the gun with powder, and he reached in his pocket, and he had a bunch of shingle nails. Put them in the gun and he aimed and fired at the fox, and he nailed the fox's tail to a tree, and the fox jumped out and left the skin. The ramrod of the gun went over his head and he killed a rabbit, and the powder, the smoke from the powder, it smothered a whole brood of partridges, and the gun kicked so hard she knocked him backward in the mud and filled his boots full of eels!

That led to general talk about old times, and I tried to steer it back to songs. *"Did there used to be much singing of these old songs around here?" I asked.

*"Oh yes," said old John, "there was some lovely old songs years ago. There was a great lot of good singers around here at one time. Old fellers, yes. Oh, and they had some good songs! . . . And there was great fiddlers then, too — old fellers that could play the fiddle, and there'd be a crowd to dance."

I wondered if he himself played.* "No, no, no," he said, "but *he* can play," motioning toward his son.

I looked over at Reggie, who gently disparaged the claim but soon gave in and got his fiddle out. Son Martin went for his guitar, and for the next half-hour the two of them filled that kitchen with "Johnny Cope," "The Road to the Isles," "Over the Waves," "Miss MacLeod's Reel," "St. Anne's Reel,"

---

[3] "Crubeen" is most likely the old Scots Gaelic word "Crùbain," which translates as "crooked, twisted, or hunched." My thanks to Dr. Michael Kennedy for this.

and a number of other pieces none of us knew the names of. Everybody was taken up with the music, feet tapping, bodies moving to the beat, asking for this or that favourite. I looked over at the father, sitting there quietly, almost a little abstracted, it seemed to me. I was soon to find out why.

There came a break in the fiddling, and to everyone's surprise — and with no introduction at all — the old man began to sing.

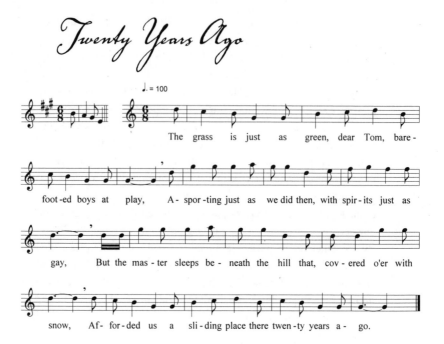

Twenty Years Ago

The grass is just as green, dear Tom, bare-foot-ed boys at play, A-spor-ting just as we did then, with spir-its just as gay, But the mas-ter sleeps be-neath the hill that, cov-ered o'er with snow, Af-for-ded us a sli-ding place there twen-ty years a-go.

1.
I wandered to the village, Tom, and I sat beneath the tree
Upon the schoolhouse playing ground that sheltered you and me.
There's no one now to greet me, Tom, and few are left who know
Who played with us upon the green some twenty years ago.

2.
The grass is just as green, dear Tom, bare-footed boys at play,
A-sporting just as we did then, with spirits just as gay,
But the master sleeps beneath the hill that, covered o'er with snow,
Afforded us a sliding place there twenty years ago.

3.
The river's running just as still; the willows on each side
Are larger than they were, dear Tom. The stream appears less wide.
But the grapevine swing is ruined now where once we played the beau
And swung our sweethearts, pretty girls, there twenty years ago.

4.

Down by a spring and upon an elm you know I cut your name—
Your sweetheart just beneath it, Tom, and you did mine the same.
Some heartless wretch has peeled the bark. We're dying sure but slow.
Just as the one whose name you cut there twenty years ago.

5.

The spring it bubbles near the hill close by a spreading beech.
'Tis very high; 'twas once so low that we could scarcely reach.
But leaning down to get a drink, dear Tom, I startled so
To see how sadly I have changed since twenty years ago.

6.

My lid has long been dry, dear Tom, but tears comes to my eyes
To think of her I loved so well—there's only broken ties.
I visited the old churchyard and took some flowers to strew
Upon the graves of those we loved there twenty years ago.

7.

Oh some are in the churchyard lie, some sleep beneath the sea,
But few are left of our old class, excepting you and me.
And wintertime has come, dear Tom, and [*when*] we're called to go
I hope they'll lay us where we played there twenty years ago.

* "I never heard you sing that before, Pop," said Reggie. The old man said nothing, but he was obviously pleased. In fact he looked like he was ready to sing another one, but the Banks children—Bonnie, Danny, and Joe, with Martin on guitar—decided they wanted to sing too and cut loose with a couple of recent country/western hits. They were great, and both Bobby and I were hoping to hear more, but the old man, deciding it was his turn again, launched into "Charles Gustavus Anderson," singing it to the same tune he had just used for "Twenty Years Ago."

I knew of this ballad, having seen it in other published collections from Maine, The Maritimes, and Newfoundland. It was one of a group of ballads telling the story of the *Saladin* mutiny of 1843, this one telling it from the point of view of an immigrant Swedish sailor who was tried and hanged in Halifax for his part in it. I had never heard it sung before and was therefore quite excited to find it.

Charles Gustavus Anderson

1.

Come all you valiant young men, with pity lend an ear,
And when you hear my feeling story, you can but shed a tear.
I'm here in close confinement, bound down in fetters strong,
Surrounded by strong granite walls and sentenced to be hung.

2.

Oh Charles Gustavus Anderson is my right and proper name,
And since I've been in custody I never denied the same.
I was raised by decent parents, although I die in scorn.
Believe me now I must lament that ever I was born.

3.

My father was a shipwright, I might have been the same.
He taught me good examples, to him I leave no blame.
Likewise my tender mother, who suffered for me sore,
And when she hears my sad misfortune, she'll suffer for me more.

4.

I shipped on board the [Sallada], all on the Spanish Main,
Bound down for Valparaisa, MacKenzie had command.
We arrived there in safety without the least dismay,
'Til Fielding came on board of us, curse on that fatal day.

5.

'Twas him that had seduced us to do that utter crime,
Although we might prevented it had we begun in time.
We shed the blood of innocents, the same we don't deny,
And stained our hands in human blood, for which we now must die.

6.

Oh dear and loving mother, if I could see your face,
I'd kiss the lips of tenderness and take my last embrace.
I would bathe you in my tears of love before my final hour,
And then commit my soul to God, to His holy will and power.

7.

Oh brothers and sisters all adieu, who's near and dear to me,
Whose face beyond the ocean, whose face I never shall see.
In happy hours we spent upon my native shore;
Farewell sweet you Zorilla, I never shall see you more.

8.

The sheriff and the officers all went to him in jail;
He knew the awful message well but never seemed to fail.
He placed the fatal halter on to end all shame and strife;
With his own hands he greased the cord that cut the threads of life.

9.

He was led up to the gibbet, placed on the fatal stand;
He viewed the briny ocean and then the pleasant land.
The rope adjusted through the ring that quickly stopped his breath;
Soon ended his career in the iron jaws of death.

Son Reggie was genuinely surprised, and so was Vivian, never having heard him sing either of those songs before. It was the kind of surprise I'd run into often enough—the children knowing nothing of the songs their parents knew—but this time it seemed especially significant, because the Bankses were a family to whom both music and "old times" were important. It was as if these songs were somehow an old man's secret treasure. Once they were vital and called for; now they were only a memory, not so much scorned as edged out by more insistent forms, but when someone like me came around actively looking for them, once again, however briefly, there was a forum for their presentation, and out of the dark they came, a little time-worn, perhaps, but still clear and still shining.

We left the Banks family just before sunset, full of the bonhomie that comes when you've had a great time sharing music with new friends, and drove down to Poole's Corner to check in at the one motel there. Bobby decided to call home just to see if all was well. She had only just begun to talk. Suddenly, "Oh, my God!" she said. And then again, "Oh, my God!"

"What?" I said, all attention.

"When did it happen?" she said.

"*What?*" I said insistently.

She looked at me. The bonhomie was gone. "Martin Luther King's just been assassinated," she said.

Nineteen Sixty-Nine

I WAS HOPING AND PLANNING to get back up to P.E.I. in the summer of 1968, but it didn't work out that way. The next opportunity came as it had the year before during my University's 1969 spring vacation break. Once again, that had the disadvantage of being the height of mudtime, making travel on the Island back roads chancy, but once again it also had the advantage of being when farm people were at home with time on their hands and glad to see even strangers with questions and tape recorders. Unfortunately it snowed for the first two days we were there, keeping us housebound, but the third day dawned fine and cold—no danger of the clay roads thawing—and we took off for Kings County.

Monday, March 31[1]

Several people had mentioned Jack Farrell to us, even sending us directions to his home in St. Georges ("Can't miss it!"). Of course we *did* miss it a couple of times, but it turned out that was just as well, because when we finally found it Farrell was just driving into the yard. Had we been earlier, we might have missed him.

"Oh yes," he said enthusiastically when I introduced myself. "I saw your letter in the paper, and I was going to write you, but I just never got around to it, I guess."

"Well," I said, "it doesn't matter. You've got neighbours who told us about you anyway, and here we are."

"My father knew Lawrence Doyle well," he said. "Boarded with him for a short while. Come on in."

The house was cold, the heat having been off for several hours while he was out, but we all sat close to the stove and kept warm enough, the only problem being that the stove had been converted to kerosene, and the blower kept up a muted roar throughout the whole interview. That was less than ideal for tape recording, but the trade-off was heat or a quiet ambience, and we chose heat.

Farrell's father, Patrick William (generally known as Will) had a place in Iona, where he raised his considerable family of fourteen (Jack was the fourth). Naturally he farmed some, but he also taught school, and it was while

---

[1]Much of the material in this section is taken quite directly from my *Lawrence Doyle*.

teaching in Farmington in the local Birch Hill School (of which Lawrence Doyle had been a trustee) that he boarded with the Doyles one winter. Jack remembered him speaking of it:

> *He [Doyle] used to work in the shop in the wintertime. He was a farmer, but in the wintertime he'd work in the shop making frames and windows and doors. And he'd be working away. My father was there; he boarded there, he taught in the school. He'd be in the shop with him on Saturdays hanging around talking to him, and he used to watch him. He was pretty observant, my father, you know, about things like that. He said you'd see Doyle getting a—you'd see a smile appearing on his face, you know, and then he'd walk over and take his pencil. He had a little book on his workbench, and he'd write some. Then he'd go back and be working away, and by and by you'd see him smiling again and then he'd go and write a little more. And he was making up a song all the time, you know, and that's the way he used to work.

The first Doyle song Jack thought of was "the one about the potato bug," a pest which began arriving on the Island in significant numbers in the late 1880s. He knew he didn't have the whole song, but what he did have gives a good picture of the farmer's desperate remedy of walking between the rows and simply knocking the bugs into a pan as he went along. (For stanzas 3 through 6, repeat the tune for stanza 2.)

The Potato Bug

1.
Now, Tom, by the way we are both getting grey
And our time in this country's not long,
But bedad while we're here we must keep in good cheer
And I'll now sing a bit of a song.

2.
It's just past ten years, how short it appears,
My stars how this time slips away,
Since I've been to town and the news spread around
That the bugs have come over the sea.

3.
It's just past ten years, how short it appears
Since we heard of that plague of a fly;
Sure, we thought 'twas the bug that laid out of our lug
When we down on our bed went to lie.

4.
Every morning I go to the drills as you know,
And I carry a pan in my hand;
Through the drills I will walk and I'll shake every stalk
And it's down in the pan they will land.

5.
But bejapers as quick they would play me a trick,
For it's out of the dish they will crawl,
And without one bit of noise they'll be over the sides
And the bugs left behind after all.

6.
But one thing I know, though it might be too slow
Would be to carry a pan of hot coals,
And scorch them a little and then let them go
And I think they'd stay quiet in their holes.

Other measures were tried, Paris Green being one of them. It was a well-known and powerful insecticide, but the cure could be as disastrous as the problem, as Jack remembered only too well:

> *But I remember being out there one day back of the barn putting
> Paris Green on the potatoes. I had it mixed with flour, you know, a
> bucketful of Paris Green and flour mixed together. And we had a pig, a
> good big junk of a pig, and he got out. . . . And while I was up the further
> end of the field he got over to this and he ate the Paris Green—he ate

the whole damn rig and what he didn't eat he spilled. So when I came up and saw it, I came in and told my mother the pig ate all the Paris Green. "Well," she said, "we'll get him in and give him all the milk we have." . . . And he drank all the milk that was about the place. And then she told me to keep after him, not to let him lie down. Get the whip and keep him moving around. And boy, after a while he started to throw up! A pig will throw up, but a cow won't.

We moved on to less emetic matters.

While Will Farrell boarded with Doyles that year, his wife stayed with her parents, Mr. and Mrs. John Moran (that's pronounced MORun, by the way) down in DeGros Marsh sixteen miles away; then on weekends, weather permitting, he'd drive down to be with her. One Saturday, time being heavy on his hands, Doyle decided to go along. *"It came up a big storm," Jack said, "and they had quite a time getting back." After it was over, the two men made a song about it.

The Visit to Morans

♩. = 60

1.

But when we got up - on the road, 'Twas then we found how much it snowed; Our jaun - ting sleigh was quite a load, 'Twas cut - ting to the ground. The horse we had was good in - deed, But snow his pros - pects did im - pede; He was as good a no - ble steed As

1. (sts. 9, 10 and 12)

an - y can be found.

1.

In the month of January, ninety-two,
When winter winds so keenly blew,
And finding nothing else to do,
We harnessed up our team;
The course we took was south by west,
The horse required but little rest,
Until we were two welcome guests,
As plainly can be seen.

2.

The sun kept up a sidelong gaze,
Enveloped in a murky haze;
It soon shut off its sullen rays,
And winds began to wail.
An omen that will plainly show
In winter season storms of snow,
But joyfully we on did go,
We feared not storm or gale.

3.

In DeGros Marsh John Moran lives,
A well-respected man he is,
A robust wife indeed is his,
Who is both good and kind;
Some of his daughters now are wives,
A few still cling to single lives,
Until the happy man arrives
In wedlock bonds to join.

4.

With these good people well content
A merry night and day we spent,
But to get home we quickly bent
Our thoughts without delay.
We harnessed Dan and bade good-bye
Through drifting snow and lowering sky,
And through the snowbanks on did fly
On that forsaken day.

5.

But when we got upon the road,
'Twas then we found how much it snowed;
Our jaunting sleigh was quite a load,
'Twas cutting to the ground.
The horse we had was good indeed,
But snow his prospects did impede;
He was as good a noble steed
As any can be found.

6.

But now to speak of Narrows Creek,
I think this place is awful bleak;
The roads they were a solid streak
Of banks from end to end.
And to avoid the banks of snow
The fences all we had to throw
And through the fields were forced to go,
Our weary way to wend.

No. 24: Peter Amberly's grave, Boiestown, New Brunswick, as it appeared in 1957. The wooden cross has been replaced by a black polished granite stone.

7.

We left McMillans' far behind,
The biting winds we did not mind,
To turn the corner there to find
The wind we had to face.
And driving on, to our surprise,
A bank of snow 'til then disguised
Loomed up between us and the skies —
It was a dreadful place.

8.

Of course the sleigh went down again,
But to the horse we laid no blame;
The harness could not stand the strain,
The horse from all went clear.
The sleigh we then did extricate,
We were not sad, it was our fate,
But patiently we there did wait
To tie our broken gear.

9.

We scarcely could restrain a groan,
Our situation there alone,
Our harness broke so far from home,
And darkness coming on.
No whisky had we, ale or beer,
Our sinking spirits for to cheer;
If we to Martins could get near
Before the day was done.

10.

But as we gave a look around,
And in the sleigh 'twas there we found
A piece of rope both good and sound —
A fortune to us then.
For with this rope we tied our gear,
And then for Martins we did steer,
Where we arrived and had our beer
Before the hour of ten.

11.

We rested there 'til morning dawned —
A splendid place, both snug and warm;
We cared but little for the storm
That raged the whole night through.
At ten a.m. the storm was o'er,
The biting wind had hushed its roar;
To start out as we did before
Was all we had to do.

12.

The journey then we did pursue,
The prospects did not seem so blue,
Because we had a track or two —
A guide to lead us on.
And very soon we did espy
That wished-for spot with joyous pride:
The cottage where we both reside
That lies in Farmington.

Even if he did help Lawrence Doyle make up this song, Will Farrell evidently never thought of himself as a songmaker. Neither his family nor his community saw him that way either, but at least once when the occasion presented itself he showed he could rise to it respectably, demonstrating the truth of Jim Whitty's statement to me that *"All the place down there years ago was full of poets. Everybody was making poems." Jack Farrell recalled both the occasion and the song:

*My father made this song. He used to play the fiddle. This dance was going on, this party, and he was away; he was in Charlottetown that evening. And they came to the house, you know, to get him to go to play. There was another fella playing there that could play . . . and [when] my mother told them that he [Farrell] was in town they asked if they could get the fiddle, and she said yes, she'd give them the fiddle. So they took the fiddle, and—oh, the [other fiddler] said it was no good. It was a good fiddle, but he was disagreeable, you know, and said the fiddle was no good [and] he couldn't play on it and that was it.

And the dance was [turning out] no good. And then after my father got home . . . they came to him again, and he went. And [the place] was called at that time Montague, Montague West—it was west of Montague about twelve miles—[today it's called] Iona. He made the song.

The Spree at Montague

♩ = 60

There were a spree in Mont-a-gue not ver-y long a-go, At a far-mer's house I need not name, a man you all do know; The boys and girls as-sem-bled to have a jol-ly time, To sing and dance as you should do when the au-tumn moon do shine.

1.

There were a spree in Montague not very long ago,
At a farmer's house I need not name, a man you all do know;
The boys and girls assembled to have a jolly time,
To sing and dance as you should do when the autumn moon do shine.

2.

The fiddle was a borrowed one from a neighbour by the way,
The fiddler said it was no good, on it he could not play;
He fixed his face and played a tune, against his will I'm sure,
But the people could not dance for it was really very poor.

3.

A stranger being amongst them all who happened there by chance,
And of course the owner of the house invited him to dance;
He said he could not dance quadrilles, but a breakdown he would try,
If the fiddler he would please play up a tune called "Soldier's Joy."

4.

The host then asked the fiddler in a coaxing sort of way
To play a breakdown for this man who happened there to stray;
The fiddler made an answer I dare not here repeat,
Which made the kind host wonder was he standing on his feet.

5.

They went then for a fiddler about a mile or so, p'raps less,
And said a little music would make a great success;
The fiddler in good humour said, "Boys, I'll go with you,"
And on the scene of action came that fiddler number two.

6.

When the shouts that marked his coming had died away and gone,
He took that very fiddle condemned by number one;
Saying, "Boys, get to your places. Ask what you want in time."
And the walls of that old mansion rang with music sweet and fine.

7.

The dance it soon got lively, each one seemed full of cheer;
The fiddler played quite willingly 'til daylight did dawn clear.
And when the party ended, each one there agreed
That the dance it was a good one though at first 'twas poor indeed.

8.

Now let us thank the farmer who treated us so kind,
And remembrance of that party shall linger in our mind;
And when you want good music, the best thing you can do
Is send an invitation to that fiddler number two.

Jack recalled that his mother's brother was a great singer, too. *"He was up in the States," he said. "He spent his last years up there, and he was a good singer. He used to sing all them songs. He had that song about the potato bug, and oh different songs. He had songs too that a fella down here made. His name was Hughie MacDonald—Hughie Lauchlan MacDonald."

I remembered that both Art Cahill and Leo Gorman had mentioned this man. *"Did you ever know any of them?" I asked.

*"He made some good songs," he said. "I never knew them at all. And I was asking Hughie's wife after Hughie died if she had any of the songs written, and she said, 'No, not a one.' But Hughie could make a song all right!"

I was disappointed, but I pressed on. *"Do you remember what songs he made up?" I asked.

*"One was 'The *Bonny Flora Clark*,'" he said, and he went ahead, singing what he knew and filling in what he didn't, making it into a *cante-fable* [2] of sorts. The song was about six young men (Hughie among them) commandeering old Donald Clark's rowboat to go up grassy little Grand River to a party in Dundas:

The Bonny Flora Clark

*It was about a trip they had, a bunch of them, you know, on the river. That's down there, Grand River. And this Clark had a boat, and they went across there and took the boat on Clark and went to a raffle [party] up at Dundas. And it was the fall of the year and there was a little ice formed on the river that night, and I guess they chafed the bow of the boat coming back. Hughie made the song about it, you know, and you'd think it was an awful big boat. . . .I don't know it all, but I know some of it. . . .

1.
Ye winding braes of Narrows Creek, come listen unto me;
I'll tell you of six sporting youths that went onto a spree.
'Twas in the chilly months of autumn when the nights were very dark,
We sailed up Grand River Harbour in the *Bonny Flora Clark*.

2.
Young Fraser was our captain, as you may plainly see,
A man that ofttimes crossed before those dark and stormy seas;
Young Steele he was our chief mate, a man both brave and smart;
MacDonald was the pilot of the *Bonny Flora Clark*.

3.
Young Bradley was our second mate, a man of courage bold;
MacDonald was our boatsman, or at least I have been told.
McCormick cooked our victuals, he's a man of features dark,
And that made up the company of the *Bonny Flora Clark*.

4
The captain gave his orders to get her under way.
"Heave on the weather braces, boys, and let her fill away."
She went along so steadily you'd swear she was the Ark,
'Til the ice came rolling o'er the bow of the *Bonny Flora Clark*.

---

[2] A story form that alternates prose and poetry (or song).

Ye wind - ing braes of Nar - rows Creek, come lis - ten un - to me; I'll tell you of six sport - ing youths that went on - to a spree. 'Twas in the chil - ly months of au - tumn when the nights were ver - y dark, We sailed up Grand Riv - er Har - bour in the Bon - ny Flo - ra Clark. 2. Young Fra - ser was our cap - tain, as you may plain - ly see, A man....

Then I don't know. There's a place there I don't know it. But anyhow they got to the raffle.

5.

But now we're at the raffle among the Dundas girls;
They gathered all around us and got us in a whirl.
Miss Pope she was our leader, she acted rude and sharp—
The captain she offended of the *Bonny Flora Clark.*

Then there's a place where they—anyhow—that I don't know, but the—

6.

The captain struck a sailor, and the row it soon began,
And all that we can blame for it is Sandy Martin's gin.

That was the same Martin [mentioned in "The Visit to Morans"]. But then they started back. It came up a storm, you know, and they got her under way. But the old fellow [Clark] at home was in bed. and he was talking to his wife, and he spoke in Gaelic. And he said "Ye'un grass un

Christie"; that's "Oh my God, Christie" I think in Gaelic (I don't know any Gaelic, you know, but that was in the song).[3]

7.
Poor Donald in his couch at home he sank in troubled sleep;
In dreams he saw his gallant craft fly o'er the stormy deep.
He heard the angry billows roar, the dark and stormy sky,
And the ice before the *Flora Clark* was flying twelve feet high.

8.
"*Oh ye'un grass un Christie*, but how the winds do roar;
I'm afraid my craft will be stranded on the Graystone Harbour shore.
That reckless crew and captain too will have to keep a look-out sharp,
Or they'll run her on those violent reefs, the *Bonny Flora Clark*."

9.
But now the trip is over, and the dangers are all past,
But the good ship *Bonny Flora Clark*, this trip will be her last;
She stood the ice for twelve long miles, but she could stand no more,
And now she lies a total wreck on the Graystone Harbour shore.

But it was a good song, you know, if you knew it all. . . . They borrowed his [boat] without his knowing it, and he was wild about it. And Hughie made up the song, and old Clark got mad. Yes, he got mad about it. He had a daughter that was named Flora, and she was a young girl at the time, and of course Hughie he called the boat the *Flora Clark* ; it was after his [Clark's] daughter. And of course Clark never called the boat that, but Hughie called the boat *Flora Clark*; he christened it the *Flora Clark* in the song. . . . Of course there was nothing in the song, you know, about the girl or Clark himself (only that he just spoke in Gaelic to the wife).

Well, Clark got mad about that song. Oh, yes! He went to Father Francis MacDonald (he was a middling old priest at that time—in fact, I don't remember him myself. He was gone before we came here). And he went to the priest about the song, and Father Francis sent the serving man and told him to go up and tell Hughie Lauchlan to come down, that he wanted to see him. So Hughie, of course, didn't know what he wanted him for, and he went down there and went into the room where Father Francis was, and here was Clark in there. Well, Father Francis said to Hughie, "Now, you made a song about this man's boat and his daughter, and I want to hear that song. I want you to sing it right here." So Hughie couldn't get out of it; he had to sing it. And he sung the song. And Father Francis said when he was finished that old Clark had nothing to complain

---

[3]According to Dr. Michael Kennedy, this is probably better rendered as "O, Dhia nan grasan Christie (Oh, God of the Graces, Christie)."

about—that there was nothing in it to hurt the man's feelings at all, or the girl's. It was praising the boat and everything!

It had been a wonderful session. No "big ballads" or anything like that, but a series of locally made songs that, taken together, give an interesting picture of the life of the time—from Doyle's matter-of-fact description of a snowstorm contretemps to Hughie Lauchlan's hyperbolic treatment of a rowboat ride. Not only that, but while people like Doyle or MacDonald were the ones a community looked to for the making of new songs, clearly people like Will Farrell could turn out a respectable product when the need arose. And, finally, though there was little occasion for singing them any more, these songs still lived in the hearts and minds of people like Jack Farrell, to be called up and shared with friends—and even with the passing and interested stranger and his tape recorder.

Nineteen Eighty-Two[1]

AS I'VE SAID BEFORE, I NEVER REALLY saw myself as a "collector" in the tradition of Helen Creighton or Edith Fowke; I was always working on a rather specific problem: local songmaking—always, in fact, working up information on a particular songmaker: Larry Gorman, Joe Scott, or Lawrence Doyle. After I had for all practical purposes completed fieldwork on these three—and especially after the books I had written on them were on the shelf—I had no immediate or pressing reason to do further fieldwork on Prince Edward Island and considerable immediate and pressing reasons to explore further my home turf of Maine. Always, of course, I had it in the back of my mind that someday I'd get back to the Island and do some *real* collecting, but I never did. I kept in touch, even went back for occasional lectures, not to mention pep talks to various administrative and faculty groups on the need for an Island folklore program and archives, but I did no more fieldwork.

Then in the fall of 1982 Harry Baglole invited me to take part in the forthcoming Island Folk Festival, an event sponsored and run by the University's Institute of Island Studies (of which he is the Director), with help from the West Prince Arts Council. Of course, in my more vealish academic years it had been rather *de rigueur* to display a scholarly disdain for "revivalists" (in spite of the fact that I had long been one) and their "folk" festivals, but now that I was almost sixty I had pretty well worked my way through that. Both Bobby and I thought the Festival was a wonderful idea, and, to make it even better, Reg Pendergast (Big Jim's son) had offered us the hospitality of his home in nearby St. Louis. We accepted both invitations.

We arrived at Reg's house under a late evening lowery sky that, while it was a little early for snow, prompted talk of it as we came into the warm kitchen. "Sometimes it takes you by surprise, though," Reg said. "A couple of years ago a big storm came so early it caught us without any wood in the house. Plenty of it all stacked and dry out in the shed, but there was that much snow we couldn't get to it for several days, but I'm ready this year, believe me."

At that point Mrs. Pendergast (Big Jim's widow—I never did get around to calling her Gertrude) walked into the room, which was great, considering we hadn't seen her for some years—not since Jim's death anyhow—and there were warm greetings all around. "How long are you home for this trip?" she asked.

---

[1]I am pleased to acknowledge that the songs in this chapter were recorded at the Festival by Jim Hornby and published by him and the Institute of Island Studies on an LP record, *Island Folk Festival* (1985).

"Just for the Festival, I'm afraid," I said, "but it's good to be here again for any time at all."

"This calls for a drink, wouldn't you say?" said Reg, and without waiting for my reply headed for the pantry. "What'll it be?"

"He means do you want whisky or moonshine!" said Mrs. P. That brought a good laugh, and so did my prompt reply of "Moonshine, of course!" Reg poured small glasses of the clear liquid all around, and we toasted each other neat. It was a wonderful way to celebrate our return to the Island.

The Festival took place next day, a chilly sixth of November, in the four-hundred-seat auditorium of Westisle High School in Elmsdale. The crowd—mostly local and predominantly middle-aged to older—was small at first, but it got larger (and younger) as the day turned to evening, and for me it was a special pleasure not only to see old friends like Edmund Doucette (now over ninety) and Mary Elbridge Cousins again, but also to have the sons and daughters of others who had sung for me years ago seek me out to say hello. For instance, John Cousins, Mary's son, was there; he'd gone on to become an active folklorist in his own right, and he's always claimed that my visit to his mother back in 1957 was what got him started. Later on in the day he would sing "John Ladner," and sing it very well. The beat goes on . . . and on.

There were "workshops" in the morning and early afternoon, but the real singing began in a late afternoon session and continued after supper until well into the evening. Like their audience, most of the singers, too, were from West Prince, but there were others like Tommy Banks from Kings County, Marie Hare from Strathadam on New Brunswick's Miramichi, and Dorman Ralph from St. John's, Newfoundland. I even sang a song myself—"The Boys of the Island" the way I'd learned it from Art Dalton—so Maine could be said to be represented, too. In addition to some fine fiddling, there were a couple of stalwart Acadian singers. Most of the audience had no French, but everyone responded enthusiastically to Imelda Arsenault's spirited *chanson* with its mouth-music refrain and *battement des pieds* accompaniment (there is simply nothing like this stuff in English-language tradition, and I love it).

Both Reg Porter and Ed Fitzgerald had for a long time been interested in the songs made up by Alec Shea of Tignish. Shea (1903–1969) was something of a latter-day version of Gorman and Doyle, making up funny, often satirical songs on local happenings, and something of a Hughie Lauchlan MacDonald in his habit of making fun of himself. Reg had given a talk on Shea earlier in the day, and that evening Ed sang his "Alec's Lament" in a very straightforward unaccompanied manner. The song was written about 1960, and it adds to the fun to know that at that time the Tignish jail was nothing more than a tiny renovated shoemaker's shop.

Alec's Lament

♪ = 96

1. Oh, come all ye jol-ly boot-legg-ers and you who han-dle brew: Be-ware of How-ard Fo-ley, or he'll play a trick on you. Be-ware of How-ard Fo-ley, boys-- now take a tip from me, Or you'll spend your night in Tig-nish jail with-out your bread and tea.

1.
Oh, come all ye jolly bootleggers and you who handle brew:
Beware of Howard Foley, or he'll play a trick on you.
Beware of Howard Foley, boys—now take a tip from me,
Or you'll spend your night in Tignish jail without your bread and tea.

2.
Now we have a keeper round the jail by the name of Albert Knox;
He's not much good to wrestle, and he's neither good to box.
He'll try for to console you, boys, until you're locked within,
And when you turn your head around he'll put on that dirty grin.

3.
Here's adieu to Tignish village and the way that it is run;
It used to be a place to drink and enjoy a good night's fun.
But Foley now is on the beat, in every hole and nook,
Just waiting for that sneaky chance to throw us in the coop.

4.
Ah, they talk about their freedoms, but there's really none for me;
For every night he's haunting me when I'm out on a spree.
He tries to stop my drinking; I'm to live a sober man,
So I'll have to leave the village and go to some foreign land.

In general, "Alec's Lament" is perfectly clear even to an outsider, but it would be far funnier to those who knew Howard Foley and had experienced

Knox's dirty grin. Like his predecessors, Shea made his songs to be sung within the local community, where their in-jokes and local allusions would have been understood and thoroughly enjoyed. Within that tradition, it would have been expected that his "new" words would be set to an "old" and familiar tune. That's exactly what Alec Shea did in the early 1960s, and it's exactly what Alton MacLean of Glen Valley did twenty years later when he made up his song "Unemployment Insurance." But where Shea drew on the old stock of Anglo-Irish come-all-ye airs for his tune, MacLean turned to the burgeoning country/western tradition for his. The more things change, the more they stay the same.

MacLean's song probably needs no explanation to Islanders, but outsiders—especially Americans—may need some help. "Pogey" is a widespread Canadian term for any kind of dole, but most particularly for "UI," the national Unemployment Insurance program (now called "EI" or Employment Insurance). Ten weeks of summer work could be sufficient for a person to file. Then—after the obligatory but painful six-week waiting period—the cheques would start coming, and they could very well carry a person through the whole winter and even up until the next summer season, but, of course, the claimant was obligated to be "actively seeking work" all that time. The song suggests that perhaps not everyone operates fully within the spirit of this program.

MacLean, a farmer who also did seasonal work at Cavendish National Park, told the festival audience how he came to write this song:

*This is a song I like to do this time of the year. It's one I wrote two or three years ago. Waiting about, I happened to hear a bunch of ladies talking one evening, whispering in the corner. [One] said, "Did you get your pogey yet?"

And the other one said, "No, I never got a damn thing!" And she said, "I don't know what we're going to do. If we don't get some groceries or oil before long we're going to be in trouble."

The other one she spoke up and she said, "I was going into Towers yesterday, and my husband had the nerve to ask me to pick up a bottle of rye—as if we didn't have [just] enough for a dozen eggs!"

There was [another] one who spoke up, and she said, "Well, I went in yesterday to file my claim," and, she said, "do you know what they asked me to do?"

"No," she said, "I don't know."

"They sent me three different places looking for work!"

The other one said, "Well, did you find any?"

She said, "No."

"My God, weren't you lucky!"

Towers, by the way, was a huge department store in the Charlottetown Mall, and the liquor store is right handy to it.

Unemployment Insurance

1. Well I'm sit-ting here wait-ing for the mail to come by; The cup-board is emp-ty, the oil tank is dry. Well it's near-ly six weeks since I filled out my claim; If I don't get some po-gey I'll be go-ing in-sane.

1.

Well I'm sitting here waiting for the mail to come by;
The cupboard is empty, the oil tank is dry.
Well it's nearly six weeks since I filled out my claim;
If I don't get some pogey I'll be going insane.

2.

Well most of us mothers work on the North Shore,
Cooking and cleaning for ten weeks or more.
Well the work it is hard and the pay it is small;
We just keep hoping we'll last 'til the fall.

3.

Well the tourists are leaving, I'm laid off again;
I go into the office to fill out my claim,
Praying to Jesus the jobs will be few;
If they got one for cooking, what the hell will I do?

4.

Soon as I get there they ask me to look
Three different places where they might need a cook.
But boy I'm sure lucky, there's no vacancy —
"Don't come back later" (they're gonna call me).

5.

Well the mailman's a-coming, my husband stops by:
"If you're going to Towers will you pick up some rye?"
I look at him, saying, "If my cheque don't come through
You'll be damn lucky if you're drinking home brew!"

No. 25: Allan Rankin.

6.

As I watch from my window I'm nearly a wreck;
Then I rush to the mailbox to look for my cheque.
I'm tripping and falling as I run through the grass—
Oh thank you, dear Lord, there's one here at last.
[*Spoken*: All ready to go!]

7.

So I take out my curlers as I warm up the car;
The gas tank is empty, I won't get too far.
But I don't give a damn what my neighbours say,
I'll be enjoying my pogey 'til the last of next May.

8.

Since I have been laid off I'm back home again;
Each Sunday morning I make church by ten.
I look up to Heaven, saying, "Dear Lord, let it be.
If you find work for someone I sure hope it's not me!"

While songmakers like Shea and MacLean generally follow the traditional pattern of setting their "new" words to "old" tunes, contemporary "singer/songwriters" are more likely to compose their own tunes, and their topical satire ranges far beyond village personalities and contretemps. Their audience is no longer a group of neighbours gathered in a kitchen, but in all likelihood a radio, t.v., or concert-hall audience, which is to say mostly strangers who will measure them against the more marketplace standards of "uniqueness" and "originality." But the impulse to speak out in song on some issue is still there, a constant, and Allan Rankin is a wonderful exemplar of its present-day continuity. When he sang his "Rough Pavement" song I knew the old tradition—changed as it may be—was still in good and loving hands.

As he sang that night, Rankin took many liberties with the tune. The second phrase, for instance, may end on D or even G rather than C, and he may shout or even speak this-or-that word for emphasis as he goes along. He treats the tune as a general plan he can play with in performance. And after all, it's not only *his* song, it's *his* tune.

Rough Pavement

1.

Oh they say on the Island potato is king;
They load them on freighters, the wharflines they sing.
Ah, but I know another whose kingdom abounds;
They call him Jack Frostbump—he's always around.
CHORUS: Singing, "Slow down, boys, beware!
Rough pavement, rough pavement! Slow down and beware!
In springtime the potholes occur everywhere.
Oh that black roller-coaster will kill me, I swear.
You can scramble an egg, count your change in mid-air—
On rough pavement, boys, beware.

♩. = 63

Oh they say on the Is-land po-ta-to is king; They load them on freight-ers, the wharf-lines they sing. Ah, but I know an-oth-er whose king-dom a-bounds; They call him Jack Frost-bump— he's al-ways a-round. CHORUS: Sing-ing, "Slow down, boys, be-ware! Rough pave-ment, rough pave-ment! Slow down and be-ware! In spring-time the pot-holes oc-cur ev-ery-where. Oh that black rol-ler-coast-er will kill me, I swear. You can scram-ble an egg, count your change in mid-air— On rough pave-ment, boys, be-ware.

2.

Now they put Jimmy Snowie to work on the roads
[*Spoken:* Somebody's laughing!]
To test the hot asphalt and count up the loads.
Oh he'd make a sharp foreman if only he could
Stop taking the flag-girls on tours in the woods.
CHORUS

3.

Now old Harry Thompson survived the Great War
In Belgium and Flanders in the Infantry Corps;
But when he takes his Pontiac out in the spring,
He swears he's right back in the trenches again.
CHORUS

4.
Now I drove to the mainland the first of the week,
But the roads were so smooth they put me to sleep.
My wife's not accustomed to such a smooth trip,
So we pulled the car over and we followed the ditch!
CHORUS

Earlier on I said I thought I had pretty well worked my way through my snobbishness in regard to revivalists and their guitars, but when it was announced that Clifford Wedge would now sing "The *Flying Cloud*," and a man about my age walked out on stage carrying a big twelve-string, I was prepared to disapprove. That old lumberwoods classic should be sung in the old way, I told myself—high, hard-voiced, and most certainly unaccompanied. That's the way I'd always heard it, and that was the way I always wanted to hear it, but it looked like that wasn't the way I was going to hear it now. I scrunched down in my seat, braced for musical calamity.

Then Cliff bent over that big twelve-string and started in. I sat up immediately, because clearly something special was happening with that old warhorse "The *Flying Cloud*," and I didn't want to miss any of it. Cliff's voice was absolutely right: strong and steady, and against the rich drone of those steel strings it was magical. He took his time, cutting no corners and never hurrying, giving the words plenty of time to do their work, even though by anyone's standard this is a long song. I have never heard that ballad sung better, before or since.

The flying Cloud

1.
Oh come all of you bold sailor boys, come listen unto me,
And you who are bound in irons strong to die for piracy.
With eighteen more I am condemned in sorrow to remain
For the plundering and burning ships down on the Spanish Main.

2.
Oh my name is Edward O'Holleran sure as you may understand;
I was born in the county of Waterford in Erin's happy land.
I being a bold undaunted youth kind fortune on me smiled;
My parents doted on me, I being their only child.

3.
Oh when I was young and innocent my heart it knew no guile;
In a happy home I lived content, my friends did on me smile.
But drinking and bad company has made a wreck of me;
Take warning now by my sad fate: beware of piracy.

♩ = 100

3. Oh when I was young and in-no-cent my heart it knew no guile; In a hap-py home I lived con-tent, my friends did on me smile. But drink-ing and bad com-pa-ny has made a wreck of me; Take war-ning now by my sad fate: be-ware of pi-ra-cy.

4.

My father bound me to a trade in Waterford's fair town;
He bound me to a cooper there by the name of William Brown.
I served my master faithfully for eighteen months or more;
Then I shipped on board the *Ocean Queen* bound for Valparaiso's shore.

5.

Oh it's when we reached Valparaiso's shore I fell in with Captain Moore,
The commander of the *Flying Cloud* going out from Baltimore.
He pressed me to join him on a slaving trip to go
To the burning sands of Africa where the sugar canes do grow.

6.

Now the *Flying Cloud* is a Spanish ship, five hundred tons or more;
She was built to outsail any ship going out from Baltimore.
Her sails were as white as the driven snow and on them was no stain,
And eighty-five brass nine-pound guns she carried on her deck.

7.

Now the *Flying Cloud* is as fine a ship as ever sailed the seas,
That ever hoisted a maintopsail before a lively breeze.
I have often seen that gallant ship with the wind abaft her beam,
And her main and topsails set aloft, most handsome to be seen.

8.

In less than three weeks' sailing we reached dark Africa's shore,
And fifteen hundred of those slaves were made to come on board.
We took them from their native home and stored them down below,
And eighteen inches to each man was all allowed to go.

9.

Oh it would have grieved your heart full sore to look upon those slaves;
'Twould have been better far for those poor souls if they were in their grave.
For the plague and fever struck our ship and took them half away;
We dragged their bodies up on deck and threw them in the sea.

10.

Then back we went a-sailing and arrived on Cuba's shores;
We sold them to the planters there to be slaves for evermore—
Their rice and coffee fields to hoe beneath a blistering sun,
And to lead a hard and wretched life 'til their sad career was done.

11.

Then when our money was all spent we put to sea again,
When Captain Moore came up on deck, and he spoke unto his men:
"There is gold and silver to be had if with me you'll remain;
We'll hoist aloft the pirate flag and scour the Spanish Main."

12.

We all agreed but five young men, and he told those five to land;
Two of them were Boston boys, two more from Newfoundland.
Oh the other being an Irish chap belonging to Erinmore—
Oh I wish to God I'd joined those men and went with them onshore!

13.

For we robbed and plundered many a ship down on the Spanish Main;
Left many a widow and orphan child in sorrow to remain.
For we made those men to walk our plank, gave them a watery grave,
For the saying of our captain, "A dead man tells no tales."

14.

Oh chased we were by many a ship, both liners and frigates too;
We were chased by every man-o-war that ever hove in view.
It was all in vain, for every time our cannons boomed aloud;
I never thought that any ship could catch this *Flying Cloud.*

15.

Until one day to our surprise the *Dungeon* hove in view;
She fired a shot across our bow, a signal to heave to.
We paid no heed to the random shot but ran before the wind,
When a chain shot stripped our mizzen mast, and we soon fell behind.

16.

"Oh clear the decks for action, boys," the Captain gave command.
The decks were cleared for action, and the bosun piped all hands.
And soon across our quarterdeck there flowed a crimson tide;
We fought 'til Captain Moore was dead and eighty men besides.

17.

Oh it's back to Newgate we were brought, bound down in iron chains,
For the plundering and burning ships down on the Spanish Main.
It was whisky and bad company that made a wreck of me.
Take warning now by my sad fate: beware of piracy.

18.

Oh fare thee well green hills and dales and the girl that I adore;
Her voice like music in my ears will cheer my heart no more.
I'll never kiss those ruby lips nor touch her soft white hand,
For I must die a scornful death in this dark and foreign land.

No. 26: Clifford Wedge at the Larry Gorman Folk Festival, 1995.

As I sat and listened at this festival, both the old songs and the new appeared to be in good hands on Prince Edward Island. So long as there was a Clifford Wedge the old would be carried forward with verve and imagination, and so long as there was an Allan Rankin the new would grow from it and keep the balance. Not to worry.

During intermission I went out to the car to get another roll of film. On my way back one of the older performers hailed me from his car across the lot. "Can you come over here for a minute?" he asked.

I thought I knew what he wanted. I walked over, and noticed that there were two other men in the car. "What's up?" I asked.

One of them held a bottle out the window. "We thought maybe you'd like a drink."

"You were right," I said, taking the bottle and tilting it back.

It wasn't moonshine this time, but that was alright.

It was good to be home.

Coda: Three That Won't Fit

CHRONOLOGY IS ALL VERY WELL, and it has given me a useful rack on which to hang the songs included in the foregoing chapters—year by year, day by day, each song tidily in its context of time and place—but when all is said and done there are three songs left over, because I never actually "collected" them on Prince Edward Island in any one time and place. The first two I knew about before I ever went there; the third is a little more of a special case, but all three belong in this book, not only because they were always on my mind, but also because they are part and parcel of Prince Edward Island.

"Prince Edward Isle, Adieu"

I knew about "Prince Edward Isle, Adieu" right from the start from reading it in Doerflinger's *Shantymen and Shantyboys*, where it bore the title "The History of Prince Edward Island" and was attributed to Larry Gorman.[1] Naturally, I started asking about it down in Maine right away. Art Dalton recalled a few lines, and several other PIs I talked with did too—especially the lines about boarding the train for Bangor, Maine. Billy Bell even recalled buying a copy of it from Gorman himself, and once I got to the Island I heard snatches of it everywhere. Everyone seemed to know *of* it, but no one really *knew* it, though several people were able to furnish me with manuscript or newspaper versions. As for authorship, as might be expected, most people had no idea who made it up, but a surprising number held definite—and various— opinions: in West Prince it was generally attributed to Larry Gorman, though several people around Lot Seven denied that, saying it was written by one James H. Fitzgerald (Campbellton's first school teacher),[2] while down in eastern Kings it was assumed to be by Lawrence Doyle. The whole situation is a muddle, and while I'm convinced that Doyle was indeed its author, I'm not about to insist on it.

The history presented by this song is both complex and partisan, and anyone interested in its details can find them in my book *Lawrence Doyle*.[3]

---

[1] See Doerflinger, pp. 256–57.
[2] See John Cousins, "James H. Fitzgerald and 'Prince Edward Isle, Adieu,'" *The Island Magazine*, No. 8 (1980), pp. 27–31.
[3] pp. 61–86.

Briefly, though, it is a Grit (i.e., Liberal) view of the political situation around 1880, showing how bad times — brought on by selfish Conservative policies — were forcing young people to leave the Island. The hardy original settlers, so the song tells us, came here to escape tyranny at home in Britain, but that tyranny followed them in the form of absentee landlords claiming rents. The present tyranny was that of the Conservatives, who had not only dragged the Island into the Dominion by building a railroad they couldn't pay for, they were subjecting it to the Dominion's policy of protective tariffs and doing nothing to develop a permanent year-round link to the mainland (a problem that never really got settled until the completion of the Confederation Bridge in 1997). As I say, it is a partisan political poem, which is why I'm pretty sure Lawrence Doyle, an active Grit, wrote it.

The song has been a significant presence in Island folklore for over a century, and perhaps I can best represent that presence by the 1950 version I found in *The Guardian*.[4] I have made a few corrections (which I have set in italic) to make it more in line with what I feel to have been the author's original intentions. The tune is from Mrs. Frank Sweet of St. Eleanors. Anyway, here is "Prince Edward Isle, Adieu" in all its partisan glory:

Prince Edward Isle, Adieu

1.
Come all ye hardy sons of toil
Pray lend an ear to me,
Whilst I relate the dismal state
Of this our country.
I will not pause to name the cause,
But keep it close in view;
For comrades grieve when they must leave
And bid this Isle adieu.

2.
There is a band all in our land
That moves in pomp and pride.
To swell their store they rob the poor
On Pleasure's wings they ride.
With dishes fine their tables shine
Like prince they move in style.
Those are the knaves that made us slaves
And sold Prince Edward's Isle.

---

[4] November 13, 1950.

♩. = 60

There is a band all in our land that moves in pomp and pride. To swell their store they rob the poor on treas-ure's wings they ride. With dish-es fine their ta-bles shine like prince they move in style. Those are the knaves that made us slaves and sold Prince Ed-ward's Isle.

3.

The father's boy, his only joy,
Must bid a sad farewell;
They're parting here, no more to meet
On Earth, for who can tell?
Far from this Isle in prairies wild,
In countries now that's new,
Content they stay and bless the day
They bid this Isle adieu.

4.

Our daughters fair, in deep despair,
Must leave their native land;
To foreign shores they're swiftly borne,
As I do understand.
The tide it flows, they all must go —
There's nothing else to do,
While parents grieve as they must leave
And bid this Isle adieu.

5.

Through want and wear and scanty fare
The poor man drags along;
He hears a whistle loud and shrill,
The "Iron Horse" speeds on.
He throws his pack upon his back —
There's nothing left to do;
He boards the train for Bangor, Maine,
Prince Edward Isle, adieu.

6.

The reason why so many fly
And leave their native home:
Because 'tis clear they can't stay here,
For work to do there's none.
In other climes there's better times —
There can't be worse, 'tis true;
So weal or woe, away they go:
Prince Edward Isle, adieu.

7.

In days of yore from *Erin's* shore
Our fathers crossed the main;
Though dark and drear, they settled here
To quit the Tyrant's chain.
With hearts so stout they put to rout
The forest beasts so wild;
Rough logs they cut to build their huts
Upon Prince Edward Isle.

8.

With axe well ground they levelled down
The forest far and wide;
With spade and hoe the seed they sowed —
The plow was left untried.
With sickle hooks they cut their stooks,
No "Buckeyes" were in style;
They spent their days, their ashes lay
Upon Prince Edward Isle.

9.

The place was new, the roads were few,
The people lived content;
The landlords came their fields to claim —
Each settler must pay rent.
So now you see the *tyranny*
That drove us to exile
Begin again *across* the main,
Far from Prince Edward Isle.

10.

But changes great have come of late
And brought some curious things:
Dominion men have brought us in —
The Island's Railway Ring!
There's maps and charts and towns apart,
And tramps of every style;
There's doctors mute and lawyers cute
Upon Prince Edward Isle.

11.

There's judges, too, who'll find a clue
To all the merchants' bills;
There's school trustees who want no fees
For using all their skill.
There's laws for dogs, for geese, for hogs —
At this pray do not smile;
For changes great have come of late
Upon Prince Edward Isle.

12.

So here's success to all who press
The question of Free Trade;
Join hand in hand, our cause is grand,
They're plainly in the shade.
The Mainland Route the *year* throughout—
Take courage now, stand true.
My verse is run, my song is done:
Prince Edward Isle, Adieu.

Peter Emberly

"Peter Emberly" was written in the Miramichi lumberwoods by one John Calhoun of Parker's Ridge, New Brunswick, in the winter of 1881, but no song has done more to carry the name and beauty of Prince Edward Island both to the other Atlantic Provinces and to Maine and even beyond. With the exception of "The Jam on Gerry's Rock," it was the ballad best known by singers all through the northeast lumberwoods, yet no one I met on P. E. I. was able to sing me more than a stanza or two, though once again it was widely recognized as "a good one" or "one they used to sing."

Part of the explanation for this apparent scarcity may have been my own attitude at the time. Since I knew the song had been attributed to Larry Gorman yet patently was *not* his work, I made no specific attempts to elicit it and may by my attitude even have discouraged singers from performing it. On the other hand, I can't believe that had some singer offered it up I would have refused it. It is also possible that it was considered a bad-luck song—something I have heard over on the Miramichi. John Cousins, who sang the version I give below and who often sang it to his P.E.I. History class, remembers one boy from Miminegash saying that he wouldn't be allowed to sing that song in *his* house. "A good many people from that area believe that it is bad luck to sing it in one's home," John added. But whatever the reasons—and whatever the risks—it belongs in any anthology of Island songs.

The song may be scarce on the ground, but there's a fair amount of local tradition about it. It is claimed, for example, that Peter was the child of his mother's previous marriage and often quarreled with his stepfather. One man claimed to have been with Peter the night before he left and even helped him hide his clothes so his father wouldn't suspect anything the next morning. And, of course, there was the house itself, a continuing and sentimental presence, which people in the area could—and did—point out to interested and sentimental visitors like me. The house is gone now, but I feel privileged that the Doucettes and Tremblays took me to see it that day.

John Cousins, Mary Cousins' son, is a well-known Island folksinger and folklorist, and he sang the present version for a record that he and fellow

No: 27: John Cousins.

folksinger Tommy Banks issued in 1976.[5] Recently I wrote him, asking where he had learned it:

> I learned it from Louise Manny's radio program from the Miramichi. My father had been a woodsman there for a good part of his life. I know he was there in the twenties, all through the thirties, and I think his last trip was in 1949 when I was four years old. My father couldn't sing. In my mother's words, "He couldn't carry a tune in a basket." He had been deaf most of his life, but he loved to hear singing. He could tell good singing from bad, but he couldn't sing himself.
>
> During the early fifties, before electricity, we had an old [wet] battery radio, and when Louise Manny came on between three and four on Sunday afternoon my father put his ear to the radio and we would turn it up as high as it would go. Then he would listen to the old songs which he had heard sung in the woods.
>
> As children, we were not impressed. Wilmot MacDonald we figured was the best of the lot, and my brothers used to sing like him in that high nasal voice. He sang "Peter Emberly" quite often, and that is how I came to learn it—and I still haven't heard anyone sing it as well as Wilmot.[6]

Thus the oral tradition leaped Northumberland Strait, and a young boy from Campbellton, living within a mile of the old Emberly house, learned Peter's song from Miramichi's greatest singer. One look at Wilmot's version, both text and tune, will show how well John Cousins had learned it.

Peter Emberly

1.
Oh my name is Peter Emberly as you may understand;
I was born on Prince Edward's Island close by the ocean strand.
In eighteen hundred and eighty-two when the flowers were in brilliant hue,
I left my native coun-te-ree my fortune to pursue.

2.
I landed in New Brunswick, that lumb'ring coun-ter-ee;
I hired for to work in the lumberwoods on the banks of the Mir'michi.
I hired for to work in the lumberwoods for to cut the tall spruce down.
And it was loading sleds while in the yards I received my deadly wound.

3.
Here's adieu unto my dearest friend, I mean my mother dear;
She raised a boy who fell as soon as he left her tender care.
'Twas little that my mother knew as she sang me a lullaby
What foreign countries I would roam or what death I would die.

---

[5] *When Johnny Went Plowing for Kearon* (Charlottetown: P.E.I. Museum and Heritage Foundation, 1976). With notes by Allan Rankin.
[6] Letter to me, c. October 25, 1997.

♩ = 120

2. I lan-ded in New Bruns-wick, that lum-b'ring coun-ter- ee; I hired for to work in the lum-ber-woods on the banks of the Mir'-mi- chi. I hired for to work in the lum-ber-woods for to cut the tall spruce down. And it was load-ing sleds while in the yards I re- ceived my dead - ly wound.

4.
Here's adieu unto my father, 'twas him who sent me here;
He treated me most cruelly, his treatment was severe.
It is not right to oppress a boy or to try to keep him down,
For it will drive him from his home when he is far too young.

5.
Here's adieu unto Prince Edward's Isle, fair island of the sea;
No more I'll roam your flowery banks to enjoy the summer's breeze.
No more I'll watch those gallant ships as they go drifting by,
Their flags a-flying in the wind far above their canvas high.

6.
Now there's one thing I do ask of you, and this I humbly pray:
To get a holy father for to bless my peaceful grave,
Far from the city of Boiestown where my mouldering bones do lay,
To await the coming judgment on the Resurrection Day.

The O'Halloran Road

As I have already pointed out, Mary Cousins had recited Dan Riley's "The O'Halloran Road" for me back in 1965, but I didn't record it, figuring there'd be an appropriate time later on. For any number of reasons—none of them very good—I kept never getting around to it, though Bobby and I visited with Mary every time we made the trip to the Island, which, if it wasn't every year, was often enough to seem like it. Then in the early seventies some film-makers used a couple of stanzas of Mary's singing of it very hauntingly in a documentary called *Passage West*. Even so, I didn't finally drag a tape recorder into Mary's house until the summer of 1996. As a folklorist I can beat my breast over this lapse—why, for God's sake, had I not recorded all that wonderful talk over the years? All I can say is that Bobby and I loved Mary; she is our dear friend, and the tape recorder simply didn't seem part of our relationship.

The song describes a family's sixty-mile winter trek in 1857 from Malpeque (where Dan Riley was born) to their new home, a fifty-acre farm about a mile from present-day Campbellton on what is still generally known as the O'Halloran Road. It was a dirt road when I first traveled it in 1957 (as were just about all the roads in West Prince at the time), and of course when Uncle Dan and his family arrived a century earlier it would have been little more than a wilderness track (according to Meacham's *Illustrated Historical Atlas of Prince Edward Island*, published in 1880, Lot Five isn't even mentioned in either the Census of 1861 or that of 1871).[7] Gavin's Cross, by the way, is present-day Bloomfield Corner (one Matthew Gavin owned the land at the intersection), where the O'Halloran Road branches off from the Western Road.

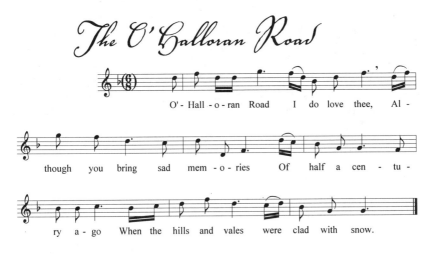

The O'Halloran Road

O'- Hall - o - ran Road   I   do   love   thee,   Al -

though   you   bring   sad   mem - o - ries   Of   half   a   cen - tu -

ry   a - go   When   the   hills   and   vales   were   clad   with   snow.

1.
O'Halloran Road I do love thee,
Although you bring sad memories
Of half a century ago
When the hills and vales were clad with snow.

2.
When I first trod your lonely way
It was on a cold Saint Patrick's Day,
With my father and my mother then
And children we just numbered ten.

---

[7]*Meacham's Atlas*, p. 11.

No. 28: Mary Cousins and Bobby Ives. *Photo taken August 1991.*

3.

Although I was only eight years old,
I remember the day; it was clear and cold.
Six Malpeque men with horse and sleigh
Conveyed us west that Saint Patrick's Day.

4.

And when we came to Gavin's Cross
Us children thought that we were lost,
For a great dense forest lay between
The Western Road and Campbellton.

5.

Just then I heard my father say,
"Here's the O'Halloran Road! This is the way.
About five miles along this road
My dwelling stands, a poor abode."

6.

O'Halloran Road I do love thee,
Although you bring sad memories
Of half a century ago
When the hills and vales were clad with snow.

*"There's another verse, I think," she said, "but I can't remember it."

*"Uncle Dan was a very mild-mannered man," she added later. "He loved to read, and he used to sing for us. Oh, when he'd come over in the evening and sat down and sang for us we were happy as kings. We thought we'd been to the opera! And you know," she added, "he had an old clock, one of those clocks that there was weights on, and it finally got so old that the weights fell to the bottom and it didn't work at all. But still that old clock would strike when somebody was going to die in the community. It'd strike and he'd give the word, and sure enough somebody *would* die. It even struck for his own death, they say."

As I write this, it has not yet struck for Mary. God be praised.

Notes to the Songs

I HAVE KEPT THE BIBLIOGRAPHICAL CITATIONS to a minimum, simply giving the name and town of the singer, the date of the singing, and where the reader can turn for further information about the song. If the song is in the Ives Collection of the Northeast Archives of Folklore and Oral History, University of Maine, its tape number is given (e.g., NA Ives 64.7). If it is also found in the Archives of Traditional Music, Indiana University, I cite its index number (e.g., ATL 2195.3), or if it is also on deposit at the Archive of Folk Culture, American Folklife Center, Library of Congress, I cite its index number there (e.g., AFC 14,820B). Three further references which occur frequently are to G. Malcolm Laws's two syllabi, *Native American Balladry* (NAB) and *American Balladry from British Broadsides* (ABBB), and my *Twenty-One Folksongs from Prince Edward Island*. For the most part, I have not repeated references given either in Laws' two syllabi or in my three earlier works: *Larry Gorman* (1964), *Lawrence Doyle* (1971), and *Joe Scott* (1978). All other works will be found in the List of Works Cited.

The additional notes contain material that, while it didn't seem to have any place in the narrative, may be of interest to folklorists and other specialists.

Alec's Lament (217)
By Alec Shea. Sung by Edward Fitzgerald at the Island Folk Festival, Westisle Theatre, Elmsdale, November 6, 1982. Transcribed from the LP record, *Island Folk Festival.* See Gledhill, 44–47.

Bachelor's Hall (39)
By Larry Gorman. Sung by Mrs. Cyrene McLellan, Grand River, June 22, 1957 (NA Ives 1.30; ATL 2156.1). See Ives (1964), 20–22, 190, to which add Szwed, 157–67 (another song by the same name).

I have added stanzas six and seven from the singing of Big Jim Pendergast.

Benjamin Deane (89)
By Joe Scott. Sung by Angus Enman, Spring Hill, August 19, 1958 (NA Ives 1.38; ATL 2164.3). See Laws, NAB, 206 (F-32); Ives (1963), 54–59, 78–79; Ives (1978), 228–66.

Benjamin F. Deane shot and killed his wife in Berlin, N.H., May 4, 1898. He was allowed to plead guilty to second degree murder, was sentenced to twenty-five years, served less than ten, returned to Berlin, remarried, and died there in 1924. The ballad, one of Joe Scott's best-known works, has been found in New Hampshire, Maine, New Brunswick, and Nova Scotia, as well as on Prince Edward Island. For an extensive account and analysis, see Ives (1978). For a further interpretation, see Renwick (1985), 412–415.

Bold McCarthy (187)
Sung by John D. Gorman, St. Charles, April 2, 1968 (NA Ives 68.4; AFC 14,820B). See Laws, *ABBB*, 154 (K 26), to which add Manny and Wilson, 224–25; Peacock, 860–61.

Bonny Flora Clark, The (20)
By Hugh Lauchlan MacDonald. Sung and recited by John Farrell, St. Georges, March 31, 1969 (NA Ives 69.1; AFC 14,823A). See Ives (1971), 187–91.

Boys of the Island, The (19)
Sung by Arthur Dalton, Rumford, Maine, January 31, 1957 (NA Ives 1.20; ATL 2148.7). See Ives (1964), 122–25, 191, to which add Cousins and Banks, 5; Dibblee and Dibblee, 44; Doerflinger, 218–19; Eckstorm and Smyth, 118–20; MacKinnon and Belsher, 22–23.

Although it is often attributed to him, there is some question whether Larry Gorman actually did write this song. I'm skeptical, but I leave the matter open. Whoever wrote it, the song gives a spirited picture of the young PI in his native homespun arriving at Bangor's old yellow brick depot on his way to the woods.

Brennan on the Moor (126)
Sung by Linus Christopher, Tignish, August 26, 1965 (NA Ives 65.6; AFC 14,801B). See Laws *ABBB* 169 (L-7), to which add Cazden et al i:414–17, ii:81–82; Gledhill, 80–84. I have transcribed the meter as 6/8 with two 4/8 infixes, but it can easily be sung as straight 6/8 all the way through.

This ballad is widespread and well-known both in America and in Britain—well enough known in the Northeast to be parodied in a local Maine song called "Bracey on the Shore" (Eckstorm and Smyth, 332–34). There is quite convincing evidence that there really was an eighteenth-century Irish highwayman by the name of Willie Brennan, but whether the ballad is an accurate account of his activities is an open question made even opener by the remarkable similarity of his behaviour to other chivalrous highwaymen like the Australian wild colonial boys Jack Dobbin and Jack Donahue and the English Dick Turpin. It is Turpin, by the way, and his famous steed Black Bess who are referred to in the second stanza.

Cabin Boy, The (147)
General outline and a fragment recalled by John Morrison, Charlottetown, August 30, 1965 (NA Ives 65.10; AFC 14,802B).

For an apparently complete text and further references, see Gardner and Chickering, 324–25.

Charles Gustavus Anderson (197)
Sung by John Banks, Poplar Point, April 4, 1968 (NA Ives 68.6; AFC 14,821B). See Laws, NAB, 170 (D-19), to which add Peacock, 867–68.

For a good brief historical account of the *Saladin* mutiny, see Doerflinger, 180–83. For other ballads on the same mutiny, see Creighton (1932), 235–42.

Cheese and Marrowbones (109)
Sung by Wesley Smith, Victoria West, July 15, 1963 (NA Ives 1.148; ATL 3155). See Laws *ABBB*, 274 (Q-2); Ives (1963), 75–77, 84, to which add Cazden et al.i:518–22, ii:99–101; Creighton (1962), 122; Doerflinger, 281; Morton, 89–90, 121, 170; Peacock, 261–62.

This song has been a great favourite, not only with Wesley Smith's friends, but all over the United States, Canada, and the British Isles. Variants have been found from Texas to Illinois and from North Carolina to Maine, and Cape Breton's John Allan Cameron's singing of it as "The Old Woman from Mabou" did a great deal to popularize it in the Maritimes. A second and almost equally popular ballad (though it doesn't seem to be known in New England or the Maritimes), "Johnny Sands" (Laws Q-3), tells the same story, except that the man's wife ties his hands instead of "blinding" him. When she falls into the water, he says he'd be glad to help her, "but you see my hands are tied."

Crazy Grey Mare, The (183)
By Hugh Lauchlan MacDonald. Sung by Leo Gorman, St. Charles, April 2, 1968 (NA Ives 68.4; AFC 14,820B).

For further information on this song and its author see Ives (1971), 182–201.

Crockery Ware, The (129)
Sung by Linus Christopher, Tignish, August 26, 1965 (NA 65.6; AFC 14,801B). See Peacock, 257–58.

Although this light-hearted song is clearly British in origin, the only other

North American version I have found to date has been Peacock's from New-foundland. On the other hand, there are several other ballads about young men who have been similarly fleeced by women they have tried to seduce. See Ives (1978), 340–50.

Cumberland's Crew, The (16)
Sung by William Bell, Brewer, Maine, December 13, 1956 (NA Ives 1.2; ATL 2136.3). See Laws, *NAB*, A-18, to which add Cazden et al, i:81–85 and ii:14–15.

The event celebrated in this ballad occurred March 8, 1862. Doerflinger (p.133) gives an excellent brief historical description of the battle itself. The ballad was a great favourite in lumbercamp tradition and—like so many Civil War songs—was well-established in Canadian tradition. Not surprisingly, it seems to have been unknown in the southern states.

Dark-Eyed Sailor, The (93)
Sung by Angus Enman, Spring Hill, August 18, 1958 (NA Ives 1.39; ATL 2164.5). See Laws, *ABBB*, 221 (N-35), to which add Fowke (1965), 30–31, 166–67; Huntington (1964), 120–22; Huntington/Henry, 318; Manny and Wilson, 230–31; O'Lochlainn, 10–11; Peacock, 513–14.

This song, a great favourite in the Maritimes, is one more reworking of the disguised—or unrecognized—lover's return, and these songs often include the theme of identification by a ring (see "The Old Beggar Man" below).

Drive Dull Care Away (81)
Sung by Charles Gorman, Burton, Lot Seven, August 18 , 1958 (NA Ives 1.37; ATL 2163.3). See Ives (1963), 46–48, 79. See also Hickerson's recording on FSI-58 and its accompanying booklet. Hickerson's note is worth reproducing here: "The song is old, but very rare. A sacred text with a different tune has been printed in B. F. White and E. J. King's *The Sacred Harp* since 1844. The only other printing is over 200 years old and was recently located by Arlene Rodenbeck while assisting Gillian Anderson in the latter's researches into song material of the American Revolutionary period. Untitled, the words appeared in the September 30, 1775, issue of *The Pennsylvania Ledger: Or the Virginia, Maryland, Pennsylvania, & New Jersey Weekly Advertiser*, with much the same secular words as those found in the present text (plus another verse) but a different verse-ending: 'Then let us constant (true friends) be/ For while we're here/ My friends so dear/ We'll fight for Liberty.'"

Drunken Captain, The (170)
Sung by Joseph Walsh, Morell Rear, September 1, 1965 (NA Ives 65.13; AFC

14,803B). See Laws, *NAB*, 265 (dD-52), to which add Leach (1965), 118–19; MacEachern, 48–49; Peacock, 871–72.

Erin's Green Shore (140)
Sung by Wesley Smith, Victoria West, August 28, 1965 (NA Ives 65.9; AFC 14, 802A). See Laws, *ABBB*, 286 (Q-27), to which add Cazden i: 266–70, ii: 53–54; Fowke (1965), 88–89, 180–81; Peacock, 362–65.

Flying Cloud, The (223)
Sung by Clifford Wedge, Miminegash, November 6, 1982, at the Island Folk Festival, Elmsdale. Transcribed from the LP record, *Island Folk Festival* (Fox House, 1985). See Laws, *ABBB* (K28), to which add Gledhill, 48–55; Huntington (1966), 34–37; Leach, 156–58; Peacock, 842–45.

Fogan MacAleer · (156)
By Lawrence Doyle. Sung by Joseph Walsh, Morell Rear, September 1, 1965 (NA Ives 65.12; AFC 14,803A). See Ives (1971), 35–46, for a full discussion, to which add Michael Kennedy's discussion of the Scottish custom of having a go-between approach the prospective bride's father to arrange for a marriage in "The Réitach in Prince Edward Island," *Tocher*, No.50 (Spring, 1995), 46–51.

   In Willie Mathieson's manuscript songbooks at the School of Scottish Studies I found a song called "The Jolly Barber," which was clearly Doyle's model for this song, as the two opening stanzas will show:

> There was a Jolly Barber and he lived in Aberdeen
> He was as jolly a barber as yet was ever seen
> He was an awful bonnie laddie he was a son of ancient paddie
> He was awful like his daddy don't you know what I mean.

> There was a gay young maiden she dressed up so fair
> She wanted this young barber to come and curl her hair
> With his curling tongs and scissors his soap box and his razor
> And to come away and shave her don't you know what I mean.

Then it carries the double-entendre to its obvious conclusion.

Ghostly Fishermen, The (79)
Sung by Edmund Doucette, Miminegash, August 17, 1958 (NA Ives 1.37; ATL 2162.4). See Laws, *NAB*, 168–69 (D-16); Ives (1963), 25–28, 79; to which add Peacock, 873–74; Leach (1965), 244–45; Creighton (1971), 223–25.

Horace Beck writes in *The Folklore of Maine* that somewhere in the 1870s the schooner *Haskell* ran down another vessel on George's Bank. After that, "Every time the Haskell put to sea and went to George's the ghastly crew came aboard. Eventually, as a result of these visitations, no one could be found to ship in her and the *Haskell* lay alongside a pier in Gloucester till she went to pieces" (p. 203). For further examples, see Creighton (1950), p.30, and Greenleaf and Mansfield, pp. 228–29. Doerflinger reports that the "original words, by Harry L. Marcy, appeared in 1874 in *Fishermen's Ballads and Songs of the Sea*, a collection of songs, poems, yarns, and useful facts compiled for the fishermen by a Gloucester stationery house, Procter Brothers" (p. 180). Where the words picked up the tune, there is no way of telling. The song has not been found outside Maine, the Maritimes, and Newfoundland, and it has never travelled very far from the sea.

Gull Decoy, The (85)
By Larry Gorman. Recited by Frank O'Holleran, Bloomfield Station, August 18, 1958 (NAIves 1.38; ATL 2164.4). See Manny and Wilson, 102–03. For a discussion, see Ives (1964), 30–35. Both sources give examples of the several tunes to which this song has been sung.

Guy Reed (96)
By Joe Scott. Sung by Wesley Smith, Victoria West, August 19, 1958 (NA Ives 1.40; ATL 2165.4). See Laws, NAB, 151 (C-9); Ives (1963), 63–68, 79–80; to which add Manny and Wilson, 104–07; Ives (1989), 183–86. For extended studies, see Ives (1978), 140–77, and Renwick (1985), especially 416f.

Guy Reed was killed just a few miles above Livermore Falls, Maine, on September 9, 1897, in a logging accident very similar to the one that killed John Ladner. In addition to P.E.I., this ballad has been frequently found in New Hampshire, Maine, New Brunswick, and Nova Scotia. Since Smith learned it before he went to Maine, it had reached P.E.I. in less than a dozen years.

Hell-Bound Train, The (163)
Sung by Joseph Walsh, Morell Rear, September 1, 1965 (NA Ives 65.13; AFC 14, 803B). See Finger, 110–13; Lomax, 402; Ohrlin, 36–37; Randolph IV, 23–24; Shay, 95–97.

Hind Horn (See "The Old Beggar Man").

Howard Carey (131)
By Joe Scott. Sung by Malvina Doucette, Tignish, August 26, 1965 (NA Ives 65.5; AFC 14,801A). See Laws, *NAB*, 187 (E-23); to which add Dibblee and Dibblee, 59–60; Manny and Wilson, 11–14. For extended studies see Ives (1978), 106–39, and Renwick (1985), 405–31 (especially 409–12).

Howard Carrick, a woodsman, aged 33, hanged himself in his room at Annie Siddal's boarding house in Rumford, Maine, on May 5, 1897. It was common knowledge among woodsmen I have talked to that he was dying of syphilis at the time, and according to Mrs. Siddal he had said that morning that he feared he would die within a few hours. Almost certainly Joe Scott knew Carrick, and his ballad, which probably appeared within a few days of the suicide, is widely known in Maine and the Maritimes.

Irish Jubilee, The (160)
Sung by Joseph Walsh, Morell Rear, September 1, 1965 (NA Ives 65.12; AFC 14,803A).

Evidently the late-nineteenth-century words to this song were written by one James Thornton, the music by Charles Lawler (who also wrote "The Sidewalks of New York"). For full sets of both words and music, see Sigmund Spaeth, *Weep Some More, My Lady*, 225–28; and Morton, 88–91.

Jam on Gerry's Rock, The (33)
Sung by Mrs. John Coughlin, Ellerslie, June 22, 1957 (NA Ives 1.30; ATL 2155.11). See Laws, *NAB*, C-1, to which add Bethke 64–66; Cazden et al, i:46–52, ii: 8–9; Fowke (1970), 95–99; Ives (1989), 26–29; Leach, 256–57; Manny and Wilson, 115–117; Peacock, 752–53. For Eckstorm's essay, "The Pursuit of a Ballad Myth," see Eckstorm and Smyth, 176–198.

"The Jam on Gerry's Rock" is without doubt the most popular lumberwoods song going. Its only rival is "Peter Emberly," but that song is pretty well confined to the Northeast, while "The Jam" has been found from Florida to Oregon—and even in Scotland. I have talked to men who located Gerry's Rock—often with considerable precision—on the Connecticut, the Androscoggin, the Penobscot, the Sou'west Miramichi…on and on, but as Fannie Hardy Eckstorm said years ago, "Nothing about the song…has been settled except that it did not occur at all the places where it has been located" (Eckstorm and Smyth, p.196). The basic story is clear enough: a jam of logs out in the centre of the river builds up out of control, and a boat crew (six men plus the foreman, all volunteers) goes out to break it up. The foreman senses danger, but his warning comes too late; the jam "hauls" and all hands are swept away. Work stops while the men search for the bodies. That's how it would go. As for the rest of the story, as William Caxton said in his introduction to *The Book of Arthur*, "ye be at your lyberté."

John Ladner (60)

Sung by Edmund Doucette, Miminegash, June 30, 1957 (NA Ives 1.32; ATL 2157.6). See Laws, *NAB* (dC-40), to which add Ives (1963), 13–17; Ives (1980), 240–45; Dibblee and Dibblee, 40–41; Manny and Wilson, 122–23. For tune parallels, see Cazden, i:73–76, ii:12–13. For a full discussion, see Ives (1980), 239–258.

John Ladner, 33, of Victoria West was killed in a logging accident in Madison, Maine, on Thanksgiving Day, November 29, 1900. He and another man were breaking in a pile of logs north of the village and rolling them into the river for use at the Madison pulp mill when some of the falling logs caught and crushed him. The late William Bryant recalled that John had a fine big funeral in Victoria West, and certainly the stone that marks his grave is one of the most impressive in the little cemetery adjoining the United Church there.

Last Winter Was a Hard One (112)

Sung by Wesley Smith, Victoria West, July 15, 1963 (NA Ives 1.148; ATL 3155.5). See Cazden, i:362–66, ii:71.

According to Cazden, this song was popularized by a singer named Johnny Roach. "The popularity of Roach's rendition," he adds, "is attested also by publication of his booklet, *Favorite Dime Song Book #95*, issued by the New York Popular Publishing Company in 1881. It bears portraits of Mrs. Reilly and Mrs. McGuiness on its cover, and it is entitled *Johnny Roach's When McGuiness Gets a Job Songster.*"

Lost Babes of Halifax, The (75)

Sung by Joseph Doucette, Palmer Road, August 17, 1958 (NA Ives 1.36; ATL 2162.1). See Laws, *NAB*, 225 (G-25); to which add Ives (1963), 37–40, 80–81; Manny and Wilson, 130–34.

Helen Creighton always said that this song should be called "The Lost Babes of Dartmouth," and she is quite right, but of course it is too late now! *In Songs and Ballads from Nova Scotia*, she prints a 19-stanza variant from the singing of Ben Henneberry of Devil's Island with the following comments: "The scene of the tragedy recorded in this tale lies about three miles from Dartmouth, N.S.... The facts recorded in the ballad are historically correct, and may be found in Mrs. Lawrence's *History of the Township of Preston*" (p. 296). Creighton also gives an interesting word picture of the circumstances under which she first collected the song (xiii–xiv). The ballad is also known as "Meagher's Children," and that name is pronounced "Marr" or Ma*har*." Sam Jagoe of Newcastle, N.B., in singing this song pronounced the name as "Migger," giving pretty clear evidence that he got the words from a printed source (see Manny and Wilson, 131).

Joe learned this ballad in New Brunswick. His tune is the same as that used by Sam Jagoe and quite different from the two tunes I have seen from Nova Scotia. The break in stanza four comes from an accidental erasure; I supply the words from memory.

Lost Jimmy Whalen, The (35)
Sung by Mrs. John Coughlin, Ellerslie, June 22, 1957 (NA 1.30; ATL 2155.12). See Laws, NAB (C-8), to which add Fowke (1970), 114–16; Manny and Wilson, 263–264; Peacock, 385–89. For a discussion of the tune see Cazden et al, i:120–24, ii:19–20 (#28).

This ballad sounds for all the world as if it ought to have come from Ireland, but since no British versions have yet been found, Irish or otherwise, it evidently originated in North America, more than likely in Maine or the Maritime Provinces, where it became a fixture in lumberwoods tradition. Through that tradition it spread to Michigan, Wisconsin, Minnesota, and Ontario, but it doesn't seem to be known beyond that area.

Michael O'Brien (52)
By Larry Gorman. Sung by Edmund Doucette, Miminegash, June 26, 1957 (NA Ives 1.31; ATL 2156.7). See Ives (1964), 43–44, 196.

Millman and Tuplin Song, The (46)
By Dan Riley. Sung by Mary Cousins, Campbellton, June 25, 1957 (NA Ives 1.30; ATL 2156.4). See Laws, NAB, 270 (dF60); Ives (1963), 42–44, 82, to which add Manny and Wilson, 195–96; Wilson, 41, 96–97; Dibblee and Dibblee, 71–72. For other songs on the Millman-Tuplin case, see Creighton (1933), 306–08; Doerflinger, 285–86; and "The Millman Murder" in the present volume. For a discussion of the various Millman/Tuplin songs see Ives (1971), 167–74. For more information on the murder, trial, and hanging, see Jim Hornby, *In The Shadow of The Gallows* (Charlottetown: Institute of Island Studies, 1998), 80–91.

The evidence for Dan Riley's authorship is strong. First of all, the dates and places figure out about right. That is, he would have been about forty at the time of the murder, and he came originally from Malpeque, not all that far from Margate. In addition, he knew the Tuplin family well. To that point, Mary Cousins remembered him talking about it. One time she was at her grandfather's farm—right next to Uncle Dan's on the O'Halloran Road—and he came in for a visit:

> *He told us the story about Mary Tuplin. He often talked about it. He said that her mother was sick in bed, and she wasn't going to get better, and he went to see her. He went to see the girl's mother, and

she was so glad that he came. She said, "Dan, I'm so glad you've come. I didn't expect you. I didn't think you'd come" (you know, on account of what happened). He said, "You should have known that I'd come to see you." And he stayed with her and talked to her. He said he thought she felt better after he talked to her. Told her that these things happen in the world, and it wasn't her fault. She had no part in it. She didn't know a thing about it.

Millman Murder Trial, The (180)
Sung by Arthur Cahill, St. Charles, April 1, 1968 (NA Ives 68.2; AFC 14,819B). See also "The Millman and Tuplin Song."

Miramichi Fire, The (62)
Sung by Joseph Doucette, Miminegash, June 30, 1957 (NA Ives 1.32; ATL 2157.8). See Laws, NAB, 224–25 (G-24); Ives (1963), 33–37, 82; to which add Manny and Wilson, 145–51.

This song has become a legend in itself here in the Northeast. That there is such a song is well known. Everyone has "heard it" and many people can tell you who used to sing it or who you should go see "because she has the whole of it." A bit of a tune here, a few lines or a couple of stanzas there, but rarely more than that and never the whole song—never, that is, the full twenty-one stanzas found in the series of printed versions.

We can reconstruct the history of the song something like this: The Great Fire took place October 7, 1825. Beginning on the Northwest Miramichi and aided by heavy winds and tinderbox conditions, it swept down to the Main River, where it raged along both banks, destroying four thousand square miles of timber and several towns, among them Newcastle. Shortly after that, John Jardine of Black River wrote a ballad about it, which he almost certainly had printed and sold. Either he or, what is more likely, later singers put tunes to it and it caught on, especially in the lumbercamps, through which it spread over to the State of Maine. The original broadsides have now entirely disappeared, but we have newsprint copies (and copies of copies) that surely represent the original rather well. Because it was long, plotless, and very circumstantial, the song was hard to remember, and, however much they may have jogged people's memories, the printed copies also reminded them that they didn't know it all. Thus we have an oral tradition somewhat awed by a written or printed one.

Odd as it may seem, such a conclusion seems to fit the facts. If we take the six variants I have found where the singer knew half-a-dozen stanzas or more, we find that in every case he got through the first five stanzas in an order that squares with the printed variants (let's call it "the original order"). From there on in nothing is certain. Long Joe sang the song for me on two different occasions over a year apart. Each time, he got as far as stanza 6 and stayed right with the original order. From there on in, though, the sequence of the stanzas bore no relation to that order, nor are the two sequences entirely consistent with each other; they were simply a series of individual stanzas on a common theme. This is not Long Joe's fault but the fault of a ballad that develops along no clear plan, making any consistent sequence a feat of pure memory. It is nothing short of amazing that the piece has survived at all, let alone for almost 140 years. And so far as I know, no one has preserved it better than Long Joe.

Comparison of all the extant tunes compounds the chaos. The majority are single-stanza tunes, but I have two that cover two stanzas. There doesn't seem to be anything that can be called the "right" or "original" tune, but Long Joe's tune bears strong resemblances in contour and phrase progression to those sung for me by James Brown of South Branch, N.B. (near Richibucto), and Stanley MacDonald of Black River Bridge, N.B. (near Chatham). At the moment, then, no tune has a better right than the present one to be called, if not the "original," at least the most widespread.

Morrissey and the Black (186)
Sung by John D. Gorman, St. Charles, April 2, 1968 (NA Ives 68.4; AFC 14,820B). See Laws, NAB, 239 H-19); to which add Ives (1989), 30–32.

My Seventy-Six Geared Wheel (151)
By Ambrose Cosgrove. Sung by John O'Connor, Hope River, August 31, 1965 (NA Ives 65.11; AFC 14,803A).

Norway Bum, The (119)
By Joe Scott. Sung by Emile Arsenault, Tignish, August 26, 1965 (NA Ives 65.7; AFC 14,801B). See Ives (1978), 282–306 for an extended discussion of this ballad.

Joe Scott wrote this ballad in western Maine somewhere around the turn of the century, and, like most of his other great ballads, it became part of standard woods repertoire and was carried to the Maritimes by singers returning home. No one was killed in the fire that destroyed much of Norway, Maine, in 1894, and there is no evidence to show that the song is based on a real person or incident, but, since Scott was not given to fiction, we can be reasonably sure that he thought his source—whatever or whomever it may have been—was factual.

O'Halloran Road, The (237)
By Dan Riley. Words recited by Mary Cousins, Campbellton, August 9, 1996. Tune is from the soundtrack of the film *Passage West*. See Cousins and Banks, 6; MacKinnon and Belsher, 71.

Old Arm Chair, The (123)
Sung by Emile Arsenault, Tignish, August 26, 1965 (NA Ives 65.7; AFC 14,801B). See Brown Collection V:411–12; Huntington (1966), 72–75, 82; Randolph III:224–27; Scarborough, 373–74; Spaeth, 205–06.

Old Beggar Man, The (72)
Sung by Edmund Doucette, Miminegash, August 16, 1958 (NA Ives 1.35; ATL 2161.1). See Child I: 187–208 (No.17); Ives (1963), 19–22; Coffin/Renwick, 41–42, 219–20; Fowke (1965), 80–82, 179.

As Bronson points out, "Variants of this tune-family with a 'Hind Horn' text are pretty well confined, so far as the record shows, to Scotland and the Northeastern seaboard of North America, taking in Maine, New Brunswick, and Newfoundland." It has been found elsewhere—and to different tunes—but within the aforementioned areas, it is a marvelous example of how stable a tune-text relationship can be.

It is tempting to speak of this ballad as "ancient" or "medieval," and it may indeed be either or both, even though no extant variants can be dated earlier than 1810. Its "official" title in Child's great collection is "Hind Horn," but its exact relation to the thirteenth-century romance of *King Horn* is problematic, and certainly there is no proof of the ballad's antiquity as a ballad. Yet if any of our extant ballads go back to the Middle Ages, this one surely does. We are on very solid ground, however, when we point out that this is simply one of a vast repertoire of ballads that develop the theme of the disguised lover's return, and in many of them the lover's identity is finally revealed by some token, often a ring.

Pat Murphy (106)
Sung by Wesley Smith, Victoria West, July 15, 1963 (NA Ives 1.148; ATL 3155.1). See Morton, 46–47.

For a New Brunswick version sung for me by Wilmot MacDonald, see Ives (1989), 98–99. Steve Roud tells me that it is quite well-known in Britain, where it is generally known as "Joe Muggins" or "I Don't Care If I Do."

Peter Emberly (235)
By John Calhoun. Sung by John Cousins, O'Leary, for the record *When Johnny Went Plowing for Kearon*. See Laws, NAB, 160 (C-27), to which add Cazden i:

52–54, ii: 9–10; Creighton (1971), 231–33; Dibblee and Dibblee, 33; Fowke (1970), 127–30; Ives (1989), 99–103; MacKinnon and Belsher, 18–19; Manny and Wilson, 160–63.

Picnic at Groshaut, The (178)

By Lawrence Doyle. Sung by Arthur Cahill, St. Charles, April 1, 1968 (NA Ives 68.2; AFC 14,819B). See Cousins and Banks, 4–5; Dibblee and Dibblee, 14–15. For a full discussion of this song, see Ives (1971), 19–34.

Plain Golden Band, The (149)

By Joe Scott. Sung by John O'Connor, Hope River, August 31, 1965 (NA Ives 65.11; AFC 14,803A). See Ives (1989), 159–62; Laws, NAB, 238 (H-17). For a full discussion of this song, see Ives (1978), 191–227.

Potato Bug, The (202)

By Lawrence Doyle. Sung by John Farrell St. Georges, March 31, 1969 (NA Ives 69.1; AFC 14,823B). For a full discussion of this song, see Ives (1971), 147–55.

Prince Edward Isle, Adieu (230)

Words published in the Charlottetown *Guardian* on November 13, 1950, from a letter sent in by Mr. J. A. Gillies. Tune from the singing of Mrs. Frank Sweet, St. Eleanors, June 25, 1957 (NA Ives 1.31; ATL 2156.9). See Cousins (1980), 27–31; Dibblee and Dibblee, 120–21; Ives (1964), 46–49; Ives (1971), 61–86; MacKinnon and Belsher, 18–19.

Rough Pavement (221)

By Allan Rankin. Sung by Allan Rankin at the Island Folk Festival, Elmsdale, November 6, 1982; transcribed from the LP record, *Island Folk Festival* (1985), and reprinted here with his permission. See also MacKinnon and Belsher, 18–19.

Sally Monroe (142)

Sung by Wesley Smith, Victoria West, August 28, 1965 (NA Ives 65.9; AFC 14,802A). See Laws, ABBB, 145–46 (K-11), to which add Dibblee and Dibblee, 88–89; Huntington/Henry, 441; Leach, 108–09; Peacock, 488–89.

Gavin Greig, the great Scottish collector, printed an interesting note with his fifteen-stanza version: "The popularity of 'Sally Monro' can easily be understood. In none of our ballads is the note of sincerity more strong and convincing. I have heard it said that James Dixon used to wander about the country till not so very long ago, sometimes playing on the flute; but that the mention of Sally Munro sent him off never to come back" (lxxiv).

Saville The Brave Man (174)

Sung by Leo Gorman, St. Charles, April 1, 1968 (NA Ives 68.2; AFC 14,819B). See Cousins and Banks, 3; Dibblee and Dibblee, 88–89; Ives (1971), 219–21.

Schooner Gracie Parker, The (136)

Sung by Mrs. Benjamin Smith, Alberton, August 27, 1965 (NA Ives 65.5; AFC 14,801A). See Cousins and Banks, 7; Dibblee and Dibblee, 49–50; Gledhill, 69–73.

The schooner *Gracie M. Parker*—72 feet long, 91 tons, built in 1869 in Essex, Massachusetts, owned by Alex McFadyen of Tignish—was wrecked off the south coast of Saint-Pierre with the loss of all hands on December 16, 1893. The *Examiner* reported it this way (22/12/93):

> No sadder event to the marine community has transpired for many a long day than that whereby eight of our sturdy seamen lost their lives in Saturday's severe gale off the cruel coast of Miquelon. But a week ago, election day, full of life and hope—and one of them quite recently married—those hardy sailors, the flower of Alberton's seamen, left that port in the splendid schooner Gracie M. Parker for St. Pierre de Miquelon, with a mixed cargo shipped by Mr. Turner of O'Leary. Josiah Doiron, Mr. Turner's man of business, went with them to dispose of the valuable cargo. A succession of heavy gales was experienced almost every day after, culminating in Saturday night's terrible storm. Next morning came the sad news over the wire that a vessel corresponding to the description of the expected Gracie M. Parker had been wrecked on the west coast of St. Pierre Island, and all hands lost. Two bodies, answering to the traits of James Daugherty and William Farrell, the captain's brother, were found on the rocky shore. The others—Capt. Farrell, Frank McAlduff, John Oliver, Alfred Matthews, and the poor supercargo Doiron—will never be found. All these men were married and leave families, many of them large and entirely dependent on their earnings…. It is needless to say that those widows and their friends are disconsolate. A heavy pall of gloom has been cast over Alberton and the immediate vicinity where the poor victims were known and lived. Indeed, the whole country has felt the shock occasioned by the sad news.

Local tradition has it that a dog standing on the wharf with his master, pointed his nose at the departing vessel, put back his head, and howled mournfully.

As a check of almost any song collection from the Maine-Atlantic Provinces area will show (see especially Peacock, 931–84), ballads about shipwreck form a genre all to themselves and most of them follow the basic pattern of the present example. They were common in Island newspapers, and perhaps

Mr. Arsenault of Tignish intended that his ballad would be so published, but my careful check did not turn it up. Clearly, though, the oral tradition kept it alive and even carried it to western Maine, where Roy Lohnes—who had never been to Prince Edward Island and knew nothing about it—recited five stanzas as he remembered hearing them in the lumberwoods.

The "educated wreck" of stanza 3 has puzzled me for years. Other versions have "He chanced to spy the wreck" or something similar. My best guess is that the man walking the beach saw wreckage that "indicated a wreck." But Mrs. Smith's keeping the line the way she heard it shows the kind of authority vested in oral tradition: one doesn't change something just because it doesn't make sense.

Shepherd, The (104)
Sung by Edmund Doucette, Miminegash, July 14, 1963 (NA Ives 1.146; ATL 3153.7). See Ives (1963), 31–32, 83.

Although this ballad bears strong resemblances to other ballads of family opposition to lovers, especially those in which the father of the girl either kills the young man or has him killed, the only other variant of it I have been able to run down is in Helen Creighton's *Maritime Folk Songs* (108). That variant comes from Nova Scotia and has two more stanzas than Edmund's, but it is sung to what is certainly a set of the same tune.

Sheriff's Sale, The (138)
Sung by Wesley Smith, Victoria West, August 28, 1965 (NA Ives 65.9; AFC 14,802A).

Stekert mentions that Ezra Barhight, a New York lumberjack, sang it for her (see Stekert, 264). Outside of that, I have no further information on this song, never having heard it or come across it either before or since.

Silvery Tide, The (107)
Sung by Wesley Smith, Victoria West, July 15, 1963 (NA Ives 1.148; ATL 3155.2). See Laws, *ABBB*, 245 (O-37), to which add Huntington (1964), 125–27; Huntington-Henry, 418–19; Manny and Wilson, 289–91.

While this ballad seems to be best known in northern tradition (particularly in the Northeast), it has also been found in Tennessee and Missouri. British variants are reported from both Scotland and England. The tune Wesley uses is not one I have seen for it elsewhere.

Spree at Montague, The (208)
By Patrick William Farrell. Sung by John Farrell, St. Georges, March 31, 1969 (NA Ives 69.1; AFC 145,823A).

Teamster in Jack MacDonald's Crew, The (165)
Sung by Joseph Walsh, Morell Rear, September 1, 1965 (NA Ives 65.13; AFC 14,803B). See Ives (1985), 74–85.

Twenty Years Ago (196)
Sung by John Banks, Poplar Point, April 4, 1968 (NA Ives 68.6; AFC 14,821B). See Moore and Moore, 356–58; Randolph, IV, 393–95; Stekert, 267.

This song works the rather common theme of reminiscence in a familiar spot. For other examples, see "The Irish Emigrant" ("I'm sitting on the stile, Mary, where we sat side by side") and "When You and I Were Young, Maggie." For the former, see Peacock, 462–64; the latter is available in any number of songsters.

Uncle Dan Song, The (48)
By Dan Riley. Sung by Mary Cousins, Campbellton, June 25, 1957 (NA Ives 1.30; ATL 2156.5). See Cousins and Banks, 7–8; see Ives (1963), 44–45, 84.

Unemployment Insurance (219)
By Alton MacLean. Sung by Alton MacLean at the Island Folk Festival, Elmsdale, November 6, 1982, Transcribed from the LP record *Island Folk Festival* (1985) and used with his permission.

Visit to Morans, The (204)
By Lawrence Doyle and Patrick William Farrell. Sung by John Farrell, St. Georges, March 31, 1969 (NA Ives 69.1; AFC 14,823A). See Ives (1971), 137–46.

Wee Cup of Tay, The (168)
Sung by Joseph Walsh, Morell Rear, September 1, 1965 (NA Ives 65.13; AFC 14,803B).

I seem to remember seeing this song in a book that was lying around in the Flanders Ballad Collection when I visited there back in 1966. Steve Roud pointed me out two parallels: "The Old Woman Drinking her Tay" in Williams, 25, and "The Tay" in Huntington/Henry, 502. And there the matter rests for the time being.

When Johnny Went Plowing for Kearon (191)
By Lawrence Doyle. Sung by John Miller, Morell, April 2, 1968 (NA Ives 68.5; AFC 14,821A). See Cousins and Banks, 1–2; Dibblee and Dibblee, 19–20; Ives (1971), 122–28.

Wild Colonial Boy, The (77)

Sung by Joseph Doucette, Miminegash, August 17, 1958 (NA Ives 1.36; ATL 2162.2). See Laws, *ABBB*, 177 (L-20); to which add Cazden i: 422–27, ii:82–84; Huntington/Henry, 120–21; Leach (1965), 148–49; Manny and Wilson, 304–05. For a study of this ballad and its congeners, see John Meredith, *The Wild Colonial Boy.*

There is a large and scattered scholarship on this ballad, much of it having to do with the identity of the hero (was he or was he not an Australian bushranger named Jack Dowling?) and the relationship between this ballad and "Bold Jack Donahue" (Laws L-22). These are interesting questions, but for our present purposes it is perhaps more important to point out that this ballad was well-known in local tradition throughout Maine and the Maritime Provinces and in lumbercamp tradition well beyond that range. It has appeared many times on folk and popular commercial recordings, which certainly helps to account for the fact that it is almost always sung to some version of the tune Long Joe uses here. For a remarkably thorough study of this tune tradition, see Cazden (cited above).

List of Works Cited

Abrahams, Roger D. (Editor). *A Singer and Her Songs: Almeda Riddle's Book of Ballads*. Baton Rouge: Louisiana State University Press, 1970.

_____, Kenneth S. Goldstein, and Wayland D. Hand. *By Land and By Sea: Studies in the Folklore of Work and Leisure Honoring Horace P. Beck on His Sixty-Fifth Birthday*. Hatboro, PA: Legacy Books, 1985.

Arnold, Byron. *Folksongs of Alabama*. Birmingham: University of Alabama Press, 1950.

Arsenault, Georges. *Complaintes acadiennes de l'Île-du-Prince-Édouard*. Ottawa: Les Éditions Leméac, 1980.

Barry, Phillips. *The Maine Woods Songster*. Cambridge: Powell Printing Co., 1939.

_____, Fannie Hardy Eckstorm, and Mary Winslow Smyth. *British Ballads from Maine*. New Haven: Yale University Press, 1929.

Beck, Horace P. *The Folklore of Maine*. Philadelphia and New York: Lippincott, 1957.

Bethke, Robert D. *Adirondack Voices: Woodsmen and Woods Lore*. Champaign: University of Illinois Press, 1981.

Boni, Margaret Bradford. *The Fireside Book of Favorite American Songs*. New York: Simon and Schuster, 1952.

The Frank C. Brown Collection of North Carolina Folklore. In seven volumes. Durham: Duke University Press, 1952–1961.

Cazden, Norman, Herbert Haufrecht, and Norman Studer. *Folk Songs of the Catskills*. In two volumes. Albany: State University of New York Press, 1982.

Child, Francis James. *The English and Scottish Popular Ballads*. In five volumes. Boston and New York: Houghton Mifflin, 1882–98. Reprinted New York: Dover Books, 1965.

Clark, Andrew Hill. *Three Centuries and the Island*. Toronto: University of Toronto Press, 1959.

Coffin, Tristram Potter and Roger deV. Renwick. *The British Traditional Ballad in North America*. Revised Edition. Austin, TX: University of Texas Press, 1977.

Cole, William. *Folk Songs of England, Ireland, Scotland and Wales*. Garden City: Doubleday, 1961.

Cousins, John. "James H. Fitzgerald and 'Prince Edward Isle, Adieu.'" *The Island Magazine* 8 (1980), 27–31.

_____, and Tommy Banks. *When Johnny Went Plowing for Kearon*. LP
      Record. Charlottetown: P.E.I. Heritage Foundation, 1976. With
      notes by Allan Rankin.

Cowell, Henry, and Sidney Robertson Cowell. *Charles Ives and His Music*.
      New York: Oxford University Press, 1955.

Creighton, Helen. *Songs and Ballads from Nova Scotia*. Toronto: J. M. Dent,
      1932. Reprinted New York: Dover, 1966.

_____, and Doreen Senior. *Traditional Songs from Nova Scotia*.
      Toronto: Ryerson, 1950.

_____. *Folklore of Lunenburg County, Nova Scotia*. Ottawa: National
      Museum of Canada, 1950.

_____. *Maritime Folk Songs*. Toronto: Ryerson, 1961. Reprinted St. John's,
      Nfld.: Breakwater Books, 1979.

_____. *Folksongs from Southern New Brunswick*. Ottawa: National
      Museum of Man, 1971.

("Cummins Atlas") *Atlas of the Province of Prince Edward Island, Canada*.
      Toronto: Cummins Map Co., c.1928. Reprinted Prince Edward
      Island Museum and Heritage Foundation, 1990.

Dibblee, Randall and Dorothy. *Folksongs from Prince Edward Island*.
      Summerside: Williams and Crue, 1973.

Doerflinger, William M. *Shantymen and Shantyboys*. New York: Macmillan,
      1951. Reprinted with additional material as *Songs of the Sailor and
      Lumberman*. New York: Macmillan, 1972.

Dyer-Bennet, Richard. *The Richard-Dyer Bennet Folk Song Book*. New York:
      Simon and Schuster, 1971.

Eckstorm, Fannie Hardy, and Mary Winslow Smyth. *Minstrelsy of Maine*.
      Boston and New York: Houghton Mifflin, 1927.

Edwards, Carol L., and Kathleen B. Manley (editors), *Narrative Folksong:
      New Directions*. Boulder, Co: Westview Press, 1985.

Finger, Charles J. *Frontier Ballads*. Garden City: Doubleday, Page, 1927.

Fowke, Edith. *Lumbering Songs from the Northern Woods*. Austin:
      University of Texas Press, 1970.

_____. *Traditional Singers and Songs from Ontario*. Hatboro, Pa.:
      Folklore Associates, 1965.

Gardner, Emelyn Elizabeth, and Geraldine Jencks Chickering. *Ballads and
      Songs of Southern Michigan* (Ann Arbor: University of Michigan
      Press, 1939; reprinted by Folklore Associates, 1967).

Gerould, Gordon Hall. *The Ballad of Tradition*. New York: Oxford University
      Press, 1932.

Glassie, Henry, Edward D. Ives, and John F. Szwed. *Folksongs and Their
      Makers*. Bowling Green, OH: Bowling Green University Popular
      Press, 1970.

Gledhill, Christopher. *Folk Songs of Prince Edward Island*. Charlottetown: Square Deal Publications, 1973.

Goldstein, Kenneth S. and Neil V. Rosenberg. *Folklore Studies in Honour of Herbert Halpert*. St. John's, Newfoundland: Memorial University of Newfoundland, 1980.

Greenleaf, Elizabeth Bristol, and Grace Yarrow Mansfield. *Ballads and Sea Songs from Newfoundland*. Cambridge: Harvard University Press, 1933.

Hamilton, William. "Ghostly Encounters of the Northumberland Kind." *The Island Magazine* 4 (Spring-Summer, 1878), 33–35.

Hickerson, Joseph. *Drive Dull Care Away. Volume I*. LP record. FSI 58. Sharon, CT: Folk Legacy, 1976.

Hoffman, Alice M. and Howard S. *Archives of Memory: A Soldier Recalls World War II*. Lexington: University Press of Kentucky, 1990.

Hornby, Jim. *In The Shadow of the Gallows: Criminal Law and Capital Punishment in Prince Edward Island, 1769–1941*. Charlottetown: Institute of Island Studies, 1998.

Huizinga, Johan. *The Waning of the Middle Ages*. (London: E. Arnold, 1924; various reprints).

Huntington, E. G. *Sam Henry's Songs of the People*. Revised, with additions and indexes by Lani Herrmann. Athens: University of Georgia Press, 1990.

Huntington, E. G. *Songs The Whalemen Sang*. Barre, MA: Barre Publishers, 1964.

_____. *Folksongs from Martha's Vineyard*. Orono, Me.: Northeast Folklore Society. *Northeast Folklore* 8 (1966).

Island Folk Festival. LP record. Charlottetown/Belfast, P.E.I.: Institute of Island Studies/Fox House, 1985.

Ives, Burl. *Burl Ives Irish Songs*. New York: Duell, Sloane and Pearce, 1955.

Ives, Edward D. "The Burning Ship of Northumberland Strait: Some Notes on That Apparition." *Midwest Folklore* VIII (1958), 199–203.

_____. *Folk Songs of Maine*. LP record. Folkways FH5323. (1959).

_____. "More Notes on The Burning Ship of Northumberland Strait." *Northeast Folklore* 2 (Winter, 1959), 53–55.

_____. "The Man Who Plucked the Gorby: A Maine Woods Legend." *Journal of American Folklore* 74 (Spring, 1961), 1–8.

_____. *Twenty-One Folksongs from Prince Edward Island*. Orono, Me.: Northeast Folklore Society. *Northeast Folklore* 5 (1963).

_____. *Larry Gorman: The Man Who Made the Songs*. Bloomington: Indiana University Press, 1964. Reprinted Fredericton, N.B.: Goose Lane Editions, 1993.

_____. *Lawrence Doyle: The Farmer-Poet of Prince Edward Island.* Maine Studies, No. 92. Orono, ME: University Press, 1971.

_____. *Joe Scott: The Woodsman-Songmaker.* Champaign: University of Illinois Press, 1978.

_____. "The Ballad of John Ladner." In Goldstein and Rosenberg (1980), 239–58.

_____. "'The Teamster in Jack MacDonald's Crew': A Song in Context and Its Singing." *Folklife Annual 1985:* 74–85.

_____. "'The Man Who Plucked the Gorby': A Maine Woods Legend Debated in Slow Motion." In Abrahams et al. *By Land and By Sea,* 137–40.

_____. *Folksongs of New Brunswick.* Fredericton, N.B.: Goose Lane Editions, 1989.

_____. "Big Jim Pendergast As I Knew Him." *The Island Magazine* 34 (Fall-Winter, 1993), 28–33.

Jolicoeur, Catherine. *Le vaisseau fantôme: legend étiologique.* Québec: Université Laval, 1970.

Kennedy, Michael. "The Réitach in Prince Edward Island." *Tocher,* No.50 (Spring, 1995), 46–51.

Kirtley, Bacil F. "On the Origin of the Maine-Maritimes Legend of the Plucked Gorbey." *Journal of American Folklore* 87 (1974), 364–65.

Laws, G. Malcolm, Jr. *American Balladry from British Broadsides.* American Folklore Society, Bibliographical and Special Series, 8. Philadelphia: American Folklore Society, 1957.

Laws, G. Malcolm, Jr. *Native American Balladry.* Revised Edition. American Folklore Society, Bibliographical and Special Series, 1. Philadelphia: American Folklore Society, 1964.

Leach, MacEdward. *Folk Ballads and Songs of the Lower Labrador Coast.* Ottawa: National Museum of Canada, 1965.

Lomax, Alan. *The Folk Songs of North America.* Garden City: Doubleday, 1960.

Lomax, John Avery. *Adventures of a Ballad Hunter.* New York: Macmillan, 1947.

MacEachern, Ron. *Songs and Stories from Deep Cove, Cape Breton.* College of Cape Breton Press, 1979.

Mackenzie, W. Roy. *Ballads and Sea Songs from Nova Scotia.* Cambridge: Harvard University Press, 1928; reprinted Folklore Associates, 1963.

_____. *The Quest of the Ballad.* Princeton: Princeton University Press, 1919.

MacKinnon, Rollie, and Gordon Belsher. *The Prince Edward Island Music Series. Volume I.* Charlottetown: Garden Music Enterprises, 1991.

MacManus, Seumas. *Ireland's Case*. New York: Irish Publishing Co., 1918.

Manny, Louise and James Reginald Wilson. *Songs of Miramichi*. Fredericton, N.B.: Brunswick Press, 1968.

McKenna, James E., Joseph R., and Peter A. *The Sign of the Stag: A Chimera*. Orono, Me.: *Northeast Folkore* XXXIII: 1997.

("Meacham's Atlas") *Illustrated Historical Atlas of the Province of Prince Edward Island*. N.p.: J.H. Meacham & Co, 1880. Reprinted Charlottetown: Prince Edward Island Museum and Heritage Foundation, 1972.

Meredith, John. *The Wild Colonial Boy*. Studies in Australian Folklore No. 3. Melbourne: Red Rooster Press, 1982.

Moore, Ethel and Chauncey, *Ballads and Folk Songs of the Southwest*. Norman: University of Oklahoma Press, 1964.

Morton, Robin. *Folksongs Sung in Ulster*. Cork: Mercier, 1970.

_____. *Come Day, Go Day, God Send Sunday*. London: Routledge and Kegan Paul, 1973.

Ohrlin, Glenn. *The Hell-Bound Train*. Champaign: University of Illinois Press, 1973.

O Lochlainn, Colm. *Irish Street Ballads*. Dublin, 1939.

Peacock, Kenneth. *Songs of the Newfoundland Outports*. (3 vols). Ottawa: National Museum of Man, 1965.

Percy, Thomas. *Reliques of Ancient English Poetry*. London, 1765 (Various subsequent editions).

Purslow, Frank. *Marrow Bones*. London: English Folk-Song and Dance Society, 1965.

Randolph, Vance. *Ozark Folksongs*. In four volumes. Columbia: State Historical Society of Missouri, 1946–1950.

Renwick, Roger deV. "On the Interpretation of Folk Poetry." In Edwards and Manley, *Narrative Folksong: New Directions*, 401–31.

Rickaby, Franz. *Ballads and Songs of The Shanty-Boy*. Cambridge: Harvard University Press, 1926.

Sandburg, Carl. *The American Songbag*. New York: Harcourt, Brace, 1927.

Scarborough, Dorothy. *A Song Catcher in Southern Mountains*. New York: Columbia University Press, 1937. Reprinted AMS, 1966.

Shay, Frank. *More Pious Friends and Drunken Companions*. New York, 1928.

Silber, Irwin. *Reprints from the Peoples' Songs Bulletin*. New York: Oak, 1961.

Spaeth, Sigmund. *Weep Some More, My Lady*. New York: Doubleday, Page, 1927.

Stekert, Ellen. "Two Voices of Tradition." Ph.D. dissertation, University of

Pennsylvania, 1965. University Microfilms, No. 66-4654.

Szwed, John F. "Paul E. Hall: A Newfoundland Song-Maker and His Community of Song." In Henry Glassie et al., *Folksongs and Their Makers* (q.v.), 147–69.

Wilgus, D.K. *Anglo-American Folksong Scholarship Since 1898.* New Brunswick, N.J.: Rutgers University Press, 1959.

Williams, Alfred. *Folk Songs of the Upper Thames.* London: Novello & Co., 1923.

Wilson, James Reginald. "Ballad Tunes of the Miramichi." Master's thesis, New York University, 1961.

Index

Titles in boldface indicate those songs for which words and (usually) music appear in the text. Page numbers in boldface show where the words and music for that song can be found. Titles in roman type indicate songs referred to in passing. An asterisk after a person's name designates an informant; for each, I have given his or her town. However, in the interest of conserving space, I have not otherwise indexed place names. Book titles are given in italic.

The body text for this book is *Electra*, designed
in 1935 by William Addison Dwiggins.
Electra, a didone or modern font,
can be recognized by the distinctive
weighted top serifs unique
to this font.

Headlines are set in *Voluta Script*, designed
in 1998 by Viktor Solt. *Voluta Script* is
based on Kurrant writing, a
cursive blackletter style
of the 18th century.